RS

To My Wife

The First Tigers

THE EARLY HISTORY OF ROCK CLIMBING IN THE LAKE DISTRICT

Alan Hankinson

MB

Melbecks Books
Bassenthwaite

First published 1972
by J. M. Dent & Sons Ltd.

Revised edition 1984
Melbecks Books,
Bassenthwaite, Keswick, Cumbria

ISBN 0 9508822 1 6

Printed in England by Titus Wilson & Son Ltd., Kendal

Contents

List of Illustrations, vi
Author's Acknowledgments, vii
Foreword by Christian Bonington, x
Glossary, xv

Chapter 1	The Golden Age	1
2	The District Discovered	22
3	The Pioneer Pillarites	35
4	The Scene is Set	51
5	The Sport is Born	56
6	The Pace Quickens	64
7	The *Annus Mirabilis*	75
8	The Gentlemen Amateurs	82
9	'The Only Genuine Jones'	98
10	Community Spirit	107
11	The Cragsman's Equipment	118
12	Some Personalities	127
13	The Dynamic Trio	136
14	Triumph and Tragedy	145
15	The End of an Era	159
16	Exeunt Omnes	172
17	Postscript	184

Bibliography, 189
Index, 193

Illustrations

Between pages 78 and 79

1 W. P. Haskett Smith
O. G. Jones
The Rev. James Jackson
2 View of Wasdale Head
3 Entrance hall of Wastwater Hotel
4 The Barn Door Traverse
5 *a.* The Y Boulder
b. A. S. Thomson and the Abrahams motoring
6 Scafell Pinnacle from Jordan Gap
7 How not to climb
8 Pillar Rock—round the Notch
9 Pillar Rock—over the Nose
10 View of Scafell Crag
11 The Collie Step
12 Scafell Pinnacle from Deep Ghyll
13 George Abraham on Gable Crag
14 Scafell Pinnacle Arête
15 O. G. Jones and a learner
16 Kern Knotts Crack
General map of the Lake District, *page xii-xiii*

Front cover: Napes Needle; climbers on the Haskett Smith route

Back cover: Wastwater Hotel

Author's Acknowledgments

Writing this book has introduced me to some delightful people and put me hopelessly in debt to them. Mr Geoffrey Abraham of Keswick, the son of Ashley Abraham who is one of the book's heroes as both climber and photographer, has been unfailingly helpful and encouraging throughout. Mrs Eleanor Winthrop Young, the daughter of one fine climber and the widow of another, was equally liberal with her help and friendship. And the one person still surviving who climbed in the period covered by this book, Colonel 'Rusty' Westmorland, recollected those early days for me with a generosity as total as his recall.

Others who have given me the benefit of their experience and expert advice in the field of rock climbing include Lord Chorley, Mr Sid Cross (former landlord of the Old Dungeon Ghyll Hotel), Dr T. Howard Somervell and Mr Tony Moulam of the Climbers' Club. On the literary side I was given valuable help, stylistic and grammatical, by several friends, particularly Mr Frank Morris of Arnside and Mr Donald MacRow of Alton, while my oldest and most learned friend, the Reverend Norman Taylor of Cambridge, tracked down and translated the Homeric quotation in chapter five. Another friend, Mr Gerald Forty of Highgate, drew my attention to the parallels between the early days of rock climbing and those of his own sport, small boat sailing.

Most of my sources of information were printed ones, books and club journals, and I am grateful to the following for permission to quote: the Longman Group for O. G. Jones's *Rock Climbing in the English Lake District*; Methuen & Co. Ltd for George Abraham's *Mountain Adventures at Home and Abroad*; John Sherratt & Son Ltd for Oppenheimer's *The Heart of Lakeland*; Jonathan Cape Ltd for the *Confessions* of Aleister Crowley; the Clarendon Press for *The Collected Letters of S. T. Coleridge*; and J. M. Dent & Sons Ltd for Ronald Clark and Edward Pyatt's magisterial *Mountaineering in Britain*.

The Fell and Rock Climbing Club of the English Lake District, the Alpine Club, the Scottish Mountaineering Club, the Climbers' Club and the Yorkshire Ramblers' Club kindly allowed me to quote from their journals. My greatest debt here is to the Fell and Rock Club's Journal whose early issues carried many articles of reminiscence and whose special 1936 edition contained a valuable 'Short History of Lakeland Climbing' by H. M. Kelly and J. H. Doughty.

The definitions in the glossary derive largely from Peter Crew's *Encyclopaedic Dictionary of Mountaineering*, published by Constable, and from Alan Blackshaw's authoritative *Mountaineering*, in the Penguin Handbook series.

I have further debts to the Fell and Rock Climbing Club—for their latest editions of the Lake District Climbing Guides and for access to their collection of Abraham photographs and the expert and unstinted help of their Custodian of Lantern Slides, Mr F. H. F. Simpson. Mr George Fisher of Keswick also helped with photographic research. And there is a further debt, too, to the Alpine Club: although this book does not always reflect flatteringly on the Alpine Club men of the late-Victorian period, their modern successors generously allowed me free use of their excellent library.

There are two Frank Singletons to thank, however paradoxical that may seem to card players. One gave me my first journalistic job when he was editor of the *Bolton Evening News*, and it was the Wasdale chapter of his book *The English Lakes* (B. T. Batsford Ltd) which first roused my interest in the early cragsmen. The other, Mr F. B. Singleton, librarian of the *Guardian* in Manchester, went to considerable trouble to seek out contemporary references for me. Mrs G. Gosling, librarian of the Highgate Literary and Scientific Institution, helped me with the Coleridge research. At the Wastwater Hotel I was allowed to browse through what is left of the old visitors' book, variously referred to in the following pages as *The Visitors' Book*, *The Climbing Book* and *The Climbers' Record*. Mr George Bott of Keswick helped me with historical information, and Mr Michael Ball of Mansfield, a grandson of Dr Joseph Collier, sent me details of his family history.

I also have to thank Chris Bonington who spared time from writing his own book to write the Foreword to mine. Alan Hill and Heinemann Educational Books Ltd. generously gave permission to use the map on pp. xii-xiii which was first published in *Camera on the Crags* and adapted by Vivien Hartley. I am also grateful to J. M. Dent & Sons Ltd. for permission to use their original typography for the main text in this new edition.

A note is necessary about the spelling. Until recently the spelling of Lake District place-names has varied according to the whim of the writer. In my text I have used the versions which are now generally accepted, but the quotations retain their original idiosyncrasies for such names as Wasdale, Scafell and the Cuillin. I do not think there is any danger of confusion.

Finally the areas of my greatest indebtedness: to my son James, whose enthusiasm has forced me to continue rock climbing despite increasing cowardice and incompetence, and whose retentive memory for routes and dates has eliminated some at least of the howlers; and, above all, to my wife, whose continuous help and encouragement has been combined with fiercely critical assaults on all the faults to which my style is prone.

Foreword

by

CHRISTIAN BONINGTON

There is a magic about one's first few climbs, one's introduction to the hills. A road-side cliff seems huge and mysterious; a comparatively easy route holds a delicious terror compounded of the unknown and inexperience. I had as much excitement and satisfaction in my first years of climbing in North Wales and Scotland, on climbs graded no harder than 'Severe', as I ever did in later years on bigger mountains and much harder climbs.

This spirit of fresh, new adventure must have been even stronger in the early days of the sport of rock climbing, born in this country towards the end of the nineteenth century. This perhaps was the real 'Golden Age' of British climbing, when techniques were being evolved from scratch, when Lakeland rock faces were as little mapped and as mysterious as Himalayan peaks are today, and, perhaps most precious of all, when only a handful of people wandered over the hills and even fewer ventured onto the crags.

The most difficult climbs accomplished in that period might seem commonplace today—even routes like Botterill's Slab on Scafell, Kern Knotts Crack on Gable, or Savage Gully on Pillar. But when one remembers the gear in use in those days, as well as the psychological 'breakthrough' that each step forward in difficulty required, the achievement of the early masters was every bit as great as, if not greater than, that of the present-day high-standard rock technician, who is backed by an armoury of technical aids. There is no doubt that the early climber accepted a considerably higher risk factor than does the modern exponent, for rope technique was rudimentary and the leader truly could not afford to fall.

In this book Alan Hankinson has captured the atmosphere of this fascinating period both through his own writing and his use of original material culled from books and journals. What makes the story of Lakeland climbing so attractive is the way local farmers and shepherds have shared in the exploration of the fells and crags. Perhaps as a result of this, there seems to have been none of the bigoted snobbery that beset the Alpine Club in the same period.

Wasdale Head became the centre of Lakeland climbing and the greater part of this book concentrates on the groups of climbers which held sway over the hotel there and on the crags around. They were an interesting collection of people. Aleister Crowley, for one, spent some time there, and provides a welcome acid commentary on his fellow climbers, in contrast to the mellow, essentially under-written comments of the majority. Born in a later age, I am quite sure these early tigers would have compared well with climbers of the present day. O. G. Jones had all the 'push and neck' of the modern climber—indeed a longer neck, for he was tackling comparatively hard climbs with few or no technical aids.

These personalities are superimposed on the Lakeland scene, the empty unspoilt fells, and through them we get a vivid picture of the social pattern of the day. The whole makes this fascinating and immensely readable book.

The Lake District

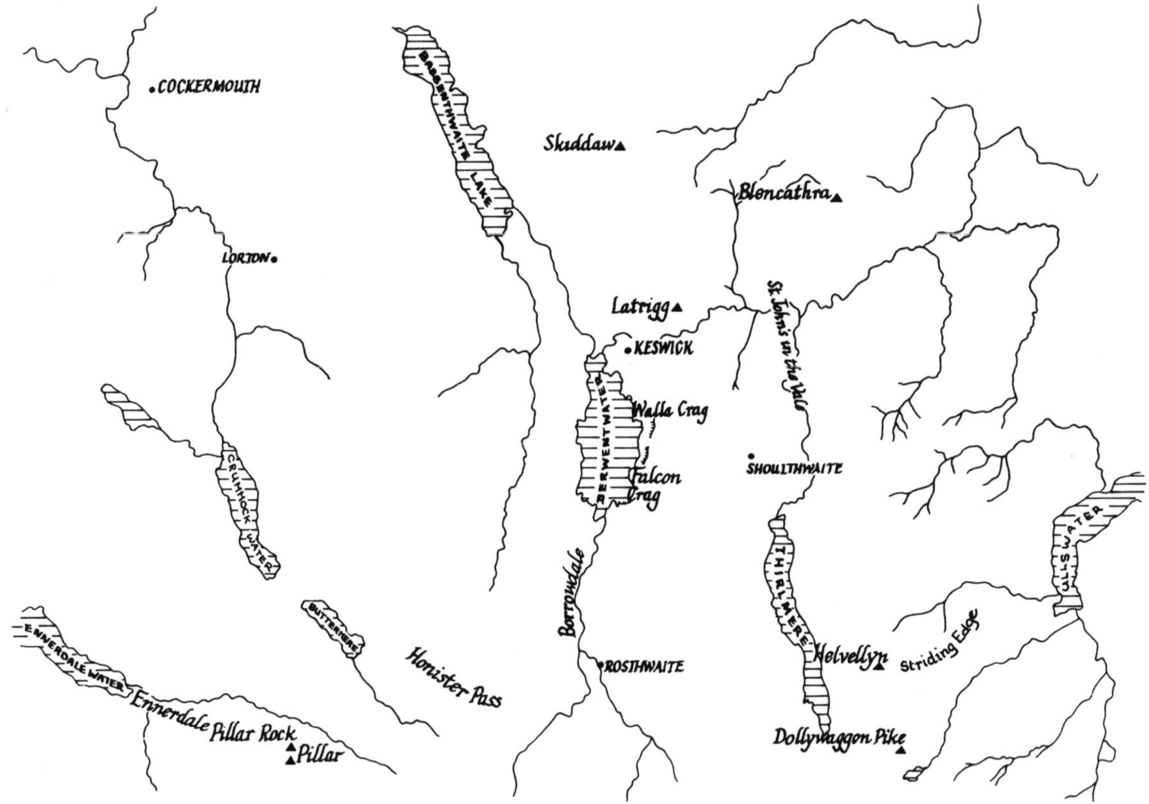

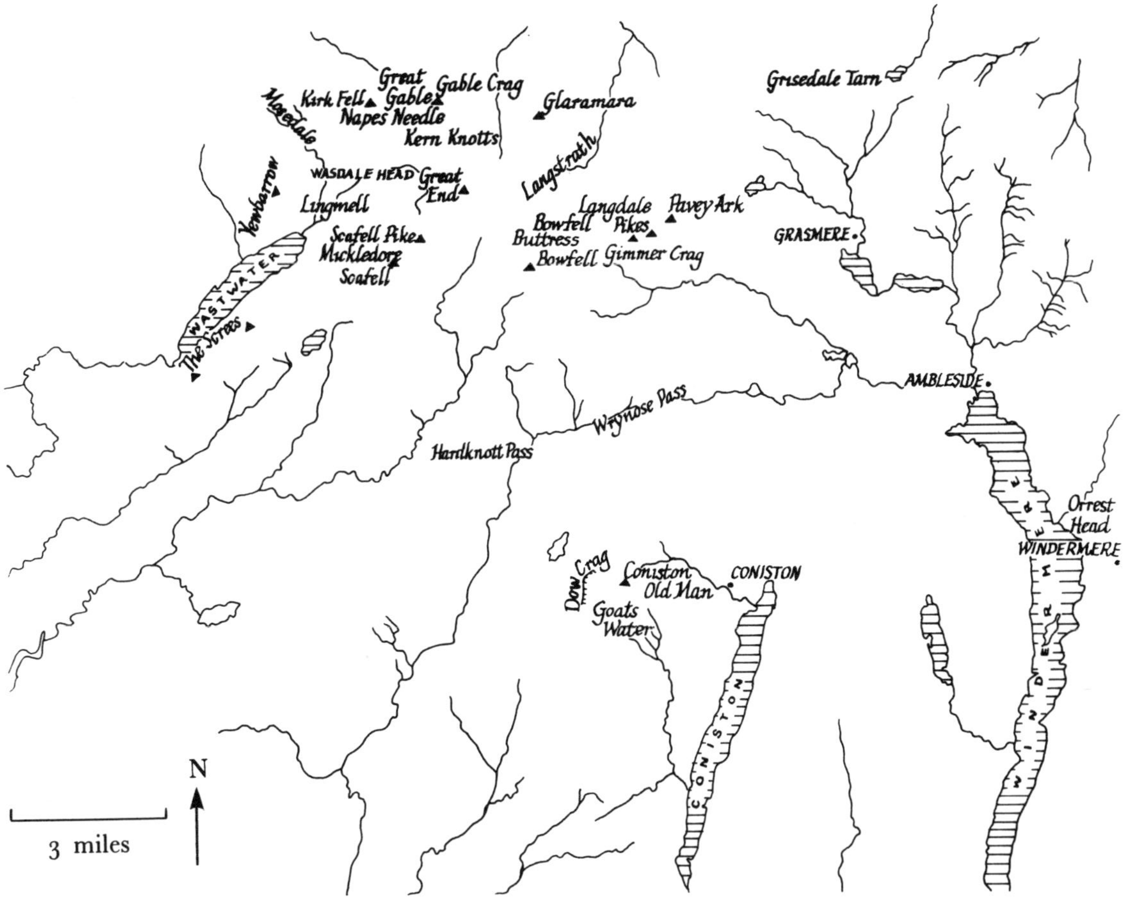
Great Gable Crag
Kirk Fell
Great Gable
Napes Needle
Kern Knotts
Glaramara
Grisedale Tarn
Mosedale
Yewbarrow
WASDALE HEAD
Great End
Lingmell
Langstrath
Langdale Pikes
Pavey Ark
Bowfell Buttress
Scafell Pike
Mickledore
Scafell
Bowfell
Gimmer Crag
GRASMERE
WASTWATER
The Screes
AMBLESIDE
Wrynose Pass
Hardknott Pass
Orrest Head
WINDERMERE
Dow Crag
Coniston Old Man
CONISTON
Goats Water
N
3 miles

Glossary

à cheval	sitting astride a narrow ridge to work your way along it
arête	a sharp and narrow ridge
back and foot	method of climbing chimneys with the back against one wall and the feet against the other
belay	(verb) the act of a stationary climber securing himself by fixing the rope round some stable rock projection (noun) the projection itself; also called the 'anchor'
bivouac	a night out in the mountains without a tent
boss	any small protuberance of rock which affords some measure of hand or foot hold
bouldering	practice-climbing on boulders where extreme difficulties can be tackled because there is little distance to fall
buttress	part of a cliff face that stands out from the rest
cairn	pile of stones set up to mark a special place or indicate a path
chimney	fissure in the rock face wide enough to admit most or all of the body
chock-stone	stone or boulder firmly wedged in a crack, chimney or gully
clinkers	boot nails of soft iron fitted round the edge of the soles and heels
col	a mountain pass; the lowest point in a ridge that connects two peaks

combined tactics	the practice of one climber physically helping another up a difficult pitch, usually by allowing him to climb onto his shoulder or head
corner	place on a cliff where two walls meet at right angles or thereabouts
couloir	an Alpine gully
course	term used by early rock climbers for a climbing route
crack	fissure in the rock face wide enough to admit the fingers or a hand, an arm or a leg, but nothing more
crag	a steep, rugged rock
crux	the hardest part of a climb
étrier	short rope-ladder used in modern artificial climbing to surmount holdless or overhanging rock
exposure	the feeling that there is a long way to go if you fall off
fell	Cumbrian term for a mountain
funnel	gully of scree or earth, often a watercourse after rain
gabbro	rough-textured granite found in the Cuillin mountains on the Isle of Skye
gardening	cleaning up a climbing route by removing loose rock, vegetation, etc.
go, will it go?	can it be climbed?
ghyll, gill	mountain stream or ravine, often both, and sometimes steep enough to become a gully
girdle traverse	roughly horizontal route across a cliff or face from one side to the other
glissade	sliding down a snow or ice slope, using the ice axe to control speed
gully	a deep cleft up a cliff face, wider than a chimney

hand traverse	horizontal movement across a rock face supported by the hands only
ice axe	implement for cutting steps or belaying in hard snow or ice, with many subsidiary uses
layback	strenuous way of climbing a corner with a sharp edge by gripping the edge with the hand, leaning back and moving the feet up the rock on the other side of the corner
needle	a sharp pinnacle of rock
nose	a jutting slab of rock
off-comer	Cumbrian term for a visitor to the area
overhang	a rock face that leans out beyond the perpendicular
pinnacle	a slender tower of rock
pitch	section of a climb between ledges or belaying points
piton	a metal peg which modern climbers hammer into cracks to make secure belays
rake	a horizontal or obliquely rising ledge across a cliff face
rappel	way of descending steep places quickly by sliding down a fixed rope
ridge	the raised line where two slopes meet
scramble	climbing on broken ground steep enough to require the use of the hands though not difficult
scree	slope of loose stones
slab	rock face inclined between 30 and 60 degrees to the horizontal
stance	place where a climber can stand or sit in reasonable comfort and manage the rope for his companion
stomach traverse	wriggling along a ledge on the stomach
top rope	a rope from above the climber which gives him the assurance that if he comes off he will not fall far

traverse	a climb across the face of a cliff, roughly horizontal
tricounis	hard steel nails with serrated edges fitted round the edge of the soles and sometimes the heels of climbing boots
turn	to avoid a difficulty by going round it
wall	rock face inclined between 60 degrees and the vertical

1 The Golden Age

One evening during the early weeks of 1881 a young Oxford graduate sat down in his rooms at Trinity to study maps of England. He had been appointed by a group of friends, students of classics and history, to decide where they should gather for the reading party they planned for the summer vacation. 'None of us,' he wrote many years later, 'had ever been to the Lakes or heard the very name of Wasdale Head, but we procured the Ordnance map of Cumberland, found that there was on it a sombre region thronged with portentous shadows, found that there was an inn at a spot which seemed the centre of all this gloom, and finally engaged rooms at Dan Tyson's for a month.'

Walter Parry Haskett Smith was twenty-two years old, a classics scholar, but more distinguished at the university for athletic prowess than for academic attainment. He never satisfactorily explained why he plumped for the point on the map where the contour lines lay thickest together, though he had already done a little mountain walking in Snowdonia and the Pyrenees. That summer, however, he and his friends read Plato in the mornings and tramped the Cumbrian fells in the afternoons, and, most important of all, they made the acquaintance of F. H. Bowring, a veteran hill walker, forty years their senior, who introduced them to the excitements of finding their way among the mountains well clear of the traditional tracks and easy paths.

Haskett Smith returned to Wasdale Head the following

summer with his younger brother. They walked up the fells one morning, turned off the footpath to take a closer look at one of the great cliffs, inspected a dark, broken gully that split the precipice from top to bottom, began to scramble up, then to climb, and finally emerged triumphant at the top.

It was the moment when rock climbing was born.

Slowly at first, but with gathering momentum as more men heard what was going on and came to Wasdale Head, and as their mounting confidence and skill led them out of the gullies into the narrower chimneys and cracks and finally out onto the open, airy faces of the great slabs and buttresses, the sport grew and flourished until its progress was suddenly halted in 1903 by a terrible accident on Scafell Crag.

The twenty-one years, from the summer of 1882 to that of 1903, carried rock climbing from its birth, through a happy childhood and a vigorous adolescence, to the final achievement of full maturity through tragedy.

The story was enacted almost entirely on the central cliffs of the Lake District, all of them within two hours' walking distance of the Wastwater Hotel at Wasdale Head. Its pervading spirit was that of the gentleman amateur—adventurous, exploring and earnest, but also friendly and free and modest. There was little of the egocentric competitiveness that has injected so much acrimony, personal and nationalistic, into the climbing story in the twentieth century. The pioneer climbers of Wasdale Head climbed because they enjoyed it—the escape, the exercise, the comradeship, the danger—and rarely for reasons of vainglory.

They called themselves 'rock climbers' and 'cragsmen'. The colloquial term 'tigers', as applied to climbers, was unknown to them, the invention of a later generation, and it would have struck most of them as embarrassingly presumptuous and ungentlemanly. It is appropriate, nonetheless. In his *Encyclopaedic Dictionary of Mountaineering*, Peter Crew defines 'tiger' as 'a mountaineer who consistently climbs at a very high standard of difficulty'.

Their achievement speaks for itself. At the height of their activity they numbered only a few score. Most of them led busy family and professional lives far away from the Lake District, and could only get to Wasdale Head briefly at Christmas and Easter and for perhaps a week or two in the summer. They were explorers in a completely new field of human endeavour, having to discover, and indeed create, the rules of the sport as they went along. By modern standards their techniques and equipment were pitifully, almost suicidally, inadequate. They ventured onto cliff faces that were dangerously littered with the debris of the ages. The public in general and the farmers of the Lake District dales both thought them mad, and many of the older generation of Alpine mountaineers condemned them as 'gymnasts' and 'exhibitionists'. Yet, in twenty-one years, they made dozens of routes on crags which had been considered impregnable until their coming. Many of their routes are still found highly exacting, Eagle's Nest Ridge on Great Gable, for example, and Botterill's Slab on Scafell; and many others, like Bowfell Buttress, the New West climb on Pillar Rock, and Kern Knotts Crack on Gable, are still regarded as 'classics' and command widespread respect and affection. All this was accomplished in a spirit of holiday companionship and, until 1903, without the loss of a single life in rock climbing in the Lake District. It can justifiably be called the 'Golden Age' of rock climbing.

No story ever had a more splendidly appropriate setting. The Wastwater Hotel stood then, as it stands today, at the head of England's most starkly impressive valley. Nowadays the motor road makes Wasdale Head easily accessible to all, but even now anyone who wants to explore further must be prepared for hard walking. Ninety years ago a visit to Wasdale Head was something of an undertaking, involving a long walk or a long carriage ride from the nearest railway station. The traveller advanced eastwards from the coastal plain, at first through undulating hill country, his eye held by the jumble of high mountains ahead, then along the shore of the black lake with its dramatic backcloth of the great Screes, and finally among the green fields of the valley head, patterned with dry-stone walls. Few landscapes in England have so successfully resisted the ravages of 'progress'. Wordsworth's description, published in 1810 in his *Guide Through the District of the Lakes*, remains accurate: 'Wastdale is well worth the notice of the Traveller, who is not afraid of fatigue; no part of the country is more distinguished by sublimity . . . the deep valley of Wastdale, with its little chapel and half a dozen neat dwellings scattered upon a plain of meadow and corn-ground intersected with stone walls apparently innumerable, like a large piece of lawless patch-work.'

From the valley head a man may 'lift up his eyes unto the hills', and see on every side a noble prospect; the shapely Yew-barrow near by and Pillar Mountain in the distance; Kirk Fell and Great Gable with its rocky promontories and steep, red-tinted screes; the hummocky hump of Lingmell; and immediately beyond it the highest mountain in England, Scafell Pike, and the country's finest cliff, Scafell Crag.

To the geologist, this is the country of 'Borrowdale volcanic' rock. Some 500 million years ago, the area lay under the sea and gradually deposits of mud and grit hardened under the pressure of the water to form a base of what is called 'Skiddaw slate'. Later, in this area, volcanoes erupted under water and poured out streams of lava which covered the slate and, in its turn, solidified into almost unbreakable rock. After many ages a great upheaval of the earth's crust lifted the rock clear of the sea, and other forces, of wind and weather and ice, went to work. For perhaps a million years the whole region lay under thousands of feet of ice; and when, 20,000 years ago, the glaciers receded, they carved out the contours of the Lakeland valleys as we see them today. In the northern areas of the Lake District where 'Skiddaw slate' predominated, the surface adapted to the pressures of the ice to create rounded shapes. But in the area of 'Borrowdale volcanic', the tough, resistant quality of the rock ensured that when it surrendered to the pressure it did so in massive blocks to create the steep precipices which are the characteristic features of the central fells. In this way, although the story has been grossly over-simplified, the crags were made ready for the cragsmen.

The first rock climbers learned their skills for the most part on three of these cliffs, Pillar Rock, Scafell Crag and the Napes face of Great Gable.

Pillar Rock, the great isolated dome of crag just below the northern shoulder of Pillar Mountain, is the only separate summit in the Lake District which cannot be gained without climbing. For this reason it was the earliest centre of interest. And because it offers routes on all four of its sides and of varying length and difficulty, it maintained its attraction throughout the 'Golden Age' and long after.

The first rock climb of all, though, was made eighty years before the appearance of Haskett Smith, on the flank of Scafell Crag, when the poet Samuel Taylor Coleridge indulged his weakness for short cuts by clambering down from Scafell summit to Mickledore gap by the route which is known as Broad Stand. In later years the Alpine men found ample scope in the gullies of Scafell Crag for winter practice in step-cutting, and the cragsmen found an inexhaustible source of challenge, at first in the gullies and later on its forbidding slabs and buttresses.

Although of the three the most easily reached from Wasdale Head, the Napes face of Great Gable was the last of them to be discovered as a climbing ground. But after Haskett Smith's solo ascent of Napes Needle in 1886, it became perhaps the most popular area of all and certainly, through the widespread publication of photographs of the Needle, the one best known to the public at large.

When rock climbing began in earnest, in 1882, what is known as the 'Golden Age of Mountaineering' was already over. This is generally taken to have begun in 1854 when Alfred Wills, a young English barrister on honeymoon in the Bernese Oberland, forsook his bride for a few days and hired four local guides to take him to the summit of the Wetterhorn. It was not the first major ascent in the Alps—Mont Blanc had been climbed nearly seventy years earlier; it was not even the first ascent of the Wetterhorn; yet it marked the beginning of a brief and intensive period of mountain conquest. English gentlemen-amateurs, most of them from the higher reaches of the upper middle class, provided the inspiration and the money, while local guides, Swiss and French, supplied the expertise. In eleven years, thirty-nine major peaks in the Alps submitted, the majority of them to that formidable partnership. By 1865 only one 4,000-metre peak in Switzerland remained unclimbed, the Matterhorn. Edward Whymper's conquest of the mountain in that year, and the tragedy that attended his descent, when three Englishmen and a guide fell to their deaths, marked the end of the Alpine 'Golden Age'.

The Matterhorn disaster shocked the small band of mountain enthusiasts and horrified mid-Victorian England. Already John Ruskin, the sharp-eyed prophet of Alpine beauty, had been driven to almost apopletic rhetoric by the activities of the mountaineers. 'The Alps themselves,' he wrote, in *Sesame and Lilies*, 'which your own poets used to love so reverently, you look upon as soaped poles in a bear-garden, which you set yourself to climb and slide down again with "shrieks of delight". When you are past shrieking, having no human articulate voice to say you are glad with, you fill the quietude of their valleys with gun-powder blasts, and rush home, red with cutaneous eruption of conceit, and voluble with the convulsive hiccough of self-satisfaction.' Now, when the tragic news reached London from Zermatt, *The Times*—much the most powerful newspaper in the world—weighed in with a battery of questions: 'Why is the best blood of England to waste itself in scaling hitherto inaccessible peaks, in staining the eternal snow, and reaching the unfathomable abyss never to return? . . . Is it life? Is it duty? Is it common sense?' And the Queen herself, though she had no time whatever for *The Times*, inquired of the Lord Chamberlain whether something could not be done to prohibit mountaineering by law.

It could not. The years that followed saw a small but growing band of Englishmen, many of them young undergraduates from the old universities, travelling to the Alps each summer in pursuit of adventure and conquest. Mountaineering, the exploration of the high regions of snow and ice, had come to stay.

It seems strange, now, that the men who pioneered the Alpine sport should have ignored for so long the opportunities for adventure among the high hills of their own country. The mountains of the Lake District, North Wales and the Scottish Highlands were more readily accessible than those of the Alps; the railways had put most of them within a day's comfortable journey of London. But the early mountaineers were, for the most part, men of wealth and leisure—university teachers, barristers, and businessmen—able to enjoy long summer holidays. The tradition of the 'Grand Tour', the young English 'milord' travelling Europe to put a final polish on his social and cultural education, still persisted. Above all, the Alpine regions of snow and ice, the peaks and passes and glaciers, offered a challenge much more immediate and obvious, and the prospect of prizes far more glittering than anything that could possibly be won from the humbler hills of Britain.

Mountaineering is senior to rock climbing both in years and in status. The mountaineer of those days was primarily an explorer, akin to the traders and missionaries and scholar-adventurers who were opening up unknown areas of Africa and Arabia at the same period. He set himself an arduous objective, involving many miles of hard going over varied and unmapped terrain, and an essential element in his skill was the ability to find the easiest and safest route. The rock climber, when he came along, confronted a limited objective, little more perhaps than a hundred feet of steep crag, and it was his special quality to seek out the hardest route of which his muscles and nerve were capable.

In an article in the *Alpine Journal* of 1890–1, W. M. Conway portrays the mountaineer as a man with 'the geographical instinct', a natural wanderer driven by the desire to find what lies beyond the skyline, an expert at route-finding, a man escaping from the soft and artificial life of urban civilization. He contrasts this man with the rock climber: 'The gymnast like "pretty bits" of rocks, with a cracklet here for a finger and a cracklet there for a toe. . . . The climbing of details is his pleasure. . . . He does not care for wandering.' The 'gymnast', he says, detests swagger, dislikes snow, is bored by easy routes, and likes to return at nightfall to the comforts of civilized living.

Conway was much more tolerant of the new breed of crag climbers than most of his fellow members of the Alpine Club. When the Climbers' Club was formed in 1897, mainly for men who climbed in North Wales, Douglas Freshfield, the arch-conservative, sneered at 'A Climbers' Club for "chimney sweeps"'. Perhaps the most extreme statement of the Alpine Club attitude was made by Walter Larden, the veteran of innumerable Alpine seasons, in his book *Recollections of an Old Mountaineer*:

> Taking the Lake mountains as an example one may state broadly that the British climber could not have learned how to climb, nor trained his judgement and nerve at all, unless he had intentionally attacked every mountain on the 'wrong side'. Thus, from the first, he had to *invent* difficulties . . . all must agree that this principle, which I take to be the guiding principle of the pure crag-climber, is a dangerous one. Once you aim at inventing and solving rock problems, where are you to stop? . . . It is the more reckless crag-climbers who are responsible for the accusations of levity and foolhardiness so often brought against climbers. . . . There are those among them who climb for the excitement only; who would far sooner spend their day climbing in a gully that affords exciting 'pitches', but makes no demand on endurance or mountaineering knowledge and lies outside the portals of the 'Celestial Kingdom', than in gaining the sublime heights of Monte Rosa or in traversing the magnificent Col d'Argentirèe. Let such recognize frankly that they don't care for the mountains, and that they are incapable of understanding that which had been the life-long passion of men who stood head and shoulders above most of us.

This kind of prejudice, the refusal to recognize as climbing anything that was done on mountains that were not Alpine in character, was characteristic of the Alpine Club in the closing decades of the nineteenth century, and did much to harm the general development of the sport and the reputation of the Club itself. Fortunately, the attitude was not universal. Many leading Alpine explorers took to Cumberland rock climbing with unashamed enthusiasm; some, Leslie Stephen and A. F. Mummery among them, acknowledged themselves dismayed by the difficulty of the climbing they found there; and many of the men who began their climbing around Wasdale Head went on to use the special skills they had learned there to advance the standards of Alpine mountaineering.

The men of Wasdale Head were too sturdily independent and too excited by the new sport to be discouraged by strictures from London or Grindelwald. They cheerfully embraced the terms that had been coined to denigrate them, 'chimney sweeps' and 'rock gymnasts'. They praised favourite crags as 'a veritable rock gymnasium', 'a fine fellow as rocks go . . . a gymnasium in itself'. When their work kept them in towns, they climbed buildings and public monuments. When the weather kept them indoors, they climbed chairs and tables and along the picture rails. If they had a spare hour or so in the valley they made new routes up the wall of a barn or refined their techniques by tackling short pitches of the greatest severity on boulders and outcrops. One route on the Y Boulder in Mosedale had, by tradition, to be climbed upside down. And Arthur Botterill, a gymnast by profession, climbed to the top of Napes Needle and stood on his head there.

Rock climbing is a narrower sport than mountaineering. It is possible to reach the top ranks of rock climbing without ever setting a boot on snow or ice or even the summit of a mountain. But it is also more concentrated and intense. On the analogy of athletics, rock climbing is an 'explosive' event, the hundred-metre sprint as compared to the marathon. It calls for the ability to exert great effort, physical and nervous, over comparatively brief periods of time. Few climbs in the Lake District are longer than 300 feet, many are less than 100 feet. It is a condition which 'concentrates the mind wonderfully'. Within these limits, the men of Wasdale Head were able to tackle routes that seemed impossible to the layman and unacceptably dangerous and difficult to the alpinist. They developed their climbing skills—the ability to move smoothly on small and awkward holds and the mental strength to accept and even enjoy the feeling of being exposed over a long drop—to standards far in advance of any climbers anywhere else in the world.

The fascination of this strange, esoteric sport brought a mixed and brilliant company of men to Wasdale Head in the closing decades of the nineteenth century. The leading heroes of the story, Haskett Smith in the 1880s and Owen Glynne Jones in the 1890s, would not be remembered today if they had not climbed the crags. But many of the supporting characters achieved eminence in a variety of fields. Professor Collie was a great scientist, the discoverer of Neon and X-ray photography; John and Edward Hopkinson were pioneers of applied electrical engineering; Professor Milnes Marshall was an eminent zoologist; Aleister Crowley achieved subsequent fame and infamy for his experiments in black magic; the Abraham brothers of Keswick live on in their superb photographs; and occasional visitors to Wasdale Head included Arthur Quiller-Couch, destined for fame as a teacher of English literature, A. E. W. Mason, the popular novelist, and Leopold Amery, who became a powerful and influential figure in politics and government.

Several distinct strands weave together to form the fabric of the story.

There was the continuing tradition of the university reading party, which year after year brought young men of high promise from Oxford and Cambridge.

There were the more enlightened members of the Alpine fraternity, who welcomed the opportunity for winter practice in snow and ice techniques in the gullies of Cumberland.

More significantly, there were the local men—not the dalesmen themselves, who distrusted the new sport and whose comments punctuate the narrative like the gloomy chorus of a Greek tragedy, but more adventurous spirits from market towns and villages on the outskirts of the mountain region. They played a key part in the embryonic years before the appearance of Haskett Smith, and again at the end of the 'Golden Age' when the Broadrick brothers from Windermere and a group of young enthusiasts from Kendal went to work on Dow Crag and Gimmer Crag.

In the central years though their role was a supporting but a vital one. They knew the fells better than the holiday visitors from the cities, known to the Cumbrians as 'off-comers', could ever hope to do. They could read the weather signs with greater acumen, and their active lives gave them greater reserves of strength. Most important of all, there was a four-square solidity and sanity about them that worked more than once as a life-saving brake on their impulsive leaders. It is no coincidence that the two most effective climbing teams involved the partnership of 'off-comer' and local man; Haskett Smith, supported by J. W. Robinson of Lorton, and O. G. Jones, supported by the Abraham brothers.

The fourth and strongest strand was formed by the holiday visitors from the cities—London, Manchester, Liverpool, Leeds and Bradford. It was from here that the vital stimulus came.

Like their Alpine predecessors, these city visitors were drawn from the ranks of the upper middle class, though generally from a point a little lower down the social ladder. Where the Alpine scientists had been professors and theorists, those who frequented Wasdale Head were more often engineers and teachers. The *Alpine Club Register* lists many clergymen, army officers of high rank and a few noblemen. Few from these categories came to Wasdale Head, which drew its recruits from the ranks of lawyers, businessmen, doctors and occasionally artists, writers and photographers. One or two had Celtic origins, O. G. Jones, for example, and the Scotsman, Professor Collie. The great majority though were English, and a surprisingly high proportion of them came from one small area. In their authoritative work, *Mountaineering in Britain*, Ronald Clark and Edward Pyatt remark on the prolific climbing families, the Hopkinsons, the Pilkingtons and the Walkers 'who lived in the triangle bounded by Alderley Edge, Liverpool and mid-Lancashire, and who dominated so many parts of the late-Victorian mountain scene'.

They were highly educated men, the products of public

school and university, steeled in the discipline of science and mathematics, the classics and the law. They approached their climbing in an academic spirit. They admired courage and skill and style. The thing they despised most of all was boastfulness. They recommended climbs to one another because they were 'interesting' or 'presented a pretty little problem'. They would debate for hours about the relative merits of certain routes, the ideal patterning of nails in their boots, whether repeated ascents made a climb more easy or more difficult. They took a lively interest in the geology of the crags, the wild life of the fells, the agriculture of the dales, the history of the Lake District and the derivations and meanings of its place-names. Their conversation, as they fought their way up difficult pitches, was often more evocative of a Senior Common Room than of a rock climb. Classicists and Senior Wranglers were much in evidence. Latin tags sprang naturally to their lips, and when Haskett Smith narrowly avoided death on one of his early climbs he found himself, by his own account, clinging to a ledge and muttering an appropriate line from Homer in the original Greek. 'Climbing then,' said Geoffrey Winthrop Young, 'had the freshness of a dawn!'

As far as is known they were men of conventional Victorian respectability. With the exception of Crowley they accepted the rigid rules of their day. Haskett Smith, O. G. Jones and Professor Collie were bachelors; the others were married and family men. None of them rebelled against the constricting formality of the middle-class way of life, but they all felt impelled to escape from its confines, briefly and occasionally, to the freedom of the fells.

By a happy chance one of the most vivid accounts of the nature of middle-class family life in the late-Victorian period is given by the daughter of one of the five Hopkinson brothers who found time, in the midst of busy and successful careers, to make a handsome contribution to the advance of rock climbing. In her book *Manchester Made Them* Katharine Chorley describes the life that her parents and her uncles led in their big houses at Alderley Edge, in Cheshire. They went up to business each day on the 8.50 or the 9.18, sitting in first-class compartments, reading *The Times* or the *Morning Post* or, most often the *Manchester Guardian*. They lunched at the Union Club, a male sanctuary. They admired brains and hard work; they saw life in hierarchical terms, and a successful career meant getting to the top of the tree. In the evenings they returned home punctually, dressed for dinner, gathered with their families in the drawing-room and devoted their energies to the observation of a complicated code of behaviour. The social system that had produced Alderley Edge was, for them, 'a fundamental article of social faith'.

To men such as they were, clever, cultured, physically strong and active, the life must have felt intolerably suffocating sometimes. Their natures cried out for escape from the smoky, overcrowded, industrial cities where they worked, and from the stuffy, controlled home-life in the suburbs, where propriety and cleanliness were the prime virtues, the rooms were cluttered with furniture and ornament, all physical work was done by servants, and where euphemism kept all vulgarity at bay and the legs of the ladies and even the tables were kept decently concealed.

Wasdale Head was a safety valve for adventurous spirits trapped in a strait jacket of social convention. The sense of release and freedom which they derived from their mountain adventures is a recurring theme of their writings. Every account of the community which formed at the Wastwater Hotel paints the same picture of a relaxed and masculine atmosphere in which a man could do as he pleased, wear his most disreputable clothes, get them filthy, argue his climbing theories interminably, sing, smoke, shout banter and play violent and noisy indoor games till a late hour, and no one would require him to 'be careful' or 'mind the antimacassar', 'change your shirt' or 'wipe your feet'.

If this book has any single hero, it is an archetype, that much-maligned figure the Victorian middle-class English gentleman. The qualities he exemplified, sturdy independence and abounding energy, curiosity and thoroughness, have fallen out of favour in the twentieth century. Yet largely because of them, he led the world in scientific and industrial development and in the building of political and social democracy; his steamships carried the world's commerce, his banks and finance houses managed its business; his Navy ruled the waves and his soldiers, administrators and traders built and controlled a vast empire. Science had revolutionized his life, making it suddenly comfortable and secure. He believed in progress and in his ability to control his destiny.

For the first time in history a large class of men found themselves with enough money and time and energy to devise elaborate sporting pastimes. Before this only the topmost layers of society had been privileged to this degree, but their conception of sport was traditionally confined to activities which involved the nurture of dogs and horses and the slaughter of most other creatures.

The Victorian middle-class gentleman took the ancient pastimes of English village life, adapted, codified and organized them, and virtually created all the sports that occupy the spare time of modern man. The Football Association was formed in 1863, the Football League began in 1888. The first county championship cricket matches were played in 1873, the first test match against Australia in 1880. The game of lawn tennis was invented in 1874, and three years later the All-England Croquet Club at Wimbledon arranged a tennis competition to raise some money. In the mid-1880s what Mr Punch called the 'Golf Stream' began to flow south from Scotland. Rugby Union received its rules in 1871, and by the end of the decade the series of home internationals had started. In 1886 Lord Queensberry drew up the code of rules which transformed fist-fighting into boxing. The Amateur Athletic Association was formed in 1880.

There were men though who craved more dangerous and individualistic sports. In the middle years of the century they invented Alpine mountaineering. Later, turning nearer home, they devised rock climbing, pot-holing and small boat sailing.

Some of the passages in R. T. McMullen's book *Down*

Channel reveal the kinship between climbing and sailing. 'I will never forget,' he wrote, 'the twelve-miles thrash to windward, with headsails sheeted like boards and the mainsheet slightly eased. It was terrible, but it was also exceedingly interesting and very grand.' And of another voyage, he said: 'In a sense of supreme satisfaction—perhaps exultation—at seeing the canvas well set, everything in its place, the beautiful surroundings, the extraordinary independence—in fact everything successful beyond almost a presumptuous expectation—I had better reason to be contented than can ever be known to anyone else.' McMullen, the inventor of single-handed ocean sailing, took pleasure too in cliffs and mountains. 'Nothing is more invigorating and delightful,' he said, 'or better calculated to make one forgetful of little ills, than landing at a picturesque spot for a few hours' scramble on cliffs and rocks.' In this way, he came to know many of the climbers' haunts, including the mountains of Arran and Skye, Ben Nevis and Glencoe.

The first rock climbers rarely tried to analyse or define their motives. Their attitude to the sport was practical and workmanlike. They professed no large and mystical sense of communion with God or nature, as their Alpine predecessors often did. Nor, in contrast to the group of leading pioneers who succeeded them in the early years of the twentieth century, the men of Pen-y-Pass in Snowdonia, did they seek to distil the essence of their feelings in poetry and fine prose. They climbed, quite simply, because they enjoyed it, and they climbed hard because it was in their nature to pursue excellence.

They wanted to be 'stretched', to be totally involved. Rock climbing is a sport that demands complete concentration, and calls into play almost the whole of a man, his muscles, balance and nerve, his courage and his mental self-control. It makes two basic challenges; the simple, physical challenge presented by steep and difficult rock routes, and the subtler, subjective challenge of retaining the power to behave coolly and sensibly in hazardous situations. Its rewards are a sense of fitness and well-being, the pleasures of companionship and achievement, and above all the feeling of being intensely alive.

The man who made the first rock climb of all, Samuel Taylor Coleridge, described this feeling more powerfully and accurately than any of the men of the 'Golden Age':

> 'I never find myself alone within the embracement of rocks and hills, but my spirit courses, drives and eddies, like a Leaf in Autumn; a wild activity, of thoughts, imaginations, feelings, and impulses of motion, rises up from within me—a sort of *bottom-wind*, that blows to no point of the compass, and comes from I know not whence, but agitates the whole of me; my whole Being is filled with waves . . . The farther I ascend from animated Nature, from men, and cattle, and the common birds of the woods and fields, the greater becomes in me the Intensity of the feeling of life.'

The gentlemen 'tigers' of the 1880s did not often commit their experiences to print, and when they did they usually confined themselves to plain narrative. Haskett Smith's pocket volume *Climbing in the British Isles: England* is an informative and academic survey of the climbing grounds of the country, but almost devoid of personal reminiscence or statement. He does, however, allow himself to say, in the introduction, that rock climbers 'experience the exquisite pleasure of forming their own plans of attack, of varying the execution of them according to their own judgment, and finally of meeting obstacles, as they arise, with their own skill and with their own strength, and overcoming them without the assistance of a hired professional'.

The next generation, the men of the 1890s, were less reticent. O. G. Jones, in the introduction to his book *Rock Climbing in the English Lake District*, wrote: 'It satisfies many needs; the love of the beautiful in nature; the desire to exert oneself physically, which with strong men is a passionate craving that must find satisfaction somehow or other; the joy of conquest without any woe to the conquered; the prospect of continual increase in one's skill, and the hope that this skill may partially neutralize the failing in strength that may come with advancing age or ill health.' For Jones the thrill of climbing became a physical need. He rarely described his feelings directly but they show clearly through his narrative. In the passage about Raven Crag Gully he says, 'when we peered up into its dark recesses we felt that good sport was at last before us'; and when the Gully is climbed he says, 'Well! we had a rare little fight; the gully had taken us an hour and 20 minutes of continuous work, and we voted it a piece of solid good business.' Most revealing of all is the picture he draws at the conclusion of his ascent of Collier's Climb on Scafell Crag. It had been a hard struggle on a steep and exposed route, but he was splendidly fit from many days of climbing and enjoyed the strong support of the Abraham brothers. Near the top he threaded the rope behind some jammed stones for greater security and sat for a few minutes on a tiny ledge with his legs dangling over the drop: 'I flung some loose stones far out into space and could only just hear a faint clatter as they touched the scree. Now was the time to appreciate the joy of climbing, in perfect health, with perfect weather, and in a difficult place without danger.'

The writings of Jones and Lehmann Oppenheimer and particularly George Abrham are alive with a swashbuckling spirit of adventure and seem to have derived their dialogue style more from Victorian stage melodrama than from life. Cries of 'What ho!' echo among the cliffs. J. W. Robinson points to Kern Knotts Crack and utters a solemn warning. 'Well, Jones, if you climb that crack I'll never speak to you again!' And Jones himself is made to cry, 'Promise me you'll never climb C Gully on the Screes! It's a deadly place!' For George Abraham, Jones is 'our indomitable leader', and capable of feats of strength and agility which the strong men of later generations have sometimes doubted. Could he really do a one-arm pull-up onto a bar with another man tucked under his other arm? Did he ever, in fact, climb up Kern Knotts Crack and down the Chimney on the other side in seven minutes?

George Abraham was the willing victim of his own enthusiasm, and loved to create or perpetuate a colourful legend. He wrote, for example, that the Pendlebury Traverse on the east face of Pillar Rock was first climbed 'by the famous Senior Wrangler after walking from Keswick in his smoking-room slippers'. The Senior Wrangler, top Cambridge mathematician of his year, was Richard Pendlebury, who made the climb with his brother William and Frederick Gardiner. Never very likely, the story was exploded many years later by William Pendlebury, who said the 'smoking-room slipper' story was 'bosh' and, in fact, the route had been led by Gardiner.

If Abraham's evidence is suspect at times for its flamboyance, that of many others suffers from too much restraint. They wrote in the mood of mellow reminiscence, courteously remembering the courage and comradeship of the times and forgetting the quarrels and acrimony. Many of the sources furthermore are obituary notices and at such a time, as Dr Johnson said, 'a man is not upon oath'.

Fortunately in this respect one visitor to Wasdale Head admitted no gentlemanly restraints, and in his outspoken *Confessions* Aleister Crowley redresses the balance in the evidence single-handed.

The fells of the Lake District offered complete freedom to walkers, scramblers and climbers. Once above the 'in-take' wall, the last contouring dry-stone wall before the open fellside, a man could wander where he pleased. Although they were private property, the fells were unfenced and open. They had been spared the fate of the Peak District hills and large tracts of the Scottish Highlands, fiercely guarded by gamekeepers for the seasonal shooting of grouse and deer.

The years that saw the emergence of climbing were formative years for the Lake District in many ways. The coming of the railway to Windermere, Coniston and Keswick swelled the tide of tourists, and the villages of the central valley mushroomed into towns of hotels and boarding-houses. The conservation movement was born to keep the railwaymen and the miners out of the heart of the mountains. From his home at Brantwood the ageing Ruskin thundered against the railways and the tourists: 'I do not want to let them see Helvellyn while they are drunk.' In 1889 the *Manchester Guardian* proposed the drastic solution of nationalization. Although they failed to save Thirlmere from the thirst of Manchester's factories, the conservationists won many battles, and in 1895 the most indefatigable of them all, Canon Rawnsley, inspired the foundation of the National Trust, which was to become the greatest landowner in the Lake District.

Mountain pastimes, complementary to rock climbing, flourished as never before. M. J. B. Baddeley's classic guide to fell walking was published in 1886 and ran into many editions. More competitive and masochistic spirits devised marathon endurance tests for themselves, and some of the rock climbers were prominent in this field as well.

The legacy of the first 'tigers' was an impressive one. They showed how much could be done in places which had, before them, been considered beyond the reach of mortal man. They also bequeathed a system of grading climbs according to their difficulty which has survived to this day.

In the introduction to his book O. G. Jones lists 'some sixty well-known courses', the popular word at that time for climbers' routes, and divides them into four sets: 'The first are easy and adapted for beginners, the second set are moderately stiff, those of the third set rank as the difficult climbs of the district, and the last are of exceptional severity.' He emphasizes that his classification refers to the climbs when conditions are good, and that adverse weather will quickly promote an easy route to the difficult class.

Jones's system, using adjectives rather than numbers to describe the categories, has proved invaluable and durable, though later progress has brought additions and sub-divisions to his list. The current guide books use twelve grades. In ascending order of difficulty, they are: Moderate; Difficult; Difficult (Hard); Very Difficult; Very Difficult (Hard); Severe (Mild); Severe; Severe (Hard); Very Severe (Mild); Very Severe; Very Severe (Hard); and Extremely Severe. It is interesting to compare some of the routes listed by Jones with their grading today:

Jones's 'Easy Courses'	*Current Grading*
Deep Ghyll, Scafell, by west wall traverse	Ungraded

Cust's Gully, Great End	Ungraded, 'useful as a way down'
Broad Stand, Scafell	Moderate
Slab and Notch Route, Pillar Rock	Ungraded, described as 'easy'
Jones's Moderate Courses	*Current Grading*
North Climb, Scafell	Moderate
Pendlebury Traverse, Pillar Rock	Moderate
Arrowhead Ridge, Great Gable	Difficult
Jones's Difficult Courses	*Currrent Grading*
Napes Needle, Great Gable	Very Difficult (Hard)
Kern Knotts Chimney, Great Gable	Difficult
Scafell Pinnacle by Steep Ghyll	Difficult (Hard)
Collier's Climb, Scafell	Severe (Hard)
Great Gully, Dow Crag	Difficult (Hard)
Jones's Exceptionally Severe Courses	*Current Grading*
Scafell Pinnacle by Deep Ghyll	Severe
Kern Knotts Crack, Great Gable	Very Severe (Mild)
North Climb, Pillar Rock, by the hand traverse	Severe (Hard)
C Gully, the Screes	Very Severe (Mild)
Eagle's Nest Ridge, Great Gable	Very Severe (Mild)

It is invidious to conclude too much from the contrast. In some places, especially where the route follows small holds on the open rock face, climbs have become harder through the wearing away of small notches and holds by the passage of hundreds of heavily nailed boots. Elsewhere the routes are undoubtedly easier now than they were. Napes Needle, for example, and the hand traverse on the North Climb of Pillar are both reckoned to have become less formidable because the pebbles and vegetation that formerly clogged the vital clefts have been scraped away. Even so Jones's classification remains remarkably valid today. Three of the climbs in his list still rate the grading 'Very Severe (Mild)'. Another climb that was made after his death but before the end of the 'Golden Age', Botterill's Slab on Scafell, is rated a notch higher at 'Very Severe'.

That, though, is almost the end of the story. For the beginning one must go back many years.

2 The District Discovered

Two hundred years ago the friendly fells and dales of the Lake District were terra incognita even to the most widely travelled of Englishmen. They knew more, from their reading, about the Americas and the East Indies, and a great deal more, from direct experience, about France and Germany, the Alps and Italy.

The tides of English history washed occasionally around the mountains but not across them. Only one army ever marched over the fells and that was nearly two thousand years ago, when the legions of Julius Agricola carried the Imperial Eagle to subdue, or at least contain, the savage tribesmen of the North. Domesday Book makes no mention of the mountain region; the border raiders of later centuries turned back north of Skiddaw or swung east or west to avoid the heights; and in 1745, when the Young Pretender marched to reclaim his royal birthright, both advancing and retreating he skirted the eastern edges of the District and engaged few Lakeland loyalties. Tucked away in the north-west corner of the country, the Lake District was not on the road from anywhere of importance to anywhere at all. It endured the ignominy, and enjoyed the advantages, of almost total obscurity over many centuries.

Unlike the high and inhospitable regions of the European Alps, though, the District was not empty of life. Neolithic man grew crops and raised animals along the Cumberland coast and up the valleys some five thousand years ago, and on the scree slopes below Pike o' Stickle he founded the area's first industry, a stone axe factory. Centuries later, men of the Bronze Age built their strange stone circles and cairns, and though they made their settlements on the lower fells, rarely more than 1,000 feet above sea-level, they knew the tracks across the mountains by the high passes and used them for trade.

At the beginning of the tenth century A.D. the Vikings arrived. They came from northern Europe by way of Iceland and the Isle of Man, first as pirates, killing, looting and burning, later as immigrants, settling the upper reaches of the dales to grow crops in the valleys and graze their sheep on the slopes above. For nearly a thousand years after this their hard-working descendants dominated the scene. Their sheep, the Herdwick, formed the sturdy basis of the mountain economy until well into the twentieth century. They called themselves 'estatesmen', later shortened to 'statesmen', but the word implied only proud independence of spirit and not any political ambition. Their language bequeathed many pebble-hard little words to English landscape vocabulary—'fell' itself, for example, as well as 'beck', 'tarn', 'rake', 'pike', 'scree', 'ghyll' and others. The extent of their occupation of the area is shown to this day in the hundreds of place-names with the Viking suffixes 'thwaite' and 'garth'.

For generation after generation, century after century, the life of the dalesmen followed the same hardy pattern. It was not until the latter half of the eighteenth century that the stirring of interest began which was to rescue the Lake District from its poverty and obscurity. The movement, beginning almost imperceptibly, was to swell to a revolution—changing the character of the Lake District almost beyond recognition, and in the wider field transforming man's whole sense of his relationship with nature.

The revolution had three stages: the advent of tourism; the discovery of the pleasures of fell-walking; and then the further discovery of the intenser pleasures of scrambling and rudimentary rock climbing. Without too serious a distortion of truth, these stages can be portrayed through the impact on general English consciousness of three poets, Thomas Gray, William Wordsworth and Samuel Taylor Coleridge.

History tells of no more unlikely revolutionary than Thomas Gray. When he left the cloisters of Pembroke College in Cambridge and took the post-chaise north in October 1769 he was already over fifty, afflicted by poor health, a retiring, sensitive spirit, respected for his carefully turned reflective poems and most notably for the famous 'Elegy written in a Country Churchyard'. Yet he also possessed qualities that made him a creator, rather than a follower, of fashion: he had a confident and independent spirit, an eye that was both busy and acute, and a mastery of English prose that enabled him to convey his finest feelings with power and delicacy. He was one of the first men to see beauty in mountain scenery.

As a young man thirty years earlier Gray had travelled extensively in Europe with his friend Horace Walpole, and had been greatly impressed by the Alpine landscape. Later, as a man of culture and language, he was aware, more than most, of the fresh Romantic spirit that was stirring in France, particularly in the writings of Rousseau and the paintings of Claude—a spirit which proclaimed the superior virtue of the natural, the simple, and the unspoilt over the old classical qualities of formal order, restraint and proportion. When Gray set off for the Lakes he took with him a vital piece of equipment, his 'Claude-glass', a convex pocket-mirror, named after the painter, which was held up to frame selected parts of the view and so concentrate the eye. He gave, as he phrased it, 'much employment to the mirror'.

The journey was made at a propitious moment. 'The time was right', Norman Nicholson says in *The Lakers*, 'for the exploration of England and the discovery of the Lakes.' The crushing defeat of the Pretender in '45 and the brutal subjugation of the Highland clans that followed effectively established the Hanoverian succession and rendered the country secure. At last something was being done about England's abominable roads; turnpikes were opening and the forces of law were gradually getting the better of the highwaymen. Only a few years later Boswell was able to persuade that almost immovable figure Dr Johnson to undertake his great journey to the Hebrides. In 1768 Gray's journey to the Lakes was equally adventurous.

During the ten days of his visit Gray travelled precisely those roads which have formed the regular tourist routes ever since. From Keswick he went to the shores of Ullswater and explored Borrowdale as far as Seathwaite; then he took the road south over Dunmail Raise, through Grasmere and Ambleside and Windermere and on towards the gentler countryside of Kendal and North Lancashire. He travelled alone and kept a detailed account of all he saw and his impressions for the benefit of a friend who had been too sick to accompany him. The resulting 'Journal' was published in 1775, four years after his death.

Many hundreds of thousands of tourists have passed that way since and many of them have published their impressions, but none has surpassed Gray in freshness and sharpness and sympathy of vision. Of his visit to Ullswater he wrote; 'Walked over a songy meadow or two, and began to mount the hill through a broad and straight green alley among the trees, and with some toil gained the summit. From hence saw the lake open directly at my feet majestic in its calmness, clear and smooth as a blue mirror, with winding shores and low points of land covered with green enclosures, white farm-houses looking out among the trees, and cattle feeding. The water is almost everywhere bordered with cultivated lands gently sloping upwards till they reach the foot of the mountains which rise very rude and awful with their broken tops upon either hand.'

Gray's reaction to the crags was typical of his time and, unfairly, it is for his more extravagant flights that he is now chiefly remembered, particularly the account of his journey down Borrowdale:

> the crags, named Lodoor-banks, now begin to impend terribly over your way. . . . Soon after we came under Gowder-crag, a hill more formidable to the eye and to the apprehension than that of Lodoor; the rocks atop, deep-cloven perpendicularly by the rains, hanging loose and nodding forwards, seem just start-

> ing from their base in shivers; the whole way down and the road on both sides is strewed with piles of the fragments strangely thrown across each other and of a dreadful bulk. The place reminds one of those passes in the Alps, where the guides tell you to move on with speed, and say nothing, lest the agitation of the air should loosen the snows above, and bring down a mass that would overwhelm a caravan. I took their counsel here and hastened on in silence.

On reaching Seathwaite at the head of the valley, and contemplating the path up to Stockley Bridge and Sty Head, he succumbed completely either to the power of his over-heated imagination or, which is more likely, to the dalesman's relish for humbugging the visitor, which was not in those days so widely suspected;

> all farther access is here barr'd to prying Mortals, only there is a little path winding over the Fells, and for some weeks in the year passable to the Dales-men; but the Mountains know well that these innocent people will not reveal the mysteries of their ancient kingdom, the reign of Chaos and old Night.

The publication of Gray's 'Journal' was the beginning of the tourist boom. The Lake District, having lain unremarked through the centuries, became suddenly fashionable, the obligatory journey for all who had claims to an up-to-date aesthetic sensibility. Guide-books and illustrated maps were rushed through the presses, indicating all 'the stations', those points at which the visitor was advised to stop his carriage and get out out to assess the view. Pleasure boats were introduced on Windermere and Derwentwater. New inns sprang up and old ones were refurbished. The dalesmen revealed unsuspected talents for enterprise and showmanship. At Patterdale and Lodore small cannon were installed to amaze the tourist with startling echo effects 'at trifling expense'. Mr Pocklington of Derwentwater organized spectacular regattas and mock sea-battles, had many follies built and a 'Druids' Circle', and employed an old crone to lend character to the Bowder Stone. He advertised for a hermit who, for half a crown a day, would agree to live in a specially contrived hut for seven years, speaking to no one, never washing and allowing his hair and nails to grow unchecked; but there were no takers. At Keswick Mr Peter Crosthwaite laid out a path to the summit of Latrigg and opened his remarkable museum where tourists could exclaim over a most heterogeneous collection of articles, including a variety of rocks and coins, Indian bows, caps and ornaments, and a Chinese gong.

Although the revolution came quickly in terms of the rhythm of Lake District life in the preceding centuries, it was spread over a generation and did not gather full momentum until the closing years of the eighteenth century. Even then the fells themselves were hardly disturbed. The fashionable visitors kept to the valley roads. Their quest was for 'the picturesque', for that perfectly composed but natural picture which had a foreground of fields and trees and, above all, water, set off against a noble backdrop of mountains and sky. The exercise they sought was not for the legs but for the eye and the fancy and, doubtless, the tongue. Like Thomas Gray before them and that subtler analyst of the mountain scene, John Ruskin, in the next century, they rarely swerved from the belief that the most aesthetically satisfying vantage point is found in the valley. Like most of those who visit the District to this day, they felt no urge to explore higher ground.

There were, however, exceptions, and none of them more exceptional than that bucolic old campaigner Captain Joseph Budworth. Hardened by years of service in India, and undeterred by the loss of an arm at the Siege of Gibraltar, he visited the District in the summer of 1792 with a friend, Mr William Noble of London. In his book, *A Fortnight's Ramble to the Lakes*, Budworth wrote: 'We were exactly one fortnight with constant fine weather, during which we walked upwards of 240 miles, besides boat and chaise conveyance.'

The Captain brought a new attitude to 'Laking'. He had a sharp eye for a pretty girl or a local character; he also had a capacious belly and devoured Gargantuan meals. But between whiles, he took to the fells. With local guides to show the way he clambered up Helm Crag and Coniston Old Man, Dollywaggon

Pike, Helvellyn and Skiddaw. 'He was the first of all the travellers to begin to see the fells as a physical challenge', says Norman Nicholson.

Budworth's account, except when he lapses into Augustan verse, conveys the enormous gusto of the man. On their way down Helm Crag, when it began to rain, he 'could not help expecting and wishing we could have had a thunderstorm'. And of a later ascent he writes, 'The air upon the mountains is so clear, I fancied myself as brisk as the sheep around me; and the hilarity I enjoyed was such as I have felt after drinking champagne, with the difference of a longer continuance without the relaxation it occasions.'

The Captain conquered no peaks that could not be managed by a modern schoolgirl in three or four hours of easy trudging. His spirit seems remarkable only when it is contrasted with that of his climbing contemporaries. Their descriptions of their mountaineering experiences carry 'Gothick' fantasy up to and sometimes beyond the point of outright dottiness. When Mr William Hutchinson of Barnard Castle ascended Skiddaw and a thunderstorm came on, the guide lay on the ground 'terrified and amazed . . . accusing us of presumption and impiety'. Another, beginning the ascent of Blencathra by way of Scales Fell, '. . . was suddenly taken ill and wished to loose blood and return'. Dr John Brown looked across Derwentwater and saw '. . . rocks and cliffs of stupendous height, hanging broken over the lake in horrible grandeur, some of them a thousand feet high, the woods climbing up their steep and shaggy sides, where mortal foot never yet approached'. And two years after Captain Budworth's visit, Mrs Ann Radcliffe the novelist made her celebrated ascent of Skiddaw from the Keswick side on horseback: 'Sometimes we looked into tremendous chasms, where the torrent, heard roaring long before it was seen, had worked itself into a deep channel, and fell from ledge to ledge, foaming and shining amidst the dark rocks. These streams are subline, from the length and precipitancy of their course, which, hurrying the sight with them into the abyss, act as it were in sympathy upon the nerves, and, to save ourselves from following, we recoil from the view with involuntary horror. . . . The air now became very thin, and the steeps still more difficult of ascent. . . . About a mile from the summit, the way was indeed dreadfully sublime, lying, for nearly half a mile, along the edge of a precipice.'

To the dalesman, accustomed for centuries to roam the mountains without fear, these accounts must have seemed ludicrously extravagant. And for all Captain Budworth's pioneering *élan*, the sport of fell walking owes its original inspiration and impetus to a man who was born on the fringe of the Lake District and brought up among the fells.

William Wordsworth was born at Cockermouth in 1770. He was sent to the grammar school at Hawkshead and it was on the open fell-sides of that region that he formed the habits of hard walking and observation and communion with nature that were to sustain him through his long life.

In the early chapters of his great autobiographical poem, *The Prelude*, he portrays this formative period of his life with a vigour and a vividness that he never surpassed:

> I held unconscious intercourse with beauty
> Old as creation, drinking in a pure
> Organic pleasure from the silver wreaths
> Of curling mist, or from the level plain
> Of waters coloured by impending clouds.
> . . . .—the earth
> And common face of Nature spake to me
> Rememberable things.

Wordsworth found in walking an unfailing joy. At the age of twenty he took a university friend, the Welshman Robert Jones, on an extensive walking tour in France, the Alps and Italy (Mont Blanc had been climbed for the first time some four years before). It was a most eccentric thing to do. The poet's biographer Mary Moorman, writes: 'Their acquaintances at Cambridge prophesied disaster. "Pedestrian tours", on such a scale at least, were then unknown among "gentlemen", who if they went abroad at all did so generally as tutors to some nobleman's son making the "grand tour". Wordsworth and Jones may be regarded as the pioneers of the great company who, from their day to the hikers and ramblers of our own, have claimed the right to walk for pleasure over hill and dale.'

Like Felix, Wordsworth kept on walking—all his life. When he finally settled at Grasmere with his sister Dorothy he gathered around him a company of friends and admirers—Coleridge, de Quincey, Southey and others—whose daily and often nightly pleasure it was to walk and talk together among the mountains. Their enthusiasm and stamina were prodigious. Dorothy's Journal is, to a large extent, a record of endless rambles, which ranged from gentle evening strolls along the verges of Grasmere and Rydal Water to major excursions when the poets, Wordsworth and Coleridge in particular, would tramp for days on end to explore the remoter valleys and passes of the District. When Coleridge lived at Greta Hall in Keswick, thirteen miles or so from Dove Cottage in Grasmere, no one thought twice before setting off in the morning for a neighbourly call, to return home under the stars that same evening.

Wordsworth was a great walker but not a graceful one. Few men had had their appearance more closely and more critically scrutinized, analysed and described than his was by Thomas de Quincey. According to de Quincey the local people said Wordsworth 'walked like a cade', a cade being 'some sort of insect which advances by an oblique motion'. He recalls walking one summer evening in Langdale alongside Dorothy and a little behind William and how she was shocked and mortified at the droop-shouldered 'meanness' of her brother's gait. 'He was, upon the whole,' writes de Quincey, 'not a well-made man. His legs were pointedly condemned by all female connoisseurs in legs; not that they were bad in any way which would force itself upon your notice—there was no absolute deformity about them; and undoubtedly they had been serviceable legs beyond the average standard of human requisition; for I calculate, upon good data, that with these identical legs Wordsworth must have traversed a distance of 175,000 to 180,000 English miles—a mode of exertion which, to him, stood in the stead of alcohol and all other stimulants whatsoever to the animal spirits; to which indeed he was indebted for a life of unclouded happiness, and we for much of what is most excellent in his writings.'

Those ungainly legs had served Wordsworth in their time for something more adventurous than hard walking. In the first book of *The Prelude* he remembers birds-nesting among the crags when a schoolboy:

Oh! when I have hung
Above the raven's nest, by knots of grass
And half-inch fissures in the slippery rock
But ill-sustained, and almost (so it seemed)
Suspended by the blast that blew amain,
Shouldering the naked crag, oh, at that time,
While on the perilous ridge I hung alone,
With what strange utterance did the loud dry wind
Blow through my ear! the sky seemed not a sky
Of earth—and with what motion moved the clouds!

It is the first suggestion in literature of the exhilaration and the heightened perception that rock climbing gives.

The young Wordsworth was following local custom when he clambered about the cliffs. For centuries shepherds and farmers, huntsmen and quarrymen, as well as exploring boys, had put their strength and nerve to the test in steep places. In Borrowdale, as in other valleys too, they kept 'a long and strong rope, by subscription, for the purpose of letting men down into the rocks to take the nests and young of eagles'. Thomas Gray talks of meeting the farmer 'that last year plundered the eagle's eirie . . . he was let down from the cliff in ropes to the shelf of rock'. But though the dalesmen were prepared to venture onto the cliffs to discourage birds of prey or rescue crag-bound sheep, and though they must at times have felt something of the thrill which Wordsworth recollected so powerfully in tranquillity, it never occurred to them that this could become a sport in its own right.

The first man to have intimations of this was Wordsworth's friend and companion, Samuel Taylor Coleridge. A few years before, each inspiring the other, they had explored the nature of poetry and poetic language together and swept away the old classical conventions. Now they explored the fells. In this pursuit it was Coleridge who was the more adventurous, despite his heavy burden of trouble; he was in poor health, already addicted to opium, and his marriage had turned sour. Wordsworth liked to talk as he walked; Coleridge preferred to walk alone—'I *must* be alone', he said, 'if either my Imagination or Heart are to be enriched.'

At the beginning of August 1802 Coleridge set off alone from Keswick on a remarkable walking tour. He called it his 'circumcision' and described the journey in letters to the woman he loved, Sara Hutchinson:

'On Sunday August 1st—½ after 12 I had a Shirt, cravat, 2 pair of Stockings, a little paper and half a dozen Pens, a German book (Voss's Poems) and a little Tea and Sugar, with my Night Cap, packed up in my natty green oil-skin, neatly squared, and put into my net Knapsack, and the Knapsack on my back and the Besom stick in my hand, and off I sallied. . . .'

He tramped over the north-western fells, across to the sea at Egremont, then up to Wasdale Head. On 4th August, 'this first downright summer Day that we have had since the beginning of May', he climbed Scafell and sat down to write again to Sara—'surely the first letter ever written from the top of Sca'Fell'.

About four that afternoon he began his descent, and made inadvertently the first rock climb on record:

> 'There is one sort of Gambling to which I am much addicted; It is this, When I find it convenient to descend from a mountain, I am too confident and too indolent to look round about and wind about 'till I find a track or other symptom of safety; but I wander on, and where it is first possible to descend, there I go, relying upon fortune for how far down this possibility will continue. So it was yesterday afternoon. I passed down from Broadcrag, skirted the Precipices, and found myself cut off from a most sublime Crag-summit, that seemed to rival Sca'Fell Man in height, and to out-do it in fierceness. A ridge of Hill lay low down and divided this Crag (called Doe-crag) and Broad-crag. . . . I determined to go thither; the first place I came to that was not direct Rock, I slipped down, and went on for a while with toler-

> able ease—but now I came (it was mid-way down) to a smooth perpendicular Rock about 7 feet high—this was nothing—I put my hands on the ledge and dropped down—in a few yards came just such another, I dropped that too—and yet another, seemed not higher—I would not stand for a trifle so I dropped that too, but the stretching of the muscles of my hands and arms, and the jolt of the Fall on my Feet, put my whole Limbs in a *Tremble*, and I paused, and looking down, saw that I had little else to encounter but a succession of these little Precipices—So I began to suspect that I ought not to go on but then unfortunately though I could with ease drop down a smooth Rock 7 feet high, I could not climb it, so go on I must . . . every Drop increased the Palsy of my Limbs—and now I had only two more to drop down—to return was impossible—but of these 2 the first was tremendous, it was twice my own height and the Ledge at the bottom was so exceedingly narrow, that if I dropt down upon it I must of necessity have fallen backwards and of course killed myself. My Limbs were all in a tremble—I lay upon my Back to rest myself.

When he had calmed down a little, Coleridge says he began to laugh at himself for a madman. Then, in a state of 'almost prophetic Trance and Delight' he blessed God out loud for the powers of reason and the will, 'which remaining, no Danger can overpower us'.

'I arose . . . at the bottom of the third Rock that I dropt from, I met a dead Sheep quite rotten. . . . I glanced my eye to the left and observed that the Rock was rent from top to bottom—I measured the breadth of the Rent and found there was no danger of my being *wedged* in, so I put my Knap-sack round to my side and slipped down as between two walls, without any danger or difficulty.'

Coleridge's nomenclature is shaky but there can be no doubt that he had descended Scafell by the route which is now known as Broad Stand and which is still graded as a rock climb, although only of a 'moderate' standard of difficulty.

His spirits were uplifted by the adventure. As he walked down to Eskdale that evening he was caught in a sudden thunderstorm: 'O how I wished for Health and Strength that I might wander about for a Month together, in the stormiest month of the year, among these places, so lonely and savage and full of sounds.' He came to a spot where the cliffs above him sent back a resounding echo, so he shouted out the names of all his friends, then those of his children, then 'Joanna' in honour of the heroine of a new Wordsworth poem, and finally the name of 'Dr Dodd', a notorious forger of the time, was sent rebounding about the crags.

It is a superb picture, this solitary, wet and already slightly portly figure, in the words of de Quincey 'the largest and most spacious intellect, the subtlest and most comprehensive that has yet existed among men', a mind capable of grappling with the most convoluted intricacies of German metaphysics, yet capable also of responding with animal high spirits to the splendour of wild places and wild weather. Had his career and ill health and domestic misery not taken him inexorably away from the mountains in the years that followed, Coleridge might have become the father of rock climbing. In the event, that title was not to be earned until eighty years later.

A few weeks after his 'circumcursion' Coleridge visited Buttermere and set off, in pouring rain, to clamber up Moss Force on the northern slopes of Robinson. He wrote to Sara: 'I climbed up by the waterfall as near as I could, to the very top of the Fell—but it was so craggy—the Crags covered with spongy, soaky Moss—and when bare so jagged as to wound one's hands fearfully—and the Gusts came so very sudden and strong, that the going up was slow and difficult and earnest—and the coming down, not only all that, but likewise extremely dangerous. However I have always found this *stretched and anxious* state of mind favourable to depth of pleasurable Impression, in the resting places and *lownding* Coves.'

3 The Pioneer Pillarites

During the early years of the last century the Napoleonic Wars effectively denied European travel to the English, and the Lake District profited. The tourists rarely deviated from the traditional north–south route through the centre of the District. The more enterprising of them would take the carriage across the sands of Morecambe Bay and proceed through Coniston and Hawkshead to join the mainstream at Ambleside. But hardly any visited the remote and starker valleys of the west, Ennerdale and Wasdale, where rock climbing was to be born.

For fifty years after Coleridge's visit, the sport made little progress. The single notable event was the conquest of Pillar Rock.

The summit of Pillar Rock is the only one in the Lake District which cannot be gained without some climbing, without using the hands and feeling some sense of exposure. Known to the dalesmen of those days as 'The Pillar Stone', towering like a great dome above the Ennerdale valley, black and forbidding yet challenging as well, it was a general ambition among the dalesmen to be the first to stand on its summit.

The 1825 edition of Otley's *Guide to the Lakes* described it as 'unclimbable'. Within a year a shepherd, John Atkinson, set off alone up the long valley of the Liza to establish the honourable climbing tradition whereby predictions about the impossible are promptly confounded. The outcome was recorded in *The Cumberland Paquet and Wares Whitehaven Advertiser* of 25th

July 1826: 'On the 9th inst. Mr John Atkinson, of Croftfoot, in Ennerdale, succeeded in attaining the summit of the rock called the Pillar Stone, and although the undertaking had been attempted by thousands before him it was always relinquished as hopeless. . . . His dog, the faithful attendant of the shepherd, lay by his staff at the bottom, and, as if conscious of the danger his master was incurring by the attempt, uttered the most piteous cries during his absence. The only precaution he took for his descent was placing pieces of moss on the track by which he ascended.'

Before the year was out three more shepherds had climbed the Rock, J. Colebank, W. Tyson and J. Braithwaite. It is not recorded which route was taken by those early 'Pillarites', but the 'Old West' seems likeliest, the easiest line and one which modern guides disdain to grade for difficulty.

The next known ascent, this time definitely by the 'Old West', was made by Lieutenant Wilson R.N., of Troutbeck, in 1848, 'the first amateur who ever scaled the Pillar Stone', according to Haskett Smith. He was also the first to leave his name on the summit, in a ginger beer bottle. C. A. O. Baumgartner, who climbed the Rock two years later, wrote: 'In the small cairn on the summit I found a glass bottle, well corked, placed upright (I believe), neck downwards, between the stones, containing a paper recording the names of the previous visitors. The bottle was about one-third, perhaps less, full of water, which I poured out; and having added my own name to the visitor's list, I restored the bottle to its place.'

This summer visit by Baumgartner was doubly significant: it is the first time that a mountaineer of some dedication appears on the scene; and the first time the name of William Ritson of Wasdale Head enters the story.

Baumgartner was born in Geneva in 1825, educated at Rugby School and Oriel College, Oxford, and at the age of twenty-two became the first man to scramble along the Crib Goch ridge of Snowdon. He was twenty-five when he came to Wasdale Head. Long after, in a letter to George Seatree, he described the visit:

> Having from earliest infancy had a propensity to climbing—even *before* I could walk, I am told—and having ascended most of the mountains of any note in the Lake District, as well as most of the break-neck places I could find wherever I went—I was naturally attracted by the fame of the 'Pillar Stone' or Rock . . . I went to Wasdale Head and made known my intentions to try the Pillar Stone; and was accompanied by William Ritson and another man to the Pillar Mountain. They were sceptical as to my chances of success; and, to test my powers, they diverge a little on the route, to a small but rather perpendicular rock, not more than 10 or 15 feet high, I think, and requested me to climb that. It was not very easy—I forget the precise nature of the difficulty—but I succeeded in surmounting it. They then said it was all right: I could climb the 'Pillar Stone'. . . . Ritson then took me to the top of the Pillar mountain and to the cleft or gap that separates it from the Pillar Stone. There we descended to the bottom of the cleft—beyond which Ritson would not go. Here he pointed out to me a narrow track on a level ledge of rock winding round the side of the Pillar Stone. This I followed till it brought me to the north side of the rock, losing sight of Ritson, who sat down on the side of the Pillar Mountain, awaiting the result. When I reached the back of the Rock, or rather the *front* of it, looking towards Ennerdale and Buttermere, it was simply a matter of climbing up by the hands more than by the feet, wherever the perpendicular faces of the stones and rocks appeared most practicable and presenting the best chance of access to the next stage above. On the way up, if I remember right, I occasionally piled a few stones here and there on prominent points, to serve as landmarks for the descent. . . . I found no serious difficulty in reaching the top, where I gladly responded to Ritson's shouts of congratulation.

It seems from this as if Baumgartner made a new route, up the east and north sides of the Rock by what came to be called 'The Old Wall Route', another line which is now regarded as too easy to be graded.

Baumgartner, a strongly built man of Swiss extraction, was an adventure-seeker. Soon after his ascent of Pillar, he was working on the Bendigo gold fields in Australia as a digger and then as an assayer; but he was back in England, living in Hammersmith and keeping his muscles in trim with heavy dumb-bells, in time to climb a little with Haskett Smith in the 1880s. By his visit to Wasdale Head in 1850, when he also climbed Broad Stand on Scafell, he became the inaugurator of a distinguished line of educated and intelligent men who went to Cumberland to seek out more testing routes on the crags.

The next three decades transformed the scene at Wasdale Head. The tiny trickle of climbers grew into a steady stream; gradually the near monopoly of local people, seeking a day's escape from the town for pleasurable exercise on the rocks, gave way to the growing number of men from farther afield with more serious ambitions.

The detailed history of this period would have been lost but for the work of George Seatree. Born in the mining village of Alston, he moved to Penrith, where his job as a corn dealer took him to all parts of Cumberland and Westmorland. He started climbing, on Pillar Rock, in the 1870s and continued, always with Pillar as his chief interest, until well into the twentieth century. He also, fortunately, made it his business to gather as much information as he could about early climbs and climbers. His statistics on Pillar Rock show the skeleton of the developing story:

1826–1850	6 ascents
1850–1866	22 ascents
1866–1873	31 ascents
1874	10 ascents
1875	50 ascents

There were several reasons for the growth of interest in climbing which now brought enthusiasts to Wasdale Head in increasing numbers. For one thing, mountaineering was 'in the air' at this time; it was the period of the Alpine 'Golden Age'. In addition the western valleys of the Lake District had become much more easily accessible; the coastal railway which linked Maryport, Whitehaven, Ravenglass and Barrow opened in 1848; nine years later a triumph of the new engineering skills created the Furness line which joined Barrow, by way of Morecambe Bay, to Carnforth and the main line to the south;

in 1875 the narrow-gauge line to Boot in Eskdale began to carry the iron-ore to the coast and people to the mountains. And there was a third important element, the personality of Will Ritson.

Ritson was born in 1808 at Row Foot, the Wasdale farm which he later inherited. He grew up, in Seatree's words, 'into a fine type of dalesman, tall, muscular, heavy-boned and athletic'. He was a hard-working and successful farmer, a passionate fox-hunter, a champion wrestler in the Cumberland style, and an invaluable guide and companion on the fells. As a young man he must have seen Wordsworth and Professor Sedgwick and de Quincey when they walked across to Wasdale, and he made fast friends with that 'modern Athenian', Professor John Wilson of Elleray, near Windermere. Wilson was Professor of Moral Philosophy at Edinburgh University, a high Tory, a poet, and, under the pen-name of 'Christopher North', the writer of savage criticism and satire for *Blackwood's Magazine*; but he was just as active physically, and when he went to camp at Wasdale Head he joined in the local field sports with a will and considerable skill. They sailed and fished on the lake and Wilson played elaborate practical jokes on them; he challenged Ritson to a jumping contest and beat him, clearing '12 yards in 3 jumps, with a great stone in each hand—Ritson could only manage 11 and three-quarters'; Ritson beat him at wrestling 'and threw him twice out of three falls, but he owned that the Professor was "a varra bad un to lick"'. In the evenings they drank and told stories and the Professor amused them by improvising irreverent songs.

By the middle of the century Ritson was undisputed 'King o' Wasdale'. He was married by now—to Dinah Fletcher, whose family was said to have lived at Nether Wasdale for over 700 years—and had two sons. He built a small wing onto the south end of his farm to accommodate visitors. About 1856 he acquired a licence and his own pack of hounds, called his place the Huntsman's Inn, and became rapidly famous as an eccentric but incomparable host. 'Ritson,' says Seatree, 'reigned supreme. He was land-lord, waiter and customer by turns. As the nights wore on, the fun became fast and furious, the company being kept in fits of laughter by his quick-witted jokes, banter and racy stories.'

It was Ritson's boast that Wasdale had 'the highest mountain in England, the deepest lake, the smallest church, and the biggest liar'. The liar was himself; according to legend he once made himself outright winner of a lying competition by claiming that he could not enter because, like George Washington, he could not tell a lie. 'The lees Aa tell,' he said, 'isn't malicious; they're nobbut gert big exaggerations.'

Ritson stories are many, and happily preserved in Seatree's book *Lakeland Memories*. The most famous of them has the authentic note of north-country callousness: 'Ritson used to tell of a farmer in Nether Wasdale who had finished the building of a high hay-stack, and his servant-lad shouted down from the top, "Ah say, maister, hoo is Aa to git don?" The farmer looked up at him and shouted in reply, "Shut thee 'ees and walk aboot a bit".'

There is a strong element of 'one up-manship' in many of the stories, especially bespeaking the dalesman's love of deflating the pretentious 'off-comer'. To one city visitor who had been discussing his plans to marry for money, Ritson made the classic rejoinder: 'That's t' varra warst thing thoo cud think o' deein'. Oor auld Dinah theer had a five pund nwoate, an Aa nivver 'eeard t' last on't.'

No one at that time knew the high fells better than Will Ritson. As shepherd, huntsman, guide and hard walker he had amassed a knowledge and experience of the tracks among the central mountains and much farther afield that was without rival. But he saw no sense in the new craze for scrambling up the crags. Though he took Baumgartner to Pillar Rock, he did not accompany him up it; one account quotes him as explaining, 'Aa'd mair nor mysel' to think on now, an' it was ower big a risk.'

When Seatree arrived on his first visit to Wasdale he found Ritson reluctant to give any information about the Rock. And a young girl who spent a holiday in the dale with an adventurous brother recalled years afterwards, 'Auld Will Ritson was furious with us if he saw us on the rocks at the top of Yewbarrow . . . he was rough in manner and not attractive to children, and was always prophesying danger, and had no sympathy with our desire to climb.'

Ritson made his definitive pronouncement on rock climbing in 1874 when Seatree asked him if he knew of a climb they had just done on Scafell Crag to the right of Mickeldore, the 'North' or 'Penrith' climb. Ritson's reply was, 'No, an' if it's t' seeam pleeace as Aa mean Aa doan't think ye've been up. Nowt but a fleein' thing cud git up theer. What's makkin' ye fellas fash yer'sels seea mich aboot climmin' t' crags? Isn't t' fells big eneugh for ye?'

Even his opposition though was not enough to stem the rising tide. Entries in the hotel visitors' book, on these pages which have survived subsequent vandalism, bear witness to the spreading passion for hard walking and scrambling:

> Aug. 2, 1866. Arrived last night from the Crown Inn, Coniston, by Walna Scar, Ulpha and Boot. Off this morning to Buttermere by Scarf Gap and Black Sail. William Harrison, Bradford, Yorks.
>
> Jan. 1867. The Rev. J. M. Elliott of Bright. On Jan. 11 walked over the Screes from Irton Pike to Sca Fell. Weather bright and frosty; brisk wind blowing. Thermometer on top of Sca Fell showed 10 degrees Fahrenheit (or 22 degrees of frost) at 3.30 p.m. On the Screes it showed 16 degrees Fahrenheit or 16 degrees of frost at 1.30 p.m. in the shade.

Julius Elliott, who was later killed on the Schreckhorn, was a pioneer of marathon fell walking.

The next year brought an anonymous ascent of Broad Stand and the first attempt to use the visitors' book to guide the steps of possible successors:

> Oct. 1868. To ascend Scafell from Scafell Pike turn to the left when you come to the cliff that rises above Mickledore and about 15 feet below the ridge you will find a narrow cleft penetrating the rock horizontally. This is the point to begin the ascent which is quite simple. The whole thing is perfectly prac-

ticable for an active man in any weather and I do not think there is a single point where a slip would be fatal.

And in the following year another significant entry brings the first mention of Deep Ghyll on Scafell Crag:

> Aug. 1869, T. H. Murray Browne, Lincoln's Inn, London. Did Scawfell Pike by Piers Gill, and Scawfell by the direct route from Mickledore, also Pillar Mountain and Rock. The attention of mountaineers is called to a rock on Scawfell on the right (looking down) of a remarkable gill which cleaves the rocks of Scawfell and descends into Lingmell Gill. It looks stiff. Piers Gill should certainly be visited.

In 1869 two new routes were made on Scafell. Major Ponsonby Cundill of the Royal Engineers, whose favourite 'scrambling ground' was St Sunday Crag, climbed the 'North' or 'Penrith' route, the climb which Ritson was still refusing to believe possible five years later. And C. W. Dymond climbed Mickledore Chimney and published an account in *Prior's Guide*: '. . . there is no special difficulty until you are near the top. Here the gully of which the chimney forms the lower section, is effectually blocked for some distance, and the only alternative is to climb out of it by the rock which forms the right wall, and which is about 12 feet high, the lower 6 vertical and the upper a steep slant. This, which can only be scaled à la chimney-sweep, is exceedingly difficult, as is also the gymnastic feat of escaping to terra firma from the narrow shelf on which the shoulder and hip work lands you.'

The favourite crags though were still those on Pillar Rock. The 'first habitué of the Rock' was Dr Whitehead, a surgeon from Whitehaven. He made his first ascent in September 1850, only a few weeks after Baumgartner; three years later he climbed the Rock again and reported that 'the ginger beer bottle left by Lt. Wilson was still there, but the papers were gone and in their place a nest of black beetles! These were dislodged and in their place a piece of paper was put in the bottle with "God Save the Queen" written on it.' There was something about the summit of Pillar Rock which moved many early visitors to loyal protestation.

Newcomers began to find new lines. In 1861 the keeper of St Bees lighthouse and four friends made the first known ascent of the east side by the route that was quickly to become the most popular, the 'Slab and Notch', which is now graded 'Easy'. C. W. Dymond followed in 1865 with some Cambridge companions, and gave a detailed description: 'To ascend you pass the chasm and cross a small sloping slab of slate by means of a shallow horizontal crack at its surface. This is the most dangerous feat in the ascent, as the slab terminates at its foot in a precipice. You then immediately begin to escalade the rock.... Arrived in view of the cleft, wriggle round (a business which seemed to me the worst feature in the whole climb) as well you may, off the rock onto the green floor of the cleft, where your way is barred by a fallen rock, jammed in. A bit of tugging will, however, raise you over this, and then you easily run up to the top. This rock has one peculiarity, its descent is at least as easy as its ascent.'

In 1869, a fourteen-year-old boy, Lawrence Pilkington, was taken to the top by his elder brother Charles; these two were destined to play important roles in three allied sports, British rock climbing, guideless mountaineering in the Alps, and marathon fell racing.

The first woman to gain the summit of Pillar Rock was Miss A. Barker of Gosforth in 1870. She was followed three years later by Miss Mary Westmorland of Penrith, who was escorted to the top in rain and cloud by her brothers Thomas and Edward. A further sister, Annie, waited at the bottom 'with watch in hand', while the three stayed long enough on the summit to defy the elements with a rendering of 'God Save the Queen'. The episode was recounted in doggerel by Tom and published, under the title 'A Summer Ramble', by a local newspaper. Six years after this the Westmorland brothers built their famous cairn on the summit plateau of Great Gable to mark what in their opinion was the finest view-point in the Lake District.

The pioneer scramblers were of middle-class background and behaviour and respected the convention of leaving their names, or cards, in the summit bottle. Sadly for the historian in June 1876 two navvies climbed the Rock—it is the only appearance in this story of 'the lower orders'—and the bottle and its contents disappeared for ever.

There are two strands in the development of climbing in these embryonic years. One was formed by day picnickers from the towns around the mountains, Penrith, Whitehaven, Gosforth and so on; the other by the Alpine mountaineers, who quickly discovered that the railways had put them within easy reach of mountain country that was not necessarily beneath their notice.

Charles Packe, the Pyrenean pioneer and inventor of the sleeping bag, started tramping the fells in the early fifties, and by the close of the decade was bivouacking on the mountain tops. He introduced several leading Alpine men to the hills of Cumberland—John Ball, Thomas Hinchcliff and William Longman among them. In 1859 Professor Tyndall came up from London to climb Helvellyn in a storm. In the *Saturday Review* he wrote: 'Here was surely an antithesis to the heavy air of a London laboratory. . . . It was a day of wondrous atmospheric effects—indeed we had scarcely seen anything grander among the Alps themselves.' He was not much impressed though with Broad Stand: 'a pleasant bit of mountain practice and nothing more.' Another great Alpinist, Leslie Stephen, could not afford to be so dismissive, for in 1863 he failed to find a way up Pillar Rock: 'The atmosphere of the English Lakes,' he complained, 'is apt to be enervating.'

Some Alpine men formed more permanent associations. During the sixties and seventies the influential Harrow schoolmaster John Stogden paid regular midwinter visits to Ritson's inn to practise his step-cutting in snow and ice. Near Christmas 1869 he and two friends were exploring the summit of Great End for a likely slope to glissade down, when one of them, 'X', slipped out of control down a 45-deg. ice slope, over some rocks, then head first down another ice slope, halting himself at last by grabbing a rock. 'In about three-quarters of an hour,' Stogden said, 'we came to him terribly shaken and almost frozen, with his clothes very much torn and his right leg almost unable to move. The next three hours were not pleasant; every step had to be cut for a considerable time, and X's feet to be put in them. . . . Exercise brought back the use to his leg and the steadiness to his limbs in a way that I could not have believed possible after such a fall. Fortunately the moon came out, and by its help we managed to find our way down to Wasdale, and appeared at the hospitable doors of Ritson about 8.15 p.m.'

The following March Stogden described this incident and the holiday as a whole in a paper he read to the Alpine Club. It was published in the next edition of the Club's Journal, the first time the Journal had recognized the existence of British hills, although there had been articles about the mountains of Spain, the Carpathians, the Caucasus and the Himalayas. Stogden ended his paper with the words: 'I am sure that anyone who will make the experiment of a winter expedition for himself will find most ample reward. The mountaineering on the higher summits is everything that can be wished, crevasses excepted. The only thing is it has to be sought to a certain extent.'

The attitude of the Alpine men was not calculated to lead them to great achievements in the Lake District. Many thought the fells altogether unworthy of attention, and many others followed Stogden in seeing in them nothing more than the chance of a little off-season practice in snow and ice technique. In the late seventies and early eighties Eustace Hulton, a Manchester merchant, organized spring meets of the Alpine Club in the Lake District and North Wales, but they were more sociable than serious and the presence of 'the ladies' inhibited exploration.

Even when proficient Alpinists paid summer visits to the crags their achievement was not impressive. The Pendlebury brothers, for example, William and Richard, failed in their first attempt to climb Pillar Rock. When they next tried, in September 1872, with another Alpinist, Frederick Gardiner of Liverpool, they succeeded and even made a variation on the 'Slab and Notch' route, the 'Pendlebury Traverse', which was regarded with awe for a while but is now graded no higher than 'Moderate'.

In the event rock climbing was to owe its birth neither to the Alpine men nor to those dedicated scramblers from the market towns bordering the Lake District; it was to prove the work of young men without Alpine experience who lived and worked, for the most part, in cities.

Before that moment came, however, one remarkable and original ancient strode onto the scene, the Reverend James Jackson of Sandwith, near Whitehaven, in Cumberland.

The climbing parson was a familiar enough figure already. Several of the Alpine pioneers had been clergymen of the new school of muscular Christianity, seeking communion and fulfilment among the noblest of God's works. Snowdonia too in the middle years of the century received regular visits from a hard-walking man of the cloth, who tramped the hills inexhaustibly in all weathers, usually alone, and aided only by an eight-foot pole. His aim, according to J. H. Cliffe, was 'to follow the sky-line . . . no rocks, however rough, no precipices, unless perfectly inaccessible, ever daunted him'; his name is not on record.

There was nothing anonymous, however, about James Jackson—he saw to that. It is difficult to conceive of any other age producing such a man. He took the classic Victorian qualities—physical vigour, moral earnestness, ineffable self-confidence—and raised them to the brink of absurdity. He was saved from becoming ludicrous by his immense appetite for life, an abounding gusto which seemed to increase as he grow old.

Jackson was born at Millom in West Cumberland in 1796. He joined the Army in time to take the field against Buonaparte. He travelled widely in Europe and North America. He was vicar of Rivington, near Bolton in Lancashire, from 1823 to 1856, but his long service is remembered for one thing only, and that quite unconnected with pastoral duties. When the weathercock on the church steeple threatened to come away and the local masons shrank from going up to repair it, Jackson did the job himself 'under circumstances', as he described them, 'of terror which made the workmen recoil from the task, and gazing rustics turn sick with horror at the sight'. Safely back on the ground again, he composed 'a commemorative epigram':

> Who has not heard of Steeple Jack,
> That lion-hearted Saxon,
> Though I am not he, he was my sire,
> For I am Steeple Jackson.

An enthusiastic and ingenious versifier; all the work of his that has come down to us though is in praise not of God but of himself.

When he retired, Jackson returned to Cumberland and devoted himself to tramping the fells of the Lake District, which he loved deeply and knew extensively: 'I have knocked about among the mountains ever since,' he wrote, 'till I may almost say "I knaw iv'ry craag"'.

He was a tall, straight man, soberly garbed in clerical grey, with a bushy white beard and a bald head. Like his Snowdonian predecessor, he generally travelled alone, and the sole companion of most of his journeys was a long fell-pole. Few others could have kept pace with him. In his sixty-ninth year he walked forty-six miles in fourteen and a half hours; two days later he covered fifty-six miles in eighteen hours; then after a further day's rest, running into top form, he knocked off sixty miles in under twenty hours.

The triumph of his mountaineering life came in the early summer of 1875, when Jackson was seventy-nine years old. He had often by his own account cast 'wistful glances at the Pillar Rock'. In April of this year he determined to conquer the Rock and sought information about the best route from George Seatree of Penrith, who had launched his long career of Lakeland rock climbing the previous year with ascents of Pillar by the 'Slab and Notch' and the 'Curtain' routes. Jackson assembled an armoury of equipment—ropes, spike nails and a hammer; he had none of the inhibitions about using artificial aids which afflicted so many subsequent climbers.

With a single companion, John Hodgson, the old man journeyed up Ennerdale to make his first assault. Unfortunately they were both exhausted by the time they reached the climb. They drove four spike nails into a sloping rock (presumably the start of the 'Slab and Notch') and Hodgson went up a little way 'by means of a rope', but he soon ran into difficulty and they decided to postpone the attempt.

On 31st May they were back again. Jackson later sent a full account to the *Whitehaven News*. He told how this time a third man came along, a relative of John Hodgson's, but he refused the ascent:

> . . . but the intrepid Hodgson had no qualms of any sort and was equal to the occasion; and the wiry old man followed in his track. The spikes, driven previously into the face of sloping rock, were fortunately in the right place, and when by the aid of the rope we had mounted about the space of 6 yds, the chief obstacle was overcome, and the victory all but gained. Nothing was now wanted but a good head and a good heart, and I and my avant courier were possessed of both. After proceeding a few yards on a narrow, heath-covered ledge, Hodgson disappeared from my sight, and I awaited, in a hopeful mood, the result. At last a cry significant of success struck mine ear, and without hesitation or fear I began to climb and successfully joined my leader on the summit of the Pillar Rock. At that moment we were 'quite up-lifted' and the Queen had no two prouder or more joyous subjects in her Realm.

It was at this moment that 'Steeple Jackson' accorded himself a new title, 'The Patriarch of the Pillarites'. He left a card in a bottle, acquainting the world with his new title and achievement and, of course, his age. He also left 'some titbits of travel from Rome, Vesuvius, Loretto and Niagara in the bottle', and another card with the inscription, 'Jacobus Stylitus, with John Hodgson, ascended the Pillar Rock on the last day of the fifth month AD 1875. Written on the summit without spectacles.'

'Our last act,' his report to the paper goes on, 'in the descent was a legacy to the Pillarites of the future. Unslinging my hammer from my neck, I directed my companion to drive a long iron hold-fast into the rock for present and future use. On this we hanked the bight of a rope, Hodgson first descended, then I followed.'

The new achievement called forth a fresh outburst of self-congratulation in verse:

If this in your mind you will fix,
When I make the Pillar my toy,
I was born in 1, 7, 9, 6,
And you'll think me a nimble old boy.

A year later Jackson made his second ascent of the Pillar Rock. This time, aged eighty, he went alone. He had a cold breakfast at Ritson's hotel at Wasdale Head and set off up Mosedale at 4.20 in the morning. He was on the summit at 7.30 and back at Ritson's just after 12 noon for a celebration lunch. The equipment he took on this occasion included an embryonic *étrier*. He described the ascent in a letter to George Seatree:

> After duly surveying the route I had to pursue I was soon at the rock with the transverse nick, which has to be traversed; then I scrambled to the sloping rock which is about 6 yds in extent, and may be called the 'pons asinorum' of the climb. Into this rock I drove a spike, on which, by means of my staff, I raised a loop of a rope ladder with four rungs, hanging it on the spike; as an additional security a hand-rope was also attached to the same point, and with these appliances I gained, without slip or injury, the narrow, heather-coated ledge. About 6 yards is the horizontal extent of this ledge, when you have again to mount upward for 20 yards. Here I left my staff with its point in the ledge below, to indicate the precise place to which I should go in my down-ward course. With ungloved hands I grasped the rugged rock and in 5 or 6 minutes I stood proudly on the summit and a second time asserted my claim to be the Patriarch of the Pillarites.

The old man got a lot of fun from his exploits. On another formidable scrambler, second only in seniority to himself, Mr Maitland, he conferred the title 'Patriarch Presumptive of the Pillarites'. Jackson's ascents had been on the shorter, eastern side of the Rock, so he playfully wondered whether his title might be questioned by 'the western division of the Order of the Pillarites' and considered securing his claim by climbing the western side as well.

This, however, was not to be. On 30th April 1878 he set off from Ritson's inn to tackle Pillar Rock for the third time. He had spent the previous evening at the inn 'narrating his own mountain exploits and reciting the verses in which he celebrated them'. He went off that morning with another four-line doggerel tribute to his own prowess ready in his pocket:

Two elephantine properties were mine
For I can bend to pick up pin or plack;
And when this year the Pillar Rock I climb
Four score and two's the howdah on my back.

By nightfall the glorious, vainglorious old man had not returned. Will Ritson organized a search and three days later the body of the Patriarch was found at the foot of the Great Doup, a steep area on the northern side of Pillar mountain. Almost certainly he had fallen to his death on his way to the Rock.

Two young hill walkers were staying at the hotel at that time and had watched Jackson setting off 'with slow step' in the early morning light. One of them, Henry S. Salt, wrote many years later: 'It has been said that his vigour was unimpaired, and that the same accident might have happened to a boy, but to us, who were strangers to him, he gave the impression of much physical weakness, and, as the sequel proved, so far from being in a fit state to scale a dangerous crag, he was not capable of crossing the easy ridge which gives access to it.'

James Jackson received one posthumous honour which would have delighted his self-regarding spirit. The first book about rock climbing in England, Haskett Smith's, contains a full and friendly account of his career under the heading 'Patriarch'. He is the only individual so honoured in this rather dry and academic work; he is praised as 'a man of no ordinary stamp'; most flattering of all, he is accorded two pages more than Great Gable.

4 The Scene is Set

The claim of Walter Parry Haskett Smith to the title 'Father of English rock climbing' is not challenged. In so far as the invention of the sport as a pastime to be pursued and advanced over succeeding years was the work of any single man, he was that man. But there can be no doubt either that even if Haskett Smith had never been born the sport would have been, somewhere in Britain some time in the closing decades of the nineteenth century.

This particular 'tide in the affairs of men' was rising to its flood in the years before 1880, most evidently perhaps around Wasdale Head, but unmistakably also on the other great cliffs of this country. It cannot have been by chance that the fascinations of the sport were discovered independently and with little or no cross-reference by a number of men in a number of different regions over the next few years: J. W. Puttrell on the gritstone of the Peak District; A. F. Mummery and Aleister Crowley on the chalk of Beachy Head; A. W. Andrews and his sister on the granite cliffs of Cornwall. Nor can it have been simple coincidence that other sports of adventure were emerging at the same time; small boat sailing around the coast, and the exploration of the limestone pot-holes beneath the Pennines.

By the 1870s Alpine mountaineering was entering a new phase. All the great peaks had been conquered, most of them by that formidable combination the determined English gentleman and the experienced local guide. The next step was to find harder routes and to dispense with the guides, and the first to do this were the two young men from Lancashire Lawrence and Charles Pilkington, who climbed Pillar Rock in their teens.

They came from a cadet branch of a prosperous south Lancashire family which owned several collieries in the Prestwich and Haydock areas, and which had already established the tile factory that was to develop into the great glass works at St Helens. They had an appetite for mountain exertion. Soon after their climb of Pillar Rock Lawrence inaugurated the masochistic sport of fell running, and recorded 12,900 feet of ascent in the Lake District in twenty-one hours ten minutes. The brothers turned their attention to the Alps, and in 1878 joined forces with Frederick Gardiner of Liverpool, the true begetter of the 'Pendlebury Traverse'. In a few fine seasons in the Dauphiné they established guideless Alpine climbing as a legitimate sport. In 1879 they accomplished their greatest feat, the first guideless ascent of the Meije. Their activities aroused the prompt disapproval of the stuffier traditionalists of the Alpine Club, but when Arnold Mumm wrote his brief history of the Club many years later he paid them high tribute: '. . . the real commencement of guideless climbing on the grand scale was made by the brothers Pilkington and Frederick Gardiner. . . . It is note-worthy that they attributed their success largely to having wandered much together among the hills of the English Lake District at all periods of the year, especially in winter. Of their most prominent successors a large proportion acquired skill and self-reliance in the same training ground.'

The Pilkingtons and Gardiner, the first in a long line of eminent Lancashire men who were to make weighty contribution to the sport, epitomized the qualities of that group—particularly in the questing and generous-spirited passion that involved them in all types of climbing in many mountain ranges, and in their self-effacing modesty. They stayed at Ritson's hotel several times in the 1870s but the visitors' book records only their names against the single word 'Lancashire'; there is no record of their achievements.

In 1880 the brothers discovered the climbing possibilities of the Cuillin of Skye. The highest point of the great ridge Sgurr Alasdair had been gained seven years before by Sheriff

Alasdair Nicolson. Now the brothers tackled 'The Inaccessible Pinnacle'. Lawrence described the day for *The Scottish Mountaineering Club Journal*:

'I first visited Skye in 1880 with my brother Charles. We had only one day's climbing there as we were on our way to fish in the Hebrides with an older brother who did not climb. We had an Ornance Map with us; on it was marked 'The Inaccessible Pinnacle'. We made the first ascent. I shall always remember that as the noisiest climb I ever had. There was a foot or more of loose rock which had been shattered by the lightning and frost of ages. This formed the edge of the pinnacle and had to be thrown down as we climbed up. The noise was appalling; the very rock of the pinnacle itself seemed to vibrate with indignation at our rude onslaught.'

The brothers were impressed by the Cuillins, and Charles, who seems to have done most of the leading on their climbs, wrote to the august editor of *The Alpine Journal*, the Rev. W. A. B. Coolidge, describing their climb and concluding: 'If ever you are in Scotland be sure and visit the Coolin hills; nearly all the mountains have one inaccessible ridge, and some of them can only be got up on one side. They are like Dauphiné on a small scale and nothing in Great Britain can touch them.' Coolidge was unmoved, however, and the Alpine Club was not made properly aware of Skye until seven years later when Charles read a paper on 'The Black Coolins' and urged members to go there.

In North Wales too things were on the move. 'In January, 1882,' wrote T. W. Wall, 'from the summit of Crib Goch, Mr A. H. Stocker and myself were struck by the grand appearance of the Lliwedd cliffs, and hearing from Owen, the landlord of the Pen-y-Gwryd Hotel, that the northern face had never been climbed, the desire to make the first ascent naturally came upon us.'

Wall was a member of the Alpine Club and sent a full account of their conquest of Lliwedd to *The Alpine Journal*. On 10th January 1882 he and Stocker forced their way about 150 feet up the great central gully of the face, but rain and the severity of the great central gully of the face, but rain and the severity of the route drove them back. Their holiday was over, but they were so anxious that they gave an addressed postcard to Henry Owen and made him promise to let them know if anybody else succeeded in climbing Lliwedd. The postcard was never sent, and next winter found them back at Pen-y-Gwryd 'with 80 feet of rope and our trusty axes'. On the morning of 4th January 1883, they stood again at the foot of the cliff and decided to try the rocks to the west of the central gully.

Wall's account is the first detailed description of a difficult rock climb in Britain:

> Three bits in particular may be mentioned as far the hardest, although they are more or less typical of these crags, which nowhere offer 20 consecutive yards of easy rock-work. The first difficulty which presented itself was where the ledge was broken by a bold face of rock. One of us was pushed to the top of the smooth part, and finding that he could not descend to the ledge on the other side, he ascended a little higher, anchored himself firmly to the rocks, assisted his companion up, and let him down to the required ledge; then, throwing the rope over a pinnacle, he gave both ends to his companion to hold tight, and slid down the 40 feet of rope to join him. After a few yards of easier work we came to a ledge about 6 inches wide and 4 yards long; the rock above was nearly perpendicular, with no handhold and there was nothing below. It was the only way; we could not turn it, and somehow we got over, but neither of us wishes to be there again. From that ever-to-be-remembered ledge the climbing was grand work up to the point where we had to turn from a westerly direction to go straight up the face. Here there was a nasty corner. A narrow ledge about 2 inches wide had below it a sloping face of rock with 3 minute cracks in it. One of us had crossed this in safety, and so assumed a position in which the rope would have been of very little use. He was then opposed by a steep bit, topped by 4 feet of perpendicular rock, with a very steep slope of heather above. At the moment that his last foot left the highest peg of rock his other knee slipped, and the heather, grass and earth began to give way in his left hand. It was an awkward moment, for the other man was not well situated for supporting a jerk at the end of 30 feet of rope, which would mean a fall of about 50 feet. Happily the other knee got

on the heather and the axe held firm in the earth. Our difficulties were then over.

The climb was ahead of its time. Wall's account shows an attitude remarkably similar to that of the Lake District pioneers of a few years later; phrases like 'the climbing was grand work' and 'it was an awkward moment' were to be echoed many times in the writing of George Abraham and others. And in their careful and sophisticated use of the rope they taught a lesson which the men of Wasdale Head took another fifteen years or more to learn. Strangely, this path-finding climb on Lliwedd did not lead on to further advances. Wall and Stocker, and indeed Snowdonia itself, fade from the picture for some time, and the spotlight swings 150 miles north to Wasdale Head.

5 The Sport is Born

'A healthy mind in a healthy body' was high among the cherished tenets of Victorian belief, and in academic circles it was widely held that vigorous exercise for the body in the clear mountain air could induce vigour and clarity of thought. It was in no way remarkable then that Haskett Smith should seek out the most closely contoured area on the map when he was asked to arrange a reading party for some Oxford friends. He chose Wasdale Head, and in the summer of 1881 he spent two months there.

Walter Parry Haskett Smith was twenty-two. Born at Trowswell, near Goudhurst, in Kent, he had been educated at Eton and made there the first of his 'first ascents', up the high wall that borders one side of the famous playing fields. He went to Trinity College, Oxford, to study classics and made a name for himself as an athlete. Proficient in hurdling and throwing the hammer, he as outstanding in the long jump—one leap of more than 24½ feet failed to go down in the university record book only because it had been achieved in practice and not in competition. In 1880 he took a second class degree in Classical Moderations; when he came to Wasdale Head the following year he was reading for his degree in Literae Humaniores.

He and his friends spent their first month at Rawhead, Dame Tyson's teetotal farm; 'and this', Haskett Smith said, 'was a great stroke of luck, for here we found and became acquainted with Mr. F. H. Bowring'.

Although Bowring was nearly forty years older than Haskett

Smith, they found their outlook and interests so similar that a strong friendship was immediately formed. Frederick Herman Bowring came of a West Country family, propserously engaged in the clothing business. At Cambridge he studied the classics and mathematics, gained distinction as a high though not the Senior Wrangler, and was elected a Fellow of Trinity. He read for the bar and practised chiefly before the Privy Council. Like Haskett Smith, who was also to go on to a career at the bar, he was a university athlete of note and a specialist in the long jump—he once cleared twenty-one feet, an impressive achievement in the primitive conditions of the 1840s. 'He was a man,' Haskett Smith said, 'of exceptional elasticity.' He was also a man of exceptional and undiminished vigour, mental and physical. A tireless hill walker and explorer, he had roamed the wilds of Exmoor and Dartmoor, the limestone hills of Derbyshire and the mountain regions of North Wales and the Lake District. Not a man to content himself with tourist paths, he was a pioneer explorer of the gullies on the north side of Cader Idris and of many of the easier gully routes in Lakeland, including those on the cliffs of Lingmell.

Bowring's meeting with Haskett Smith in 1881 was providential and germinal. The younger man, although he had been on a walking holiday in the Pyrenees with Charles Packe and had spent the previous summer vacation in Snowdonia with Oxford friends 'reading hard and walking hard', was ignorant of the delights of hard scrambling and rudimentary rock climbing. In Bowring, he said, 'we soon found an exhaustive catalogue of every rock and every gully in the county. For eight hours in every day we absorbed Aristotle and Plato; for six or seven we scoured the surrounding fells and climbed furiously. In this way we soon began to develop a fine taste in gills.'

Nearly forty years on, when he composed Bowring's obituary, Haskett Smith recalled the elderly gentleman's manner and appearance with vivid affection:

> He was then not far short of 60, but he still walked with a splendid swing, and climbed with great vigour and precision. His long legs were clad in thick trousers; his fine head (which strik-

> ingly resembled that of the poet Tennyson) was covered with a felt hat, the wide brim of which had been reduced to limpness by his habit of securing it in windy weather by means of an immense blue kerchief tied under his chin. The 'Norfolk' jacket was too modern for him and his usual coat bore somewhat bunchy tails with huge pockets, which contained, as a minimum, maps, compass, string, field glasses, sandwiches, the aforesaid blue bandana, gloves, a large grey woollen comforter, and several books, besides abundant materials for smoking. In his hand was a stout six-foot fell-pole with a forked spike, which he thought less liable to slip on rocks. He used his pole skilfully in descending slopes and in leaping the becks.

The summer vacation of 1881 served only to introduce Haskett Smith to Bowring and to the pleasure of scrambling up steep gullies. It was not until a year later that he made the essential break-through.

In the meantime, at Easter 1882, another small party of Oxford classicists gathered at Wasdale Head. They included Arnold Mumm, who was to become a prominent Alpinist and chief historian and registrar of the Alpine Club, and Charles Cannan, recently appointed a Fellow of Trinity, whose powerful influence was to bring many of the most brilliant young men of the day to Wasdale Head during the next decade. The men on this Easter party were aspiring Alpinists. After a hard morning's reading they went out each day to practise step-cutting in the gullies. They were favoured with an unusual amount of snow; it lay so deep that Mumm and a Christ Church man, J. E. King, later to become headmaster of Clifton School, walked one day down Deep Ghyll on the face of Scafell without needing to use their hands or ice-axes and without realizing that they had done anything remarkable.

Recalling those days many years afterwards Arnold Mumm wrote of Haskett Smith: 'I had known him for some time but thought of him as a classical scholar and an athlete and had never connected him in any way with climbing. . . . The great name to us was that of Pendlebury . . . we believed rather vaguely that he had done something remarkable on Pillar Rock.'

Summer brought Haskett Smith back to Wasdale Head, accompanied this time by his younger brother Edmund, and it was now that he began the systematic search for new routes up the big cliff faces that was to make this the year when rock climbing was truly born.

His achievement in a few short weeks of August and September in 1882 was phenomenal. The bare bones of the story may be gleaned from the lists of first ascents, recorded in the current Climbing Guides of the Fell and Rock Climbing Club:

Scafell Group:	Central Gully, Great End South-east Gully, Great End
Great Langdale Group:	Great Gully, Pavey Ark North Gully, Bowfell Buttress North-west Gully, Gimmer Crag
Pillar Group:	West Jordan Climb, Pillar Rock Central Jordan Climb, Pillar Rock

He also explored the lower pitches of Deep Ghyll on Scafell Crag, and on the Ennerdale face of Great Gable 'found that it was an easy matter to coast along the face of the cliff at about two-thirds of the height of it'.

These routes do not command high respect among modern climbers; Great Gully on Pavey Ark and the two routes on Pillar are graded 'Difficult', the others are dismissed as 'Moderate' or not categorized at all. Their significance lies not in any individual severity, but in their collective import. Here for the first time was a young man who went out day after day with a single objective, to find and master new rock routes. He was not interested in bagging summits or in following lines already established. He climbed for fun—for that esoteric enjoyment which springs from the powerful stretching of muscle and nerve and mind and the revelation of just how far a man can venture into the realm of vertical difficulty and danger. More than eighty years earlier Coleridge had noted the 'depth of pleasurable Impression' which resulted from a 'stretched and anxious state of mind'; others had undoubtedly experienced it since then; but Haskett Smith was the first to transmute the pleasure into a continuing passion.

One incident in the holiday illustrates more forcibly than anything else the speed with which Haskett Smith's climbing ambition had grown. He made an attempt, unsuccessful and nearly fatal, on the formidable north wall of Pillar Rock. Defeated by the steepness of the face, he was descending to his brother at the foot when he found he had to slide round the outside of a large block which was balanced precariously against the cliff wall. As he clung to it with his right hand the whole block, weighing about a ton, began to heel over away from the wall and onto him. 'Letting go with my right hand,' he wrote, 'I rolled over on my left side, wrenched my waist-coat free of the stone, and hung over the precipice by my left hand only. If the stone did not fall quickly I was lost. It seemed to hesitate but then came slowly over. My right hand seizing the tottering mass and weighing heavily upon it, eased for a moment the strain upon my left; then as the great stone dipped for its first plunge, my right foot swinging up onto it and kicking viciously downwards gave sufficient upward impetus to enable my right hand once more to clutch the hold above. It was a near thing; but a moment later I swung into the cleft just vacated by the stone. My arms were benumbed, my lungs empty, my mind an utter blank. I felt, rather than heard, my late enemy thundering down into the valley, and meanwhile someone near me grunting and gasping out "autis — epeita — pedonde — kulindeto — laas — anaides". The grunter was myself!'

The quotation, if it did indeed come out pat like that, was apt. It is taken from the eleventh book of Homer's *Odyssey*, when Odysseus is in Hades and watching Sisyphus at his interminable task of trying to push a great boulder to the hill-top. Each time Sisyphus is foiled at the last moment, when the boulder's weight triumphs and, in the words of Dr Rieu's translation, 'the misbegotten rock came bounding down again to level ground.'

It was this encounter with the 'misbegotten rock' that first moved Haskett Smith to wonder whether it would not be wise to use a climbing rope. Until then he had rejected the idea with the argument which every subsequent generation of rock climbers has used against every subsequent advance in equipment: 'In those days,' he said, 'we were heretical in our attitude towards the use of the rope. Not having one ourselves, we were inclined to scoff at those who had; and in the gall of bitterness we classed ropes with spikes and ladders, as a means by which bad climbers were enabled to go where none but the best climbers had any business to be.'

Mountaineering hazards were causing anxiety at this time. Earlier that summer the Rev. J. Pope had fallen to his death on the Ennerdale face of Great Gable, having stumbled when he jumped down from one ledge to another. In the Alps there had been three serious climbing accidents. Queen Victoria grew concerned, and on 24th August her private secretary wrote to her Prime Minister, 'The Queen commands me to ask you if you think she can say anything to mark her disapproval of the dangerous Alpine excursions which this year have occasioned so much loss of life.' Mr Gladstone's reply was placatory but discouraging: 'I do not wonder that the Queen's sympathetic feelings have again been excited by the accidents, so grave in character, and so accumulated during recent weeks, on the Alps. But I doubt the possibility of any interference, even by Her Majesty, with a prospect of advantage. It may be questionable whether, upon the whole, mountain-climbing (and be it remembered that Snowdon has its victims as well as the Matterhorn) is more destructive than various other pursuits in the way of recreation which perhaps have no justification to plead so respectable as that which may be alleged on behalf of mountain expeditions. The question, however, is not one of wisdom or unwisdom; but viewing it, as you put it, upon its very definite and simple grounds, I see no room for action.'

Alpine mountaineering was too firmly established to be stayed by royal disapproval; and by now its junior, if yet unrecognized, relative was beginning to flourish in the Lake District. It is happily appropriate that the birth year of rock climbing should have seen the introduction to the crags of the man who was to be its most loyal and loving and best-loved servant for more than twenty years to come. One day during that summer John Wilson Robinson walked up Ennerdale with his friend the Quaker headmaster J. E. Walker, and climbed Pillar Rock by one of its easier routes. For Robinson it was the first of more than a hundred ascents of the Rock, the first of many hundreds of climbs on the crags of Cumberland.

Robinson was a dalesman. He was born in 1853 at Whinfell Hall at Lorton, the tiny village where the north-western fells decline towards the Derwent valley and the market town of Cockermouth. The family were devout Quakers, and the boy was sent to the Friends School at Ackworth and remained a Quaker all his life, eschewing tobacco and alcohol. After school he took over the management of his father's farm, worked hard and prospered, married, and played an active part in local government. He became a mighty fell walker—Seatree records that he once covered seventy miles over all the principal summits of the District within twenty-four hours—and this, combined with an instinctive eye for routes and a photographic memory for landscape, gave him an unrivalled acquaintance with the fells. A normal day's holiday for him would involve rising at 3 a.m., tramping down the Vale of Lorton past Crummock Water and Buttermere, striking across country in the early morning light to meet a friend to climb all day on Gable, returning home by the same route that same evening. The fells were his adventure playground, and they later became in part his responsibility, for in 1895 he began a new career, as an estate agent based in Keswick, and acquired the management and oversight of many large estates, including the one that covered the Napes face of Great Gable.

Robinson was a Lake District man whole-heartedly and exclusively. Only once did he climb elsewhere; in 1898 he went to the Alps and climbed several mountains, among them the Matterhorn. He was not impressed and did not go again.

But although his mountaineering interest was circumscribed, and despite his puritanical upbringing and beliefs, John Robinson had a nature so tolerant and unforced and friendly that he won the affection of all. He climbed with all the pioneering 'tigers', and he climbed too with hundreds of unremembered people. George Seatree wrote: 'J.W.R.'s diary tabulates between 30 and 40 ladies who have been under his kindly escort to the summit of the Pillar Rock, and the roll of the sterner sex he has led and helped up there, on to Scawfell Pinnacle, and the climbs of the Great Gable must be legion. He was never happier than when engaged in bringing strangers and novices to his favourite shrine, the Ennerdale Pillar Rock.' Baumgartner admired 'his entire freedom from any jealousy of rival climbers'. Even the waspish Crowley wrote affectionately of him. And Haskett Smith, who could also be waspish, said, 'Never was there a man more utterly unselfish, never one who so cleverly continued to give the impression that he and not you was the person benefited.'

Robinson's appearance was described by his friend Richard W. Hall: 'a well-built figure, sandy side-whiskers, extremely bald and shining head and merry blue eyes . . . His clothes were quite unorthodox, ever the same yellowish brown tweeds and breeches.' He was a neat man and his climbing style was both neat and cautious; according to Hall 'painstaking to a degree'. His qualities were to make him an invaluable foil to the greater impetuosity of Haskett Smith when the two came together, two years later, in the first formative partnership between Cumbrian and 'off-comer'.

6 The Pace Quickens

The early rock climbs were gully climbs. 'It is one great merit of a climb,' Haskett Smith wrote, 'if it clearly defines itself. . . . If you climb just to amuse yourself you can wander vaguely over a face of rock; but if you want to describe your climb to others, it saves a lot of time if you can say—"There, that's our gully! Stick to it all the way up!"'

It is an ingenious explanation but there were better, more basic reasons for this initial concentration on the gullies. They offered the most obvious lines of weakness up the cliff face; and their enclosing walls and wide ledges reduced the climber's sense of exposure. Only as the cragsman's skill and experience grew, as he tackled steeper and more ferocious gullies and found himself increasingly forced out onto the slabs, did he discover that routes could be made on small holds on the open rock face and that a man could accept and even learn to enjoy the feeling of being delicately poised over a long drop.

The disadvantage of Lake District gully climbing is that it is usually very wet and dirty and often very cold as well. Gullies collect deeper snow and retain it longer than anywhere else; in wet weather they become waterfalls and in the driest periods they are rarely free from moisture and the soggy, slimy vegetation that flourishes in such conditions. In addition, they are assembly grounds for all the loose rocks and boulders which the ravages of frost and storm have prized away from the cliffs above over the centuries. 'Chimney-sweeps' was promptly coined as a term of Alpine Club contempt; but it was adopted with equal promptness by the men of Wasdale Head, who took a masochistic pleasure in the dirt and discomfort of their surroundings and in the heavy 'gardening' they had to do to make their routes possible.

This kind of climbing put a premium on physical strength, especially in the arms, and on sheer drive and scrabbling capacity—qualities in which both Haskett Smith and O. G. Jones excelled. Later, when the need for new challenges squeezed the climber out onto the airy rock face, the subtler skills of balance, smooth movement and pinpont precision came into play.

In 1883 Haskett Smith took his finals and gained a third class in Literae Humanieres; he did not go to Cumberland. John Robinson continued to walk the fells and on Whit Tuesday he climbed the west side of Pillar Rock alone 'in 11 minutes'.

The year is most notable for a fatal accident on Pillar on Good Friday. According to Haskett Smith's account, two climbers from Bolton had been stuck for some time in the area of zordan Gap; they called for help to a young man of seventeen named Walker who was above them: 'He [Walker] thereupon endeavoured to join them by sliding down on the snow; but he had miscalculated the pace, and when he reached the rock at which he had aimed, it was only to find that his impetus was too powerful to be arrested. He shot off to one side, rolled over once or twice, and then darted away down the steep east scree, passing the Bolton men, who could not see him owing to their position, and disappeared over the precipice.' Ever since, the steep gully between Shamrock and the north-east face of Pillar Rock has been known as 'Walker's Gully'.

The following year brought two serious accidents, though neither of them was fatal and each, by coincidence, proved the beginning of an enduring friendship.

The Pilkington brothers were climbing in Piers Ghyll, the fierce and watery chasm above the head of Wasdale. Fortunately for them another group of Lancastrian brothers, the five Hopkinsons, were exploring in the same area. The day was described seventy years later by Katharine Chorley, daughter of Edward Hopkinson: 'It must have been 15 years before I was born,' she wrote, 'that father and his brothers while on holiday in the Lake District had carried Mr Lawrence Pilkington on a farm gate down to Wasdale Head from Piers Ghyll on Scafell. . . . Mr Pilkington had been making a route up the deep clefts of Piers Ghyll when a fall of stones had caught him and smashed his thigh. While one young man clattered down Wasdale on a borrowed horse to fetch a doctor the others did what they could to make the injury comfortable. So began a friendship between the two climbing families, the Pilkingtons and the Hopkinsons, which lasted through their lifetimes.'

The Hopkinson brothers were just at the start of their remarkable climbing careers; but this was the end of serious climbing for Lawrence Pilkington.

The other serious accident of 1884 occurred on the steep broken ground between Mickledore Chimney and Broad Stand, where a young medical student from Edinburgh called Petty slipped and fell 100 feet onto the scree below Mickledore. A companion ran to Wasdale Head and was lucky to catch 'an eminent surgeon' who was on the point of leaving. The surgeon published a clinical account in *The British Medical Journal*:

> The Integuments of the head and face were scraped and ground dreadfully. They were damaged to an extent exceeding anything of the kind I have ever before witnessed. The scalp and integuments of the forehead and face were hanging in tatters over the ears and eyes. The nasal and superior maxillary bones were denuded of covering, indented and bruised. The lips and chin were in rags, the eye-lids torn and livid, and all the soft parts covered with a sandy grit embedded into their substance. He was in a state of semi-coma from shock and haemorrhage, with two ribs fractured and a deep laceration on the buttocks; but, fortunately, there was no fracture of the skull. I had no appliances but pure cold water, and no instruments but a common sewing needle and some silk. After carefully picking, scraping and wiping the parts with a clean rag, dipped in the mountain stream, I stitched the different parts of the skin together with numerous and close sutures, pressed up into shape the indented nasal bones, and bound up the head and face with a wet bandage. There was no other treatment but cold water and simple diet.

The makeshift surgery proved marvellously effective. Two weeks later Petty was well enough to go home. John Robinson walked over from Lorton and, with the help of Haskett Smith and a rough handbarrow, wheeled him down from Burnthwaite at the very head of the dale to the road below the inn where a carriage was waiting.

The introduction of Haskett Smith to John Robinson was the work of F. H. Bowring. After they had seen Petty safely on his way, the three of them walked at Bowring's suggestion towards Great Gable and the scree funnel known as Hell Gate. Here Bowring left them and the two younger men began to traverse the face of the Napes cliffs on the first of many climbs together.

Until this time the Wasdale face of Great Gable had scarcely been contemplated. 'In those days,' said Haskett Smith, 'climbers had never really looked at the Napes. The vast slopes of cruel scree below them not only kept explorers away, but gave the impression that the whole mass was dangerously rotten.' Two years earlier, though, during his initial burst of exploration in 1882, when he had been investigating the Piers Ghyll area, Haskett Smith had chanced to look across the valley towards the Napes at a moment when the mists parted briefly, and had been intrigued to notice 'a slender pinnacle of rock, standing out against the back-ground of cloud without a sign of any other rock near it and appearing to shoot up for 200 or 300 feet'. Robinson knew something of this pinnacle too; more than fifty years earlier his father had found it and drawn a sketch of it. It was, of course, Napes Needle. Now as they moved across the cliff together the two men kept a sharp look-out: 'It was a jolly climb,' Haskett Smith reported, 'and before long we came rather suddenly into full view of the rock which we were seeking. Robinson's delight was unbounded, and he eagerly inquired whether any Swiss guide would be ready to tackle such a thing.'

Certainly the two new-found friends were not yet ready to tackle it. They 'threaded the Needle', passing between the pinnacle and the main Napes cliff, then scrambled up Needle Gully to the summit. Back in the hotel that evening Haskett

Smith wrote in the visitors' book, drawing attention to 'these excellent rocks'.

A few days later they climbed Needle Ridge, now graded 'Very Difficult', but, as Haskett Smith pointed out, they did it 'in a somewhat desultory fashion', avoiding the more difficult parts.

They were still moving with great caution; they were unroped and it seems likely that Robinson exercised a restraining influence. Nonetheless, they achieved notable advances on Scafell. On 3rd September Haskett Smith, on his own, gained the top of Scafell Pinnacle by the short climb from Jordan Gap, which is now known as 'the easy way'. On the 20th, this time with Robinson, he reached the same point by a much more exacting route, from Rake's Progress via Steep Ghyll and Low Man. The current climbers' guide describes this as 'a remarkable performance whatever route was taken'.

Haskett Smith also maintained his interest in Pillar Rock. He made a first ascent of the 'East Jordan Climb', though not by the route which is now followed and graded 'Hard Severe'. He took another look, too, at the 'North Climb', where he had dislodged his Homeric boulder two years before. This time, once again with his brother in attendance, he ascended about 220 feet and reached the famous 'stomach traverse' before being forced back.

The traverse was given this name because when it was first visited the narrow chimney, bending to the right, was so packed with earth that the climber had to wriggle round as best he could on his stomach. 'When the name was given,' Haskett Smith wrote many years later, 'every hold was buried under hard earth and to get round was a tough job. Now all the earth has been dug or washed out and the climber stands perfectly secure in a deep rift.'

The development of the sport was given considerable impetus this year when the popular magazine *All the Year Round*, founded by Charles Dickens and edited by Charles Dickens junior, published a long article entitled 'the Climbs of The English Lake District'.

This was the work of an engineer turned journalist, C. N. Williamson. He had no first ascents to his name, but had done a good deal of rock climbing and much research into its history. He painted a lively picture of life at Wasdale Head: 'Either at the inn, or at Mrs Thomas Tyson's famous farm-house, climbing men linger through the summer. Some come in winter, and then the surrounding peaks offer excellent practice for Swiss mountaineering. They are enthusiastic fellows, these climbers. They ascend their favourite mountains time after time; they are unwearied at finding new ways up everywhere, and their talk, when they get together, is of nicks and notches, ladders and ledges, gullies ghylls and chimneys, and even of cols, arêtes and couloirs. All Cumberland and Westmorland is familiar to them.'

Williamson's article is a clear and comprehensive survey of the rock climbs achieved, and bubbles with the optimistic, thrusting spirit of the time. Dalesmen thought Piers Ghyll would never be climbed; Robinson himself had declared that it could not be done 'by fair climbing'; but Williamson knew better: 'When we speak of climbing Piers Ghyll we do not mean merely penetrating into the fissure till further progress is barred and then climbing out up one of the sides. The Ghyll cannot properly be said to have been climbed until all the obstacles in the ravine have been overcome and the climber emerges at the top under Lingmell crags. In all probability this feat will soon be achieved.' Piers Ghyll was climbed eight years later.

Haskett Smith did not visit the Lake District in 1885; he went instead with his old friend Charles Packe to the Pyrenees, to sleep out among the mountains and look for chamois. But the year brought one powerful and influential new recruit to Wasdale Head.

William Cecil Slingsby was a man of rare quality. This is how Geoffrey Winthrop Young, who became his son-in-law, described him: 'In appearance he was a thorough Yorkshire dalesman, stalwart, broad-shouldered, full-bearded, with a classic profile, a fine complexion even in age, and shrewd, laughing, grey-blue eyes. But an abnormal endowment of vitality, of joyous active response to the passing moment seemed to surge through him, expressing itself in a continued liveliness of controlled movement, and an emphatic almost southern grace of gesture.'

Slingsby was a favourite of fortune, in his abundant natural gifts and in his circumstances. He was born in 1849 into an old and well-to-do family of Yorkshire landowners, who had reinforced their prosperity by going into textile manufacture. As a child he grew to love the moors and particularly the Craven hills around his home. He was educated at Cheltenham School.

When he was twenty-three he visited Norway with a friend and was immediately captivated by the grandeur of the mountains and the friendly simplicity of the people. A millennium or so before, Viking people from these high latitudes had raided and settled many parts of northern England; the folk of the Yorkshire Dales still retained in their dialect many of the words and sounds of the old language, and still prized the ancient virtues of forthrightness, honesty and independence; it was natural, therefore, that the young man from Craven should strike an immediate rapport with the Norwegians and return, summer after summer, to explore the glaciers and passes and high ridges of their mountains.

Slingsby learned to speak Norwegian; he learned to ski—indeed it was he who introduced ski-ing to the Alps and who taught the Norwegians themselves to see it as a sport; he became the 'Father of Norwegian mountaineering'. He made many expeditions, and first ascents without number. In one outstanding season, that of 1876, he conquered six fine peaks, widely separated, in six days, and on the last day, when his two companions refused to attempt the final 500-foot rock wall of the Store Skagastolstind, he went on and triumphed alone.

Two years later he paid his first visit to Switzerland and after this his summers were largely divided between Norway and the Alps. With A. F. Mummery and Geoffrey Hastings and Norman Collie he formed one of the most skilful and adventurous teams ever to confront the mountains.

Slingsby was a superb all-round mountaineer. He had the strength and suppleness, the steady nerve and neat precision for work on the steepest of rocks; he had acquired all the skills needed for fast safe movement on snow and ice; and he possessed to an almost uncanny degree an instinctive understanding of the lie of mountain terrain, invaluable in the exploration of unknown regions.

Although he was staunchly Conservative in politics and traditionalist in his social views, his spirit totally rejected the exclusive attitudes of the Alpine Club 'Old Guard'. He embraced action and adventure and participation of every kind. He was widely read, in history and travel and poetry; he loved music and was the organist at Carleton church for many years; and among the mountains he was interested not only in the climbing but in the wild life to be found there and the history and customs of the local people.

It was inevitable that such a man would quickly join the ranks of the pioneer cragsmen. His first recorded visit to Wasdale Head was in March 1885, with Geoffrey Hastings, his companion on many climbs in Norway and the Alps and a fellow-Yorkshireman, engaged in the worsted spinning industry at Bradford. They tried to climb Deep Ghyll but were defeated by ice-glazed rocks below the first chockstone. They were to return the following year.

In the summer of 1885, John Robinson and George Seatree had a camping holiday in the mountains. It was a double first—the first time men had taken a tent so that they could sleep close to the crags, and the first time that rock climbers had taken a proper rope with them in the Lake District.

They had an eventful time, and by good fortune a detailed account has survived in letters which Robinson wrote to his friend Fred Jackson, which convey more graphically than anything else the fresh spirit of the time.

They met at Robinson's home at Whinfell Hall in Lorton and persuaded a young man from Workington, Ernest Peile, to join them and help to carry the gear. Robinson continues the story:

Father drove us nearly to Buttermere and we crossed Scarf Gap. . . . We boiled the kettle at the Liza and made some tea and then on again to Great Doup; as we neared Pillar Rock and could see the ridge near the mountain top some-one called and we guessed it was F. H. Bowring come to meet us. I had told him the way we would come. We threw down our loads some little distance above the foot of Walker's Gully and soon Bowring joined us; the tent was fixed and tea made on the best place we could find, but it turned out to be sadly uneven that night. . . . Bowring started off to Wastdale via 'High Level' and we three for Pillar Rock via Great Chimney and the Screen or Sham Rock, our way lay under a curious arched rock with steep scree and then a fearfully rotten piece of chimney, every hold was loose and great blocks newly loosened looked ready to fall; look out, and down came the scree in continuous stream and rushed thro' the arch while we stuck like clegs to the sides of the chimney. Mr B. was still in sight and eagerly watched thro' his glass, thinking one of us had come down with it. S. was first and we tried again, but no, it was too risky, and we turned and went round by the gully farther up. Over the 'notch' we went for our first climb and entered our names as usual. I then ran down and tried Pendlebury's Crack . . . and thought it rather easy. We hung the rope down at the corner as a precaution, but it was not used. I then again descended and attacked the 'Corner'. HS and I had both been a little way up on a former visit. . . . It is 2 chimneys and they miss each other and this makes the only real difficulty at that point. I drew myself up by hands entirely. Seatree and I then went up right Pisgah. S. went first and had a tightish struggle. Says he nearly caught at the safety rope once—he is very proud of this climb and considers it beats North Climb (on Scafell) hollow in point of strain and difficulty—from the top we went down East climb and I went into Great Chimney to look at HS's climb. It looked very bad and rocks were wet—I then found I had left my rope on the top and went up climbing direct to slab and then over notch. We went to mountain top and saw Peile off to Wastdale.

They got little sleep on their rocky ledge, so early next morning they struck camp, and moved over to Wasdale Head, where they found an excellent site in a meadow at the foot of Lingmell.

The inn was now in the charge of Dan Tyson; 'Auld Will Ritson' had retired a few years earlier and gone to live down the

Ritson' had retired a few years earlier and gone to live down the valley at Strands. Tyson's view of the climbing mania was much the same as his predecessors. Seatree wrote later: '. . . we took an Alpine rope with us, the first we had seen in Lakeland. We soon found its value. Dan Tyson chaffed us about it, and wanted to know "if theer was gaahn to be a hangin' job on?"'

Here they were reunited with Bowring and Peile and joined by 'a young tourist named Walter, a cockney who had climbed trees he said but nothing else but who developed great climbing powers'.

The party explored Piers Ghyll, climbed Lingmell and studied Scafell's Steep Ghyll through 'the glass'. Next day they went up Brown Tongue and clambered about the lower pitches of Steep Ghyll, where Bowring, who was 62, impressed them with his strength and agility. They traversed along Rakes's Progress and Seatree led them up the 'North Climb'—all except Peile whom Robinson forbade because 'he had no nails in his boots'.

After lunch on Mickledore, Bowring and Peile went up Broad Stand while the other three climbed Mickledore Chimney. Near the top of the climb they had a narrow escape.

> I was standing, [Robinson wrote] on the edge and shewing Seatree the holds, Walter standing behind him. I heard the voice of F.H.B. and a noise of falling stones, it seemed to come from the direction of Broad Stand—my heart stood still for I thought either he or Peile had fallen. The noise increased to a deafening roar and we realized in a moment that large masses of falling stones were coming down our chimney. I cried 'look out' and ducked under a crag with my face turned towards the edge above me over which it must come. I could not see the other two, they got a little higher towards the great over-hanging rock. Those were awful moments; Seatree says he hopes never to go thro' such again; he thought the great rock might give way too. The next moment a great stone about 18 inches square came bounding over, dancing from side to side as it came down and making great stars on the sides of the chimney where it struck. It was followed by a great fall of fragments of every size and shape across the entire chimney, more or less, and the air seemed darkened for a few moments. These went clattering

> you hurt? No. Mr Bowring are you there? 'Yes. We are alright.' Who set it off? 'Peile. He is in the chimney above.' 'What did he go up there for, tell him to sit where he is or he may set off another.' We were a good deal shaken and I fastened the rope as a safeguard for them to come up by.

They were near the spot where Petty had fallen the year before. They scrambled on to inspect the Pinnacle, 'but after what had happened, gave up any idea of an ascent. Seatree was very sorry; he was in splendid form before the fall of stones.'

Later in the holiday Robinson and Seatree returned to Pillar and climbed the 'Old West'; it was Robinson's fifteenth ascent of the Rock by ten different routes. On their final day Bowring took them, together with Peile and Walter, up 'Bowring's Chimney' to the summit of Great Gable, where they congratulated him on his hundredth ascent. Robinson and Seatree walked down to Rosthwaite for lunch and a 'crack' with the local guide, Jackson, who asked them about the climbing on Scafell Pinnacle and delivered his judgment; 'In my opinion yon Askatt Smith will break his neck upon some of yon crags before long.' Then they walked down Borrowdale to Keswick, pitched their tent in Mr Abraham's back garden and adopted 'Boyhood of Raleigh' poses for a commemorative photograph.

7 The *Annus Mirabilis*

If any single year stands out above all others of the 'Golden Age' of rock climbing it is 1886, for in June of that year Haskett Smith returned alone to Napes Needle and climbed it. It did not take long, the Needle is not very high; yet this was possibly the most significant short climb ever accomplished, and some see it as the true beginning of the sport.

The year saw other advances. At Easter Slingsby and Hastings were back at Wasdale Head, and on 28th March, with J. Mason, they once again confronted Deep Ghyll on Scafell Crag. Slingsby described the climb in detail:

> After a couple of hundred steps had been cut in the snow in Lord's Rake and at the bottom of Deep Ghyll, we reached the first block—a large rock perhaps 15 feet square, which overhangs the ghyll and so forms a cave. Below the rock the snow was moulded into most fantastic shapes by occasional water-drips from above. At the right hand of the big rock a few small stones are jammed fast between it and the side of the ravine, and they afford the only route up above the rock. . . . Hastings and I got on the stones. He then stood on my shoulders and, by the aid of long arms and being steadied by me, he reached a tiny ledge and drew himself up. Mason and I found it no child's play to follow him with the rope. Some 200 more steps in hard snow brought us to the only place where we could attack the second block. Here three fallen rocks stop the way, and on the left hand is the well-nigh ledgeless cliff which terminates far away overhead in the Scaw Fell Pinnacle. . . . On the left hand of the ghyll, a small tongue of rock, very steep, juts out perhaps 40 feet down the gully and

> forms a small crack and this crack is the only way upward. From the mountaineer's point of view the stratification of the rocks here is all wrong. The crack ends in a chimney about 20 feet high, between the wall and a smoothly polished boss of rock. Hastings, still leading, found the crack to be difficult, but climbed it in a most masterly way. All loose stones, tufts of grass and moss had to be thrown down, and, in the absence of hand and foot hold, the knees, elbows, thighs and other parts of the body had to do the holding on, whilst, caterpillar-like, we drew ourselves upward bit by bit. The chimney is best climbed by leaning against the Pinnacle wall with one's back and elbows, and, at the same time, walking with the feet fly-like up the boss opposite. From the top of the boss a narrow sloping traverse, perhaps 12 feet long, leads into the trough of the ghyll. With a rope this is an easy run; without one it would not be nice. A stone thrown down from here falls over both blocks and rolls down the snow out of the mouth of the Lord's Rake on to the screes far away below. The crack, chimney and traverse, short distance though it is, took us about an hour to pass.

They then scrambled on the top of the Ghyll and climbed from there to the summit of Scafell Pinnacle. The climb is not a particularly difficult one; at least two parties had previously descended that way. Its importance lies in the sequel, for Slingsby immediately wrote a brief account of the climb; this was read to a meeting of the Alpine Club on 6th April and published in the next edition of *The Alpine Journal*, and it concluded with the call: 'Do not let us be beaten on our own fells by outsiders, some of whom consider ice-axes and ropes to be "illegitimate". Let us not neglect the Lake District, Wales and Scotland whilst we are conquerors abroad.'

Slingsby paid tribute in his paper to Haskett Smith as 'a gentleman who has done much brilliant rock climbing in Cumberland and who, unfortunately, is not in our club'. Soon after Haskett Smith wrote to the 'Journal', giving more information about Deep Ghyll and the Pinnacle, and modestly concluding: 'Let me thank Mr. Slingsby, through you, for what he says of me; he makes, however, far too much of my little scrambles, never made except when the ice factor of difficulty "banishes".'

For all this, Haskett Smith was still the outstanding pioneer. Slingsby and Hastings, the veterans of many epics in Norway and the Alps, were content with an easy gully climb on which they used the full complement of axes, rope and combined tactics. When Haskett Smith went off to tackle Napes Needle, it was with no companions and no climbing aids, and the route he made, 'The Wasdale Crack', is still graded 'Very Difficult (Hard)'.

He spent only a few days at Wasdale Head that summer, between visits to Scotland. On the last day of the holiday, at the end of June, he rose early to take some friends up a climb on Buckbarrow and then help them to carry their luggage to the foot of the lake. His account of what happened next, written many years later and published for the first time in *The Journal of the Fell and Rock Climbing Club* in 1914, has become the most widely anthologized passage in the story of Lake District climbing:

> The long walk in the sun left me with a headache by the time I got back to the Inn. The afternoon was cooler and it occurred to me to stroll over into the head of Ennerdale and have a look at the cliffs on that face of Gable. These had never been climbed at any point.
>
> The marks of a recent stone-fall drew my attention to a part of the cliff where I found a very fine gully and climbed it, not without difficulty, being impeded by a long fell-pole. Coming out on top of the mountain I thought of the ridge beside which Robinson and I had come up two years before and made for it, intending to follow the edge down as strictly as might be. This proved to be quite feasible, though at one point my pole gave me a lot of trouble by dropping down a deep and narrow crevice However, the ridge was so steep at that spot that some 20 feet below, on peering into the crack, I espied my stick stuck upright, and by thrusting my arm in was at length able to reach it with my finger-tips and finally to draw it out.
>
> Continuing down into the gap and now warmed by exertion, I forgot my headache and began to examine the Needle itself. A deep crack offered a very obvious route for the first stage, but the middle portion of this crack was decidedly difficult, being at that time blocked with stones and turf, all of which has since been cleared away. Many capable climbers were afterwards

turned back when trying to make the second ascent not by the sensational upper part but by this lower and (under present conditions) very simple piece.

From the top of the crack there is no trouble to reach the shoulder, whence the final stage may be studied at ease. The summit is near, being as they say in Trans-Atlantic cities 'only two blocks away', but those same blocks are set one upon the other and the stability of the top one looks very doubtful. My first care was to get two or three stones and test the flatness of the summit by seeing whether anything thrown up could be induced to lodge. If it did, that would be an indication of a moderately flat top, and would hold out hopes of the edge being found not too much rounded to afford a good grip for the fingers. Out of three missiles one consented to stay, and thereby encouraged me to start, feeling as small as a mouse climbing a milestone.

Between the upper and lower blocks, about five feet up, there is a ragged horizontal chink large enough to admit the toes, but the trouble is to raise the body without intermediate footholds. It seemed best to work up at the extreme right, where the corner projects a little, though the fact that you are hanging over a deep gap makes it rather a 'nervy' proceeding. For anyone in a standing position at the corner it is easy to shuffle the feet sideways to the other end of the chink, where it is found that the side of the top block facing outwards is decidedly less vertical. Moreover at the foot of this side there appeared to my great joy a protuberance which, being covered with a lichenous growth, looked at if it might prove slippery, but was placed in the precise spot where it would be most useful in shortening the formidable stretch up to the top edge. Gently and cautiously transferring my weight, I reached up with my right hand and at last was able to feel the edge and prove it to be, not smooth and rounded as it might have been, but a flat and satisfactory grip. My first thought on reaching the top was one of regret that my friends should have missed by a few hours such a day's climbing, three new things, and all good; my next was one of wonder whether getting down again would not prove far more awkward than getting up!

Hanging by the hands and feeling with the toes for the protuberance provided an anxious moment, but the rest went easily enough, though it must be confessed that it was an undoubted satisfaction to stand once more on solid ground below and look up at my handkerchief fluttering in the breeze.

1 *a* Walter Parry Haskett Smith, 'the father of rock climbing'.

b Owen Glynne Jones, 'the only Genuine Jones'.

c The Rev. James Jackson, 'Patriarch of the Pillarites'.

A

B

C

2 Wasdale Head from above the Napes crags on Great Gable, with Wastwater in the distance and the Screes sweeping up to the left of the lake, taken in the 1890s.

3 Wastwater Hotel—the entrance hall; Easter 1895.

4 The Barn Door Traverse. A. E. Field watches Dr Collier negotiating the crux move.

A

5 *a* A boulder problem. The Y Boulder in Mosedale, climbed in the correct, upside-down posture.

b A. S. Thomson at the controls of his strange motor vehicle, the 'Stormy Petrel', with Ashley Abraham in front and George Abraham, uncharacteristically, in the rear. All three were keen pioneer motorists.

6 The top of Scafell Pinnacle. At the conclusion of the easy way up from Jordan Gap, J. W. Robinson brings up his two companions, W. Blunt and V. Blake, with an air of cheerful confidence though he is not belayed.

7 ‘How not to climb’ was the name the Abraham brothers later gave to this, possibly their first climbing photograph. The cliff adjoins Sharp Edge on Blencathra. Ashley Abraham, leading, is joined to his younger brother Sidney by a short length of washing line and they are moving simultaneously on unstable rock. The rope gave only one, salutary assurance—‘one off, all off’.

8 Pillar Rock. Rounding the Notch on the east face. The Slab and Notch route was the first way up this face and is now regarded as the easiest way down.

9 Pillar Rock. The crux move over the Nose on the North Climb. The slightly harder alternative was to climb the wall to the right of the Nose, grip the flake which is just visible below the over-hanging rock at the top of the picture, and swing round to the top of the Nose, relying entirely on the hand holds.

10 Scafell Crag, the finest climbing cliff in England.

11 Scafell Crag, Moss Ghyll. The leader, A. E. Field, is about to transfer his weight to 'The Collie Step', the foothold which Professor Collie hacked out of the rock with an ice axe. Just behind him is Dr Collier, below is A. D. Godley.

12 Scafell Pinnacle from Deep Ghyll. Ashley Abraham took the photograph on 20th April 1896, during the first ascent, in conditions graphically described by O. G. Jones in chapter 13. The route follows the curving crack, just to the right of the centre of the picture. Jones, coatless, stands at the top of the crack with George Abraham adopting a dynamic stance half way up to him.

13 George Abraham was an early exponent of the art of balance climbing, taking his weight on his feet and legs and using his hands to maintain his balance. Here he is seen in action on Gable Crag, which overlooks the Ennerdale valley. He went on using nailed boots to the end of his climbing career, long after rubber soles had come into general use.

14 Scafell Pinnacle Arête. The French guide Gaspard hauls the rope in while George Abraham demonstrates the 'à cheval' technique on the knife-edge ridge between Low Man and High Man.

15 O. G. Jones gives a tight rope to a struggling beginner.

16 Kern Knotts Crack, Great Gable. The climber has just surmounted the hardest part of the route, where the crack is widest. O. G. Jones, with the security of a top rope, only succeeded there at his fourth attempt.

It was three years before the route was repeated—by Geoffrey Hastings. The climb was much harder in the conditions then than it is today. In a second account of the climb, written in the jubilee year of 1936, Haskett Smith returned to this point: 'The main trouble lay in the cracks and crevices which were tightly packed with small stones flush with the surface of the slabs and thatched with slippery grass. . . . The Lingmell face of the top block was covered with a brown and brittle lichen which concealed whatever holds there might be.'

The climb was an early break-away from the preoccupation with gullies. But its true importance has a simpler and quite fortuitous cause: the photogenic splendour of the Needle. Elegantly detached from the bulk of Napes cliff, this eccentric flake, patterned at its base with diagonal cracks and surmounted by a large overhanging and shaky looking block, gave a dramatic effect of steepness and exposure. Its situation and shape made it unique, unmistakable; it seemed impressive and impregnable. Just as the Matterhorn had made itself the dominant challenge in the Alps simply by the thrilling beauty of its outline, so Napes Needle—on the infinitely smaller scale of Cumberland—came to represent the climbing challenge of the Lake District. Photographs of the Needle, in magazines, newspapers and books, carried the message of what was afoot on the crags more vividly than any words could do, and did more to attract adventurous men to Wasdale Head than any other single factor. Before the 'Golden Age' was over, there were three separate routes to the tiny summit; today there are six, and two girdle traverses.

Haskett Smith paid another visit to the Lake District towards the end of the year, in an October that seems to have been more than usually rainy. In a downpour he and John Robinson took George Seatree to the top of Scafell Pinnacle by 'the easy way', descending by Deep Ghyll. After lunch at the inn they walked over to Pillar Rock, 'with a novice from Oxford', for a little more climbing.

Haskett Smith was now exploring cliffs farther afield. He arranged with Robinson to investigate Dow Crag. They met in

Coniston, where the streets had become torrents of rainwater, and Haskett Smith was moved to verse in the visitors' book of the hotel, where their host was Mr Dove:

> Mr Dove is a dove of great mark;
> But the dove we have wanted of late
> Is the dove who brought news to the Ark
> That the flood was about to abate.

There was no abatement, though, and they reached Dow Crag 'in a dense fog with steady rain'. They started to climb Easter Gully but visibility was so bad that they wandered out onto the East Buttress and re-joined the main gully at the top of what later came to be called 'Hopkinson's Crack'. Little more than a flank attack, it was none the less the first climb on Dow Crag.

During the same rainy season they discovered 'a very fine gully' on Sergeant Crag but 'a high wet slab of smooth slate proved too difficult'. And on Pavey Ark, Haskett Smith climbed Little Gully.

The year 1886 held one other event that was to prove significant. On the island of Skye, a tall, well-built young man of exceptional intelligence was on a fishing holiday. One day, walking along the road at the foot of the Cuillin, he saw two figures on the face of Knight's Peak on Sgurr nan Gillean: 'Hundreds of feet above me, on what appeared to me to be rocks as steep as the walls of a house, they moved slowly backwards and forwards, but always getting higher, till they finally reached the summit. I knew nothing about climbing, and it seemed to me perfectly marvellous that human beings should be able to do such things.'

The climbers were A. H. Stocker, who had made the first route up Lliwedd four years before, and A. G. Parker. The observer was John Norman Collie, twenty-seven years old and on the threshold of a scientific career of the highest distinction.

Collie was the son of an Aberdeen businessman, who had gone to live at Alderly Edge near Manchester. He studied science at University College, Bristol, and then at German universities. He was now teaching chemistry at Cheltenham Ladies' College. Later he was to become Professor of Organic Chemistry at University College, London, and the pioneer of major scientific developments. 'If anyone ever happens to write an obituary of me,' he wrote, 'I want two things said; I first discovered Neon and I took the first X-ray photographs.' He was a pioneer, too, of colour photography.

Ronald Clark describes him as 'a lone, mystic, contradictory man, distinguished in half a dozen different fields, who brought to everything that he handled a certain personal touch of distinction'. Collie became almost a prototype for the familiar hero of many a Victorian story: a man of powerful intellect, reclusive in habit and confirmed in bachelorhood, gently courteous in manner, the valued member of many learned societies, widely read especially in the classics, a painter of talent, a collector of great taste—Chinese porcelain, jewels, Indian embroidery—and a connoisseur of food and wine and fine cigars. He wore neat and comfortable tweeds, and smoked a meerschaum. Once when he accompanied Slingsby to Norway, crowds flocked to see him under the impression that he was Sherlock Holmes.

From the moment he saw the two climbers on Knight's Peak, Collie was a convert to climbing. He wired immediately to London for a rope and as soon as he had it he began climbing. It was the beginning of a life-long obsession that was to take him to the Lake District, the Alps, the Himalayas, the Rockies, and the mountains of Lofoten, and to make him the foremost pioneer of the Scottish cliffs and especially, summer after summer for fifty years, those of the Isle of Skye.

8 The Gentlemen Amateurs

The level of intelligence at Wasdale Head in these years would have put many an Oxbridge senior common room to shame. Professor Collie had perhaps the most powerful and original brain of all, but there was something about the sport and the place that attracted several men of almost comparable calibre. Mostly they were cast in the new Victorian mould of creative and practical genius, operating in the higher reaches of science and engineering. But they were men of wide culture as well; some of their companions brought a leavening of literary interest—one of the many things which Haskett Smith and Bowring shared was a passionate concern to trace the derivation of Lake District place-names and dialect words; and throughout these years Charles Cannan, now the charismatic Dean of Trinity College, Oxford, continued to conduct his brightest classics students on Easter reading parties. Although they climbed and scrambled with enthusiasm, none of the undergraduates made any serious contribution to rock climbing; some, though, became famous in after years and left an account of their youthful holidays in the mountains.

One of them was Arthur Quiller-Couch, later to become pre-eminent as a teacher of English literature at both senior universities in turn and an elegant stylist writing under the pseudonym 'Q'. When his uncompleted autobiography *Memories and Opinions* was published in 1944, it contained this recollection:

> With Cannan and successive groups of friends I spent three Easter vacations at Wastdale Head in Cumberland. In the

> mornings we read, in the afternoons climbed alike strenuously. They stayed at Tyson's farm, where they enjoyed 'the monotony of sweet mountain mutton and 'Mr Pendlebury's pudding' (known to us as 'Pendlebags'), a delicious compound of farm milk, tapioca and raisins . . . Mr Pendlebury, though but a name to us then, was a Cambridge man famous alike as mathematician and mountaineer 'in which latter capacity' we sometimes challenged his prowess. But for climbers a part of Lakeland's charm at Easter lies in the diversities of snow and ice on the upper fells and in the gullies which may vary the difficulty from day to day, almost as the weather varies the game of boat sailing. Our feats, of course, would not for a moment compare with the dizzy achievements of today's experts in rock work. But we 'did' a few things to our own considerable satisfaction—on the Pillar, Great Gable, and at points on the dangerous face of Scafell from Mickledore—and took some pride in doing these without aid of rope; returning at times by help of precipitous glissades to dinner, another hour of reading, final talk around the hearth, then sleep to the sound of many waterfalls near and distant.

They were a varied company; Cannan's other protégés included A. E. W. Mason and C. E. Montague, who both went on to be successful writers in widely differing styles. Mason, who became a popular novelist in the heroic vein, used Wasdale Head as the setting for his first work of fiction, *A Romance of Wastdale*, which has long since lapsed into well-deserved obscurity. It is the melodramatic tale of two climbing companions of long standing who find themselves rivals for the love of a local beauty; the wicked one, Hawke, has compromising letters from the girl and threatens to use them; whereupon the hero, Gordon, takes him to climb Mickledore Chimney, murders him at the top with a knife under the pretence of trying to open a bottle of brandy ('"God," he shrieked, "it's an artery!"'), and concludes matters by throwing himself down one of the gullies on the Screes.

C. E. Montague's writing was more serious and balanced, as befitted one of the chief pillars of *The Manchester Guardian* in the days of C. P. Scott's editorship. He put his climbing experience to subsequent use in a short story, 'In Hanging Garden Gully', which recounts how a botanist, though a stranger to steep rock which recounts how a botanist, though a stranger to steep rock and only partly recovered from a broken leg, performs an 'impossible' traverse in order to bag a rare specimen. The character may have been inspired by Charles Packe, described by Haskett Smith as 'an ardent botanist who never did any climbing except in pursuit of a flower'. The story contains Montague's statement of the forces that motivate the rock climber:

> He deals, day by day, with the Ultimate Good, no doubt in small nips, but still authentic and not watered down. His senses thrill with delight to find that he is just the sum of his own simple powers. He lives on, from moment to moment, by early Man's gleeful achievement of balance on one foot out of four. He hangs safe by a single hand that learnt its good grip in fifty thousand years of precarious dodging among forest boughs. . . . The next little ledge, the object of all human hope and desire. . . . Each time that you get up a hard pitch you have succeeded in life. . . . Care will come back in the end: the clouds return after the rain; but for those first heavenly minutes of sitting secure and supreme at the top of Moss Ghyll or the Raven Crag Gully you are Columbus when he saw land from the rigging and Gibbon when he laid down his pen in the garden house at Lausanne.

In the years around 1886 a remarkable group of men appeared on the scene and made a powerful and idiosyncratic impact on the development of rock climbing. They were a surprisingly homogeneous company; they came from the affluent suburbs of the great industrial areas of south Lancashire, successful professional men, pillars and protagonists and happy beneficiaries of the booming economy of the new industrial revolution. As businessmen and family men and clubmen they accepted, without questioning, the rigid class structure and conventions of the day; their confidence and Victorian wholeheartedness brought vigorous new life to rock climbing and created, for a short time, a spirit that has never been recaptured. Theirs was the attitude of the 'gentleman amateur'. Their courage and skill and drive to explore new ground carried climbing into 'brave new worlds' of difficulty and danger. But it was all done in a casual, holiday, almost caught bragging. They kept few records and rarely wrote any account of what they had done. The greatest certainty about them is that they accomplished far more than we shall ever know.

These qualities found their most extreme expression in a family of five Manchester brothers, the Hopkinsons. Their father, following in the steps of Hogarth's 'Industrious 'Prentice', began his working life as a mill mechanic, earned promotion by hard word and ability and honesty, launched his own business, building textile mills and installing machinery, and became Lord Mayor of Manchester. He married a Yorskhire woman, a Dewhurst of Skipton, distantly related to two climbing families, the Slingsbys and the Tribes, and in the years between 1849 and 1863 she bore him five remarkable sons—in order of appearance, John, Alfred, Charles, Edward and Albert.

They were brought up according to strict Nonconformist tradition. Work, frugality and success were the watchwords. Their reading was the Bible and Bunyan and the works of Samuel Smiles, *Self-Help* and *Lives of the Engineers*. At home poetry was read aloud, Tennyson, Scott, Milton and Wordsworth; they were often taken to the Hallé concerts, but never to the theatre.

The boys were intensively educated. They all went to Owens College, Manchester, and though after that their paths diverged a little, each achieved distinction.

John was the senior in years and in accomplishment, and the others always accepted him as their ordained leader. At Trinity College, Cambridge, he distinguished himself as athlete, oarsman and mathematician; he was Senior Wrangler in 1871 and became a Fellow of Trinity after a dispute, which he won, over the signing of the Thirty-nine Articles—characteristically, he did not disbelieve the Articles himself but strongly objected to the element of compulsion.

He soon left the academic life for industry, joined a lighthouse firm in the Midlands and was responsible for many improvements in the management and equipment of lighthouses. In 1878 he moved to London and set up independently as a consulting engineer. He was one of the founders of the new science of electrical engineering; he designed Manchester's lighting system, the tramways of Leeds and Liverpool, and was consultant to Britain's first electric railway, the City and South London.

Alfred, the second brother, turned to the classics, Oxford and then the law. A barrister on the Northern Circuit, he became Professor of Law and Jurisprudence at Owens College, then Principal of the College and Vice-Chancellor of Manchester University. He was active in politics, initially as a Liberal, but when Gladstone split the party over Irish Home Rule he switched to the Unionist cause and was twice elected to Parliament. Distinguished in law, learning and politics, he was knighted in 1910, and twenty years later published a book of reminiscence and reflection which he called *Penvltima.*

Next came Charles, not so ambitious as his brothers and content, after matriculating in science at London University in 1871, to return to the family firm in Manchester to help his father and play an active role in local government. Less intense than the others in his professional life, Charles was the finest rock climber of them all.

Edward modelled his career on John's and dedicated himself to success with all the intensity of Alfred. At Emmanuel College, Cambridge, he made his mark as an oarsman and a swimmer and was tenth Wrangler of 1881. His career as an electrical engineer was almost more brilliant than John's; at Portrush in Northern Ireland he experimented on Britain's first electrical tramway, between Bushmills and Giant's Causeway, and he designed the engine for the first electrically driven underground train. He was politically involved too and was Coalition Unionist M.P. for a Manchester division for a few years after the First World War.

He is the brother best known to us now because his daughter, Katharine Chorley, wrote a brilliantly evocative book about her childhood, *Manchester Made Them.* She portrays Edward as 'a vital, unresting man, radiating energy . . . fairly tall and very lean, with broad shoulders and slight hips'. Charles was her favourite uncle and she remembers long, subtle debates between him and her father, in which each enjoyed the intellectual exercise of devising ever more convoluted and outrageous arguments. But she says too that the brothers, especially her father and Alfred, were 'charged with ambition . . . they almost worshipped brains and too readily judged a successful life in terms of getting to the top of the tree'.

The fifth and final brother, Albert, was not so hag-ridden by ambition. Family circumstances were easier when he was growing up and he was spared the pressure to win scholarships. Even so he studied medicine at Cambridge, became a surgeon in Manchester, and finally returned to Cambridge to lecture in anatomy: 'Cambridge,' he said, 'found it could not do without a Hopkinson.'

The five boys were introduced early to the pleasures of mountain travel. 'As early as the age of five,' Alfred wrote, 'I recall going up the river Aire to Gordale Scar, than which there is no more impressive scene in the country. To a young child the grandeur of it was almost over-powering. And then came the delight of climbing up the rocks at the side of the falls and crossing the moors to the great Cove above Malham. When I was six my father took us to the Lake District for the first time and we bathed in Easedale Tarn, climbed Helm Crag under his guidance, and another day reached the top of Fairfield with some friends. A boy's whole spirit was filled with the joy of the first ascent of one of the higher mountains and the widespread view round.'

During the sixties and seventies the family were actively scrambling and climbing in the Lake District, Scotland, North Wales, Norway and the Alps, but little detail of their exploits is known. 'In the early days of climbing in the British Isles,' said Alfred, 'it was out habit usually to take our climbs as it were by chance. If a ridge or a gully looked attractive it was the natural thing to go for it, and in those days records were not generally published even if any were kept.'

They roamed and climbed in a carefree spirit, doing it well because it was in their nature to pursue excellence even in their fun but not taking it too earnestly and avoiding, above all, any danger that they might be accused of boasting. They took a perverse pride almost in their modesty. Many years later Alfred wrote: 'To the best of my belief I have never written a word, not even in the old visitors' book at Wasdale, on any climb in the Lake District. I do not know or care whether any of them is classed as easy or severe. I expect they have now all become easy, but I do not know their names. The labels—Cust's Gully, Westmorland's Climb, Botterill's Slab—convey nothing to my mind. These proprietary brands . . . are sometimes a little trying to those who like to find out things for themselves.'

Some time early in the 1880s John and Edward descended the east face of Tryfan in North Wales, a considerable achievement for the time, but since they left no record the precise date and route will never be known. Ten years later they were the first to discover and climb the great cliffs on the northern side of Ben Nevis, but they only made this known some time afterwards when others were claiming the discovery. In the Lake District their attempts at obscurity were in vain. It is clear evidence of their skill that, despite all their modesty, their name is liberally bestowed about the steepest cliffs; Hopkinson's Cairn on Scafell Pinnacle; also on Scafell are Hopkinson's Gully, Hopkinson's and Tribe's Route, and the Professor's Chimney, named in honour of John; and on Dow Crag, the other scene of their liveliest pioneering, Hopkinson's Crack.

It is not known when they began serious climbing in the Lake District. They were, as we have already seen, providentially on hand in Piers Ghyll in 1884 when Lawrence Pilkington was crushed by a stone fall, and they became lifelong friends of the Pilkingtons, near neighbours in Alderley Edge, of the same social standing, and fellow spirits.

Their first recorded contribution to the sport's development came in September 1887, when the three youngest brothers, Charles, Edward and Albert, together with their cousin W. N. Tribe, forced a hard route down from the top of Scafell Pinnacle to a narrow ledge which runs across the face of the Pinnacle about half way down and 250 feet above the scree. They could find no further way down so Edward built a cairn on the ledge, Hopkinson's Cairn, which was to stand as a lure and a challenge to climbers of the highest order for years to come.

The first attempt to reach the cairn from below was made three months later, with Charles Hopkinson leading. One member of this party was Hermann Woolley, and it was probably he who wrote an account of the climb in the visitors' book: 'They succeeded in climbing 150 to 200 feet [this route is now known as Hopkinson's Gully] but were stopped by a steep slab of rock coated with ice. From this point, however, a good traverse was made into the first gully or chimney on the left. They forced their way up this gully to the top of the chimney. At the top there was a trough of ice about 30 feet long, surmounted by steep rock glazed with ice, which brought the party to a stop. They descended the chimney again . . . considered one of the finest climbs the party had ever accomplished.'

This was climbing of a new quality. The Hopkinsons—whichever permutation of brothers was climbing—were leaders of the movement out of the confining gloom of the gullies and onto the open slabs. No party succeeded in reaching the Cairn by the direct route from below until twenty-four years had passed; and the men who did it then, the legendary rope of S. W. Herford and G. S. Sansom, paid tribute to Hopkinson's attempt as 'one of the finest in the history of rock climbing'.

The 'old guard' were busy at this period too. In March 1887 Geoffrey Hastings and Edmund Haskett Smith climbed the gully on the east side of Pillar Shamrock, 'with the aid of deep snow'. The same month Haskett Smith climbed the Great Chimney on Pillar's east face by the Arête and Curtain route.

July of the following year found a formidable team at work—Haskett Smith, Slingsby, Hastings and Edward Hopkinson. On the 14th they made the first successful frontal attack on the cliffs of Dow Crag, when Hastings led them up the Great Gully. Next day the same party went to Scafell and, with Slingsby in the lead, reached the summit of the Pinnacle by way of Steep

Ghyll and the chimney which has been known by Slingsby's name ever since. The climb was important. It was an early example of the use of combined tactics, for Slingsby began his ascent of the chimney by standing on the shoulders of two companions; and it was a very long run-out of the rope for those days—110 feet were paid out to him before he could halt in security and haul the rope in as the others came up.

In the summer of 1890 the magazine *The Pall Mall Budget* carried an illustrated article about Napes Needle. It caught the eye of Norman Collie as he travelled home by train from a climbing trip to the Cuillin. Next Christmas he went to Wasdale Head and with two companions he climbed the Needle. He also climbed Steep Ghyll 'in snow and ice, one of the most dangerous climbs I have ever made'.

In July 1891 Haskett Smith fought the final round of his nine-year contest with the northern face of Pillar Rock. His companions were Geoffrey Hastings and Cecil Slingsby. Haskett Smith recounted the climb in detail in the pages of the magazine *Black and White* whose editor was C. N. Williamson:

> The starting point of the climb is 'The Terrace', a broad turf ledge which runs across the face of the Low Man (the lesser summit on Pillar Rock).... From the highest point of the terrace rises a huge rib of rock called the Pillar Nose, a feature of aquiline and terrible character. From almost anywhere between there and Walker's Gully, the climb may be begun; but, briefly, by starting as near as may be to the Gully, and only working to the right when actually forced, the climbing will be found finer, more varied, and more exciting. One of the peculiarities of this rock face consists in the frequency of mighty blocks of stone severed by a natural split from the mother cliff, and only maintained in their place by weight and by casual balance. These blocks vary in weight from a few pounds to perhaps a hundred tons, but when a man, after having seen the light gleam through, beneath, and beside one of these, has to crawl over it like a fly on sugar, he can hardly help thinking of the proverbial 'last straw', and shows considerable alacrity in crawling off again on the far side.

He must have thought too of the moment at the start of his

climbing career when one such block came away and almost carried him to his death.

At the crux of the climb, just below the Nose itself, the party turned aside from the direct route, descended into Savage Gully, and made their way to the top from there. Haskett Smith called it 'stooping to conquer'. Kelly and Doughty in their *Short History* comment: 'It is strange nowadays to think of the hero of Napes Needle being defeated by the severity of the Nose. The cause could not have been isolation or altitude—one would have thought the exposure was about equal in both cases. Possibly what is now a clean landing on sound bare rock may have been an earth-covered ledge heaped with scree from Stony Gully above.'

About this time another valuable recruit appeared, Godfrey Allan Solly, a simple, pious, rather solemn man of law from Merseyside. He was in his early thirties and already an experienced Alpinist when he first visited Wasdale Head. Educated at Rugby, he became a solicitor and in 1888 was appointed Clerk to the Justices of the Wirral, a post which he retained for fifty years, becoming in the meantime Mayor and Freeman of Birkenhead. The weighty and careful application which he brought to his professional and civic life he also brought to bear on his climbing.

Solly was a member of a large party which went to the north side of Pillar Rock in October 1891. Slingsby wanted to introduce John Robinson to the new route, and when they reached the ledge below the Nose he led Robinson down into Savage Gully to follow the exit line used by Haskett Smith three months before. Solly and Ellis Carr stayed on the ledge and looked for alternative routes. Nearly twenty years later Solly recalled: 'I got my hands onto a hold on what is now called the buttress, and thought it would go, but I was unroped and did not venture. . . . Ellis Carr from the other end noticed the crack that is now used in the Hand Traverse climb. . . . Carr then asked whether the traverse crack continued to the top of the wall, and, hearing that it did, he climbed up to it, and went along it. I followed and remember that I found it very difficult to get to the crack, having no-one below to give me a shoulder up. That was the first passage of the hand traverse. The route was discovered and first taken by Carr.'

This variation is still graded 'Severe (Hard)', and the current Fell and Rock Climbing Club guide book describes it in these words: 'From the right end of the ledge, ascend the steep wall for about 10 feet on good holds until the sharp edge of a flake is reached. Traverse left to the top of the Nose, gripping the flake with the hands and easing the strain by pressing the feet or knees on the bulging rock below.' In a hand traverse the climber swings himself along sideways by the strength of his arms alone; there are no footholds. It is a strenuous and exhilarating procedure at the best of time; in those days it was probably harder than it is now that generations of climbers have cleared away all the debris and vegetation from the rim of the flake.

Ellis Carr was another of the men from the market towns around the mountains who played such a vital role in this story. He was born in 1852 in Kendal into a prosperous Quaker family; his father was a partner in the biscuit-making firm Peek Frean. Educated at private schools in England, then by private tutors in Germany, Carr joined the business to become a partner and later a director. He was a cultured man, a keen flute player and a talented artist—his neat line drawings lend great clarity and charm to Haskett Smith's book. He was already an Alpinist of experience; that summer he had enjoyed an extensive season with Solly, Horace Walker and A. F. Mummery.

For some time the north face of Pillar remained the magnet of attention. John Robinson was soon back on the ledge beneath the Nose, with Hastings and Collie, determined to try the hand traverse. Norman Collie recalled the incident: 'The day was bitterly cold and Robinson was a short distance from the traverse. His hands were so frozen that he could not hold on or get back. He called out, 'I can't hold on any longer', and then fell straight onto the ledge below, bounded out into the air, turning a somersault backwards, and pitching onto a great projection some 30 feet lower down, hitting it with his shoulder. At the exact moment that he hit the grass, the strain came on the rope. If this had not happened, nothing could have stopped him, and the whole party would have been dragged after him. Sheer luck had saved us.'

Although it is clear from this that rope techniques were still primitive and largely ineffective, rock climbing was now confidently on the march. More and more routes of 'Severe' standard were being made; more and more 'tigers' were joining battle on the crags. Norman Collie, Ellis Carr and Godfrey Solly were already at work; now they were joined by another outstanding pioneer, Dr Joseph Collier, a leading Manchester surgeon with much mountaineering in the Alps and the Caucasus already to his credit.

Collier was an all-round athlete; as a medical student he had been a good rugby player, later he was keen on tennis, golf and cycling. He was lithe and tall and had the advantage of exceptional reach. With his friend S. B. Winser he created a series of high standard climbs in the early 1890s.

It was he who pioneered the Nose Direct on the Pillar North Climb, which is now regarded as the normal conclusion of the climb and graded 'Severe (Mild)'. Winser held him on a tight rope as he cautiously felt round the Nose for the holds which had eluded so many of their predecessors. In April 1893 the same pair completed a very fierce 200-foot route at the Mickledore end of Scafell Crag, Collier's Climb, which is still graded 'Severe (Hard)' although a rock fall at the hardest section has made it easier than it was initially. And in the same months, with two other companions, they took advantage of an almost unprecedented drought to force a route up Piers Ghyll, now graded 'Severe (Mild)'.

But the most remarkable climb of this period had been made one year earlier on the Wasdale face of Great Gable. On 15th April 1892 Godfrey Solly led his three companions up Eagle's Nest Ridge Direct, the first climb ever made which today ranks as 'Very Severe'. It was a cold day; his companions were Slingsby, G. P. Baker and W. A. Briggs; and Solly's account is characteristically modest and straightforward:

I went first and found it difficult enough to get to the little platform. When there I sat down to recover my breath with my back to the ridge and a leg dangling on each side. The party below made some uncomplimentary remark as to what I looked like perched up there, and I suggested that I was more like an eagle on its nest. That is, I fear, the very unromantic but truthful origin of the name. Those who have visited the spot that know no bird would ever build a nest on so wind-swept a ledge. Standing up, I found that the first steps of the next pitch were very difficult, and that the rock rather pushed one out. The others got out of the rope, and Slingsby, climbing up as far as possible, stood on a little step just below, with his hands on the platform. I put one foot on his shoulder and as I climbed up, making room for him, he raised himself and finally stood on the platform, helping me as far as possible. I went on and climbed the second step. Then when I came to the third I did not like it. Retreat was even less inviting, and consultation with the others impracticable. After looking round, something of a hold for each hand and foot was discovered, and I went on, with the knowledge that even if one hand or foot slipped, all would be over. Just above this the difficult part ended.

This was the new climbing with a vengeance. Even O. G. Jones was greatly impressed: 'The situation is terribly exposed for the first 140 feet and will try the nerves of even experienced mountaineers. . . . On such ledges good nailed boots and perfect confidence are essential. . . . The fact is that the ridge is not to be recommended.'

According to Solly, the climbers themselves were award by what they had done: 'Talking over the climb afterwards, amongst our party, we felt unwilling to let it become known as a route to be followed upon our responsibility. Where one climber can go, another can follow, but we agreed that the margin of safety was so narrow that we did not wish anyone to follow in ignorance of the difficulties. We therefore left our advice on record that no-one should climb it unless he had previously reconnoitred it with a rope from above.'

The question of whether the more testing and dangerous climbs that were now being forced should be made generally known was one that caused much heart-searching and controversy at Wasdale Head, and was later to create bad feeling between the Wasdale Head men, by then committed to open publication, and the climbers of North Wales. It was argued that the dissemination of such information could only induce the young and the foolhardy to venture onto pitches beyond their ability and so lead to disaster. The reply was that such people would get into trouble anyway, and it was better that accomplished routes should be fully and clearly made known to all who were interested, and their attendant difficulties and dangers given due emphasis; in this way capable cragsmen would be kept up to date and the not-so-capable would stand warned. The dispute was resolved by events quickly enough, and so overwhelmingly on the side of publication that each route is now mapped and described, sometimes move by move, and the modern climber can only hope to recapture the excitement of the pioneers if he is lucky enough to find an unexplored crag or skilled enough to make new routes on the familiar cliffs.

Two days after Solly's great climb, Cecil Slingsby led the attempt on another fine ridge on Gable, the Arrowhead. There were five men in the party, including the redoubtable veteran Horace Walker. Walker, a Liverpool merchant, began his climbing in the Alps in the 1850s and returned there season after season, climbing a great deal with Edward Whymper and taking part in the first ascent of the Brenva Ridge of Mont Blanc. He continued climbing through the sixties and seventies and eighties, became an early enthusiast for winter climbing in the Lake District, and made first ascents in the Cuillin with Lawrence Pilkington. Now he was well past sixty and, in deference to his years, Slingsby left the ridge for easier ground after reaching the recess behind the Arrow. But the old man was disappointed and in fact took part in the first ascent of the direct route, over the top of the Arrow, four years later.

Across the dale from Gable, two of the three great gullies that cleave the long central face of Scafell Crag had now been climbed and thoroughly explored. One remained, the hardest of them, Moss Ghyll. Several attempts on it had been made, most notably by Haskett Smith in 1889, but invariably they had been turned back at the cave high up in the Ghyll where the way on is blocked by a huge overhanging boulder.

At Christmas 1892 Collie, Hastings and Robinson confronted the problem afresh. First they investigated the gully from above to make sure that there was a possible route above the boulder. Then on Boxing Day they tackled the Ghyll from below and were quickly at the cave. Collie's famous account of how they passed the obstacle was published, eighteen months later, in *The Scottish Mountaineering Club Journal*:

> Over our heads the great rock roof stretched some distance over the ghyll. Our only chance was to traverse straight out along the side of the ghyll, till one was no longer over-shadowed by the roof above, and then, if possible, climb up the face of rock and traverse back again above the obstacle into the ghyll once more. This was easier to plan than to carry out; absolutely no hand-hold, and only one little projecting ledge jutting out about a quarter of an inch and about two inches long to stand on, and six or eight feet of the rock wall to be traversed. I was asked to try it. Accordingly, with great deliberation, I stretched out my foot and placed the edge of my toe on the ledge. Just as I was going to put my weight onto it, off slipped my toe, and if Hastings had not quickly jerked me back, I should instantly have been dangling on the end of the rope. But we were determined not to be beaten. Hastings' ice-axe was next brought into requisition, and what followed I have no doubt will be severely criticised by more orthodox mountaineers than ourselves. As it was my suggestion I must take the blame. *Peccavi! I hacked a step in the rock*—and it was very hard work. But I should not advise anyone to try and do the same thing with an ordinary axe. Hastings' axe is an extraordinary one, and was none the worse for the experiment. I then stepped across the *mauvais pas*, clambered up the rock till I had reached a spot where a capital hitch could be got over a jutting piece of rock, and the rest of the party followed. We then climbed out of the ghyll on the left, up some interesting slabs of rock.

The current guide grades this climb as 'Very Difficult (hard)' and says it is 'the first recorded use of an artificial aid in rock climbing', which is only true if one discounts the elaborate gear that 'Steeple' Jackson took with him to Pillar Rock. Professor Collie expected contumely, but there is no evidence of any from his Wasdale Head colleagues; Hastings and Robinson were happy to use the step he had chipped out, and Haskett Smith, in his book, gives the story in full with no hint of disapproval. Yet only a few days after the climb, Dr Collier took a party up the ghyll and proved that the step cutting had been unnecessary by finding a direct route up the vertical mossy wall to the right.

The most famous rock climber of the day paid only one visit to the Lake District and made only one climb there. A. F. Mummery came with a reputation second to none as the leader of the new school of Alpine climbing. With guides or with British friends—Slingsby, Hastings and Collie prominent among them—he had created new routes of spectacular difficulty, such as the Dent de Requin and the 'Mummery Crack' on the Grépon. In 1893 he went to Wasdale and took part in the second ascent of the Great Gully on Wastwater Screes; the first ascent had been made two years before by Collie, Hastings and Robinson. It was unfortunate that Mummery's first encounter with the Cumbrian crags should have been on rock so unstable, for he never returned. Later he delivered his judgment: 'Climbing in the Caucasus was easy and safe; in the Alps, too, it was usually easy and safe, though sometimes difficult; but climbing as practised at Wasdale Head was both difficult and dangerous.'

Two years after this Mummery went to the Himalayas with Collie and Hastings to explore Nanga Parbat. After some superb high-altitude rock climbing, he reached 20,000 feet on the Diamiri Ribs. But soon after, in the company of two Gurkhas, he was lost on the mountain and no one ever discovered what had happened to them.

9 'The Only Genuine Jones'

On Great Gable, early in the 1890s, Professor Collie encountered the new generation: 'We had just climbed the Napes Needle and come down again. Two men who had been watching us then started up it. They got to the ledge underneath the top, but could get no further so I climbed up to help them. One of them got into the crack but could not find sufficient handhold around the corner and wanted to know if there was no other way up. Finally he got on my shoulders, and I pushed him up till he got a handhold on the top; he then scrambled up. I went down and began climbing the ridge behind the Needle, but I had to come down again and once more climb up the Needle for the last man could not get off the top; I got him off safely, and the man was Jones.'

Owen Glynne Jones's meteoric career in climbing is packed with drama. Despite his inauspicious introduction to the crags, Jones was to dominate the next few years of climbing development in the Lake District perhaps more completely than Haskett Smith had dominated the opening years.

The personalities of the two men had little in common. Haskett Smith had the conventional virtues of the 'English gentleman' of the time. He had courage but it was tempered with caution and good sense; his interests were academic, his manner precise and almost pedantic; he could be shy with strangers to the point of frostiness; although his passion for climbing was continuing and strong, there was nothing competitive in his spirit—he climbed for fun and his passion stopped well this side of obsession.

O. G. Jones was coarser-grained and less restrained; his nature was warmer, more impulsive, more flamboyant and more foolhardy. Climbing was an obsession with him, and when mountains or outcrops lay beyond his reach and work confined his restless spirit to London he climbed church towers, got part way up Cleopatra's Needle on the embankment, made the traverse of the Common Room at the City of London School without touching the floor, and forged new routes among the girders which spanned the university laboratories. He once, it is said, 'girdled' a railway engine, using only the rivet-heads for holds.

Jones's climbs were more daring and dangerous than those of his predecessors; his writing about them was more personal and detailed and exciting. It was he who dubbed himself 'The Only Genuine Jones'.

Such a man was bound to incur the disapproval of his seniors, comparable to that which Edward Whymper had aroused among the Alpine 'fathers' thirty years before. Something of the feeling shows through Professor Collie's account of his first encounter with Jones. It was expressed more explicitly many years later by Haskett Smith: 'Strangely different opinions have been held of Owen Glynne Jones and yet there is an element of truth and of falsehood in them all. He has been lauded not only as a climber but also as a good designer of climbs. He has been condemned as unsportsmanlike, conceited and self-centred. . . . Self-centred he undoubtedly was, but what was mistaken for conceit was his scientific determination to speak only of what he knew. He had studied his own physical powers as a chauffeur studies his car and for that reason he talked a good deal about himself.'

The contrast between the generations is illustrated by Jones's own account of his first ascent of Napes Needle, and the striking discrepancies between his and Professor Collie's recollection. The 'Dr S.' in his account is Dr W. E. Sumpner, a teaching colleague and lifelong friend of Jones's, and yet another pioneer climber who became eminent in the field of electrical engineering:

I have a vivid recollection of walking down the Strand one wet spring afternoon in 1891, oppressed with the commonplace of our London streets and the flatness of people and things in general, and crossing over by sheer force of habit to Spooner's photograph shop. In the centre of the window, and eclipsing to my perverted vision every other object around it, was a striking enlargement from the original half-plate of Dixon's Needle. [Professor Dixon had taken a photograph, the previous year, to mark the first ascent of the Needle by a woman, Miss Koecher.] I heard a by-stander at my elbow draw his friend's attention to the figures in the picture with the remark, 'Scott! What fools!' But that evening a copy of the Needle hung in my room; in a fortnight Easter had come round and I found myself on the top of the pinnacle.

Dr S. and I travelled down to Drigg one night. We breakfasted there early and walked the 12 miles to Wastdale, halting only for a plunge into cold Wastwater. After the manner of our kind we inquired at once for the Climbing Book, to learn the latest news from the Fells. . . . In the afternoon we worked our way up to the Napes. Being the more enthusiastic, I found the Needle first, and was breathless on the top of the crack when Dr S. arrived. He threw a rope up from the small platform and came after me. The crack up the face seemed difficult that first time; most people find it so. . . . From here the route for ten feet is directly up the right edge. The holds are not numerous, but good enough when the rocks are dry, and we found ourselves on a platform or shoulder that serves as an excellent take-off for the last struggle. The terrors of the crack often scare off people from the final piece. They almost did our little party. I found my watch-chain broken—some links still remain in the heart of the Needle—and my watch badly dented. . . . I took off my boots, for they had no nails, and, standing on the shoulders of Dr S., stepped on to the right end of the ledge on which the top block rests. This corner is difficult to climb alone and exceedingly daring work, for the climber drags his body on to it over a sheer drop of a hundred feet, and feels no certainty of safety till he is up. . . . The disposition of one's centre of gravity must be carefully considered, and there is a sense of alternate peril and safety in inspiration and expiration. Once on the ledge the game was evidently in our hands, and traversing along to the left I found a rounded boss of rock 18 inches higher that offered good hold for both feet. Then the left was brought well up to a little ledge nearly an inch wide, the right hand gripped the right edge

> of the boulder, and on straightenening out the top edge could be grasped. An arm pull was helped by sundry roughnesses for the toes and I sprawled half across the top triumphantly. In a couple of minutes Dr S. was by my side. . . . We descended without seriious difficulty.

Jones was a man towards whom no one could be indifferent; his personality provoked strong and strongly contrasting reactions from the men he climbed with. The Abraham brothers held him in the highest respect and affection; the 'old guard' at Wasdale Head, and particularly John Robinson, had to admire his achievements but were often forced to deplore his attitude and manner; a few despised him both as a man and a climber, and none more venomously than Aleister Crowley, the most vituperative climber-writer of the period.

In his *Confessions*, Crowley recalls a holiday in Langdale in the summer of 1893: 'One very wet morning I started to climb Scafell, chiefly with the idea of tackling some of the gullies which I had noticed on the great cliff. I had reached the grass traverse when I heard voices in the mist above me, and a few minutes later a powerful man with red whiskers and a rope about his shoulders came towards me from the cliff. It was J. W. Robinson, a local farmer who had laid the foundation of Cumberland climbing. He offered to show me some of the easier climbs. He had started that morning with a man named Owen Glynne Jones. Jones had insisted on trying to climb Steep Ghyll, which is for the most part a shallow gully of smooth slabs set at a dangerous angle. There is no reliable hold for hand or foot on the main pitch, which is some 80 feet high. As torrents of icy water were pouring off the crags, it was sheer foolhardiness to attempt it. Robinson had refused to do so, whereupon Jones had quarrelled with him and they had parted.'

There were to be other occasions when Robinson's cautious good sense would bring him into conflict with Jones. And it was not long after this that Crowley, for the first and last time, found himself climbing with Jones:

> It was on Great Gable; the rocks were plastered with ice and a bitter wind was blowing. In such conditions one cannot rely on

> one's fingers. Our party proposed to descend the Oblique Chimney on the Ennerdale face. Robinson led the way down. The second man was a Pole named Lewkowitch, who was generally known as 'oils, fats and waxes' because of his expert knowledge of them and the personal illustration of their properties which he afforded. He had no experience of climbing, and weighed about 16 stone. It was up to me, as third man on the rope, to let him down slowly. I had, of course, to descend little by little, the rope being too short to allow me to lower him from the top. I soon found myself in the most difficult part of the chimney, very ill placed to manipulate a dangling ox. I looked up to Jones, the last man, to hold my rope so that I could give full attention to Lewkowitch, and saw to my horror that he was maintaining his equilibrium by a sort of savage war dance! He was hampered by a photographic apparatus which was strapped to his back. Robinson had urged him to lower it separately. As not Einstein nor the Blessed Virgin Mary was there to suspend the law of gravitation, I have no idea how we got to the bottom undamaged; but when we did, I promptly took off the rope and walked home, utterly disgusted with the vanity which had endangered the party. Of course, there could only be one end to that sort of thing, and Jones ended by killing himself and three guides on the Zinal side of the Dent Blanche a few years later.

The description of Jones's death is heartless and inaccurate. For the rest, however, Crowley's story is only too credible. Although he was the only one who was enough of a 'bounder' to write such things, several must have thought them.

Many of the stories about O. G. Jones make it clear that the simplest day's outing from Wasdale Head with him was liable and even likely to assume epic dimensions. Dr Sumpner, the companion of his Easter visit in 1891, wrote a revealing account for the *Gipsy Journal*, with Jones thinly disguised under the pseudonym of 'Faraday':

> Faraday and I had been ten days at Wasdale Head. The cold was fearful, even for January; but indoors we had been comfortable enough. . . . Two or three professors from a northern college had come to the end of their scanty vacation. Some schoolmasters had gone home . . . a party of Cambridge undergraduates, who had slithered down the Sty Head Pass and arrived bleeding, had departed the next day. We were alone and Faraday was in his glory. . . . The miseries I endured would

> soften the heart of the Gable Needle. I had been dragged up Deep Ghyll and pushed down Broad Stand—I had been hauled violently over one obstacle, and left to freeze for half an hour at a time while Faraday tried a fancy route over the next. I had been alternately plunged up to the neck in snow and ground to pieces on frozen scree. . . . I was all over bruises and frost-bites. My clothes were in rags and my boots cut to bits; but I was left with life and that was something. We were to leave next day, and I thought the bitterness of the thing was past; so when, after lunch, Faraday proposed a last stroll round by Windy Gap into Mosedale, I assented cheerfully. He took me straight up Yewbarrow from the hotel. It is steep, and he had an aneroid. If this instrument did not mark a sufficient number of feet every five minutes, Faraday insulted me. I arrived, perspiring. Next came a bare-faced attempt to take me to Red Pike by a course well to the left of Baddeley's. After frightful escapes we gained the top, to find a thick driving mist which shut out all the view and chilled me to the bone. We could not see more than 60 yards in any direction. My companion, however, led on confidently along the ridge, and I followed, being assured he would recognize Windy Gap in any weather. Whenever we came to a particularly bad snow-shoot, going perpendicularly down into abysmal mist, Faraday would take his axe and practise step-cutting, while I shivered . . . in about half an hour he admitted he did not know where he was, and said he must get down below the mist and take bearings. We consulted the compass, chose a likely gap, and descended some 500 feet of scree into an unrecognizable valley; then farther over rock and grass, still in doubt but beginning to gain more and more certainty that we were altogether out of our route, until finally all doubt was at an end as we opened out the profile of the Angler's Rock in Ennerdale Water, cut sharp against the sunset.

Jones was no route-finder; he had little natural sense of direction or feeling for the lie of the land, and to make matters worse he was very shortsighted. 'The fact is,' Haskett Smith said, 'to bring out his best qualities he needed a good guide not to precede but to follow him.' Haskett Smith also remarked of one of Jones's more testing routes, 'Of course, he would never have done it, if he could have seen it.' In a perverse way, his myopia was an advantage; it shielded him from realizing the true extent of his exposure and it led him into places which called forth the utmost exertion of his phenomenal strength and gymnastic genius. His capacity for getting into difficulties on the crags was more than equalled by his ability to find a way out of them. 'He was never so happy,' the Abraham brothers said, 'as when in a really tight place.' Jones seems to have needed the thrill of danger, the challenge of apparently insuperable difficulty, in almost the same degree and with much the same regularity as the heroin addict needs his 'fix'.

He took pleasure in the extremes of discomfort and danger. His stamina and powers of endurance gave him much in common with the 'hard men' of the 1950s who claimed they could only really become interested in a climb when it took them up overhanging rock with a waterfall coming down. His remedy for frostbite was to stick his fingers into boiling glue. Application of this terrible treatment in the Alps twisted some of his fingers permanently out of shape. But Jones was cheered rather than distressed because it enabled him to find a secure grip on finger-holds that were merely awkward for normal hands.

Jones's climbing style has been closely described. Haskett Smith said: 'His muscular endurance enabled him to think quietly in places where an ordinary man would have had to give undivided attention to the question of holding on or getting down again.' In his early days on the rocks Jones was a noisy climber; accorcing to Hasket Smith, when he ran into difficulties he 'indulged in all sorts of scratchings and scrapings before he made a serious attempt to advance'. Taxed with this, Jones explained, 'It helps me to think, it keeps my courage up; I always do my best when I have a full head of steam, and the scratching and scraping help me to feel that I have it.'

Though his outstanding quality lay in his muscular strength, in his hands and arms especially, the standard of climbing he attained and maintained would not have been possible without remarkable suppleness and balance. George Abraham, his most constant companion on the rope in the years of his finest climbs, said, 'The secret of his almost unequalled success as a rock climber was his abnormal finger-power, and an exceptional gift of balance on small foot-holds.' Abraham, in his book *Modern*

Mountaineering, described one of Jones's idiosyncrasies: 'He had a curious tendency, which was sometimes criticized. At the top of some exceptionally severe pitch, when the finishing hand-grip had been gained, he would fling his feet, as it were, to the winds. This was in vivid contrast to his impressive neatness and steadiness on the lower sections; but there was no element of danger or risk in this final, joyous pull; rather it was a signal to those below that the fight was won.'

The son of a Welsh carpenter-builder, Jones was born and bred in London and always made his home there. Born in Paddington in 1867, he showed an aptitude for scientific subjects, went on to the Mechanical Department of Finsbury Technical College, then to the Kensington Institution. He was a keen and serious student, took his B.Sc. at London University, and gained a first-class Honours degree in experimental physics. In 1891, having failed to secure a professorship at Aberystwyth, he became physics master at the City of London School and kept the post for the rest of his life.

As a boy he was taken to holiday in the Welsh mountains and his adventurous spirit soon led him to solitary scrambles around Cader Idris. In 1888 he accomplished his first ascent, the Cyfrwy Arête on Cader, with no nails in his boots, no rope, no companion, and really no idea. Two years later he went to Wasdale Head and began to develop, through many trials and frequent errors, the qualities of cragsmanship that were to make him the outstanding pioneer of the decade.

At Easter 1890 an Alpinist, W. M. Crook, took the tyro Jones to Pillar Rock: 'I marvelled,' he later wrote, 'at his wonderful grip of the rocks, his steady head, his extraordinary power of balancing himself on one foot in what seemed to me then almost impossible positions.'

From the beginning Jones kept a detailed diary of his climbs, written in shorthand in small notebooks. These notes were to form the basis of his book.

In the summer of 1891, the year of his Easter encounter with Napes Needle and Professor Collie, he paid his first visit to the Alps. He made his first big climb on the Dent Blanche, which was to be the scene of his last climb only eight years later. Now his life set into a pattern that rarely changed. In term time he worked hard as a science teacher; each vacation he lived his real life, among the mountains. Christmas and Easter found him, almost without fail, at Wasdale Head; each summer, with the sole exception of 1893, he spent the long vacation in the Alps. He rapidly became an accomplished Alpinist, and his list of ascents in a few seasons is prodigious.

Jones took the Alps more seriously than Wasdale Head. In the introduction to his book, he wrote: 'Personally I should always go to the high Alps when the chance offered itself, but Cumberland serves remarkably well to allay the desire for mountain air and vigorous exercise when Switzerland is out of the question.' It was fortunate for rock climbing, and for Jones's posthumous fame, that his schoolmaster's pay did not allow him to go to the Alps every holiday, for though he climbed hard he did nothing in the Alps that was epoch-making. On the shorter but more difficult climbs of the Lake District his impact was revolutionary. By the middle of the decade he was the leading spirit at Wasdale Head, both during the daytime out on the crags and in the evenings in the Wastwater Hotel.

10 Community Spirit

Wasdale Head was now the climbers' centre and at holiday times, Christmas, Easter and Whitsun, the hotel was given over to them entirely. Something about the period and the place, the character of these men and the power of their enthusiasm, engendered a community spirit that was compelling and unique. It is always possible that some such spirit may be generated when a small group of men come together, away from their normal family lives and remote from the world, to pursue a common objective. It can happen in school, in the forces, or on expeditions. It certainly happened, and to a remarkable degree, at Wasdale Head between 1890 and 1914.

Wasdale Head was still sufficiently hard of access in those days for its visitors to feel temporarily cut off from the rest of the country and freed from the tight conventions which ruled their everyday lives. Women rarely ventured to visit the hotel at these times and their absence had a liberating effect. Most important of all the community was not consciously organized; no club was formed for Lake District climbers until the 'Golden Age' was past; there were no written rules and the conventions which grew up were relaxed and tolerant.

The Wasdale Head community was what would now be called an 'in-group'. Their conversation, like that of climbers everywhere ever since, was dominated by the single subject: 'In the evening,' G. T. Lowe wrote in 1896, 'round the long dining table were gathered upwards of 30 men in strange costumes of rough tweed and as they ate with wondrous appetites, their talk was of rocks, hand-holds, traverses, aretes, and all the peculiar jargon of the mountaineer's art.' But it was not a closed society. New men could, and did, gain admittance. They did not have to be particularly young or necessarily strong; but to survive as a member, it was important to be fit and healthy, to be alert both physically and mentally, and to be enthusiastic. It was necessary too to have a taste for companionable chaos.

When the heyday of the community was over and the alchemy no longer worked its magic at the Wastwater Hotel, some of those who had experienced it tried to recapture the special spirit in books and articles. In the nature of things, none could be entirely successful, but one man wrote a powerfully atmospheric account that has the ring of truth.

Lehmann J. Oppenheimer was another Mancunian. Born in 1868, he went to a private school and then to Manchester School of Art. He became a talented artist, gifted in many media and outstanding in mosaic design. His was a gentle nature, generous, modest, self-effacing. A leading pioneer of climbing in the Buttermere area, his name appears repeatedly in the first ascents in that region in the first decade of this century but always in a supporting role. In his own descriptions of climbs he is never the hero; in other men's accounts he emerges as the ideal companion, tireless, selfless and always cheerful. He loved the life at Wasdale Head, and in his book *The Heart of Lakeland*, published in 1908, he evoked it vividly.

Oppenheimer begins by imagining a stranger approaching the Wastwater Hotel at Eastertime:

> As he nears the hotel, hungry and tired after a night in the train and a walk of a dozen miles from the coast, he bears an unwonted hum of voices, and entering the yard he finds a group looking up at, and shouting to a man who seems stuck like a fly some ten feet up the rough wall of the barn, feeling with one hand among the open joints of the stone-work for a hold higher up.

This is the famous barn-coor traverse.

Inside the stranger meets the landlord, Dan Tyson, and is

told the place is full to overflowing—'"They come up every Eastertide, a lot of 'em—a daft lot."'

Oppenheimer's stranger has greater shocks to come, beginning with the appearance of 'the Cambridge Bohemian':

> At this moment a wild-looking, unshaven individual enters, without collar or tie, and with knickerbockers well torn and patched; he gazes abstractedly at the traveller and passes on into the coffee-room. . . . Breakfast is proceeding merrily; the talk at the table is loud and jovial, for the majority in the room have met at least half of those present before, either here or at Pen-y-Gwryd or amongst the Alps, and have plenty of tales ton tell and experiences to compare. . . . Most of them wear jerseys or coarse flannel shirts without collars; some are breakfasting without their jackets which are still at the fire recovering from the vicissitudes of the previous day. . . . Much of the conversation at breakfast takes the form of speculation or prophecy; various parties are inquiring how much the barometer has fallen and discussing whether the day will be better for rocks or snow, ridges or gullies.

A perennial topic is under discussion between 'the Christ Church dandy' ('the scars on the backs of his hands show that he has had plenty of close acquaintance with the rocks') and a member of the Alpine Club. The Alpine Club man speaks:

> 'I must confess that I like these little English climbing expeditions better in many ways than the Swiss ones. A good English breakfast and a night's rest at the back of it are delights to begin with. You go out into the fresh morning air readier to enjoy the mountains than after having been rudely awakened at one or two at night and tramping for an hour or two along interminable moraines and glaciers by the feeble light of a candle.' Furthermore, he says, 'While there isn't the hundredth part of the danger, the standard of difficulty is higher here.'

The 'dandy' concurs and finds an added attraction in the freedom from guides:

> 'There is a great charm about the compulsory reliance of two or three firm friends on each other here; I shall feel far more delight if we succeed in getting up the crack today by ourselves than if Simond or Burgener led the way. . . .'

> How long this conversation will continue seems doubtful: the room is becoming deserted, and we will follow the deserters into the hall. In it stand three pairs of well-blacked shining boots, and some 40 or 50 others streaming with oil; strong and heavy, the soles and heels completely surrounded by curious shaped nails. All the men who can crush into the little standing room left are trying to discover their belongings; outside some are hammering fresh nails into gaps made the previous day, and on the stairs others are attempting to extricate their ropes from the many which wind up the staircase. . . . In groups of two, three, four or five the climbers stroll off with their ropes and ice-axes, and their pockets swollen with lunch. A couple of hours more and the cliffs of Sca Fell and Great Gable will be ringing with voices and the hotel will have resumed its wonted quietness.

Three tourists, bewildered by what they have seen at the hotel, amble towards the lake, admiring the view and wondering what can be the motives of the mad climbers: '"Brag, sir, merely brag, that, I have no doubt, is their enjoyment . . . men struggling to degenerate into apes."'

Meanwhile, back on the crags, Oppenheimer and two companions clamber up Steep Ghyll, enveloped in cloud and hindered by wet rock and snow-covered ledges, and gain the top of Scafell Pinnacle. They lunch on 'bread and butter, potted meat, raisins, prunes, chocolate, crystallised ginger and brandy'. A familiar voice is heard, a cry of 'What ho!', and 'turning round we see the merry face of the Photographer appearing over the ledge of the rocks, followed rapidly by four others'.

The 'Photographer' is presumably George Abraham, or his brother Ashley, or an amalgam of both. His party has ascended Moss Ghyll. They talk about routes and reflect that Steep Ghyll, considered a hard route when Haskett Smith discovered it, is now 'the easy way'.

> Soon those anxious to make ascents in new ways will have to adopt the tactics of an old hand at the game, who last year succeeded in climbing a famous boulder, near Wasdale, feet uppermost. . . . By the time we have descended from the Pinnacle another party has joined the Moss Ghyll group, and Sca Fell presents a lively scene. My two friends suddenly start a wrestling match in memory of Professor Wilson. One of the

Photographer's companions bursts into song, and the Photographer himself tells us all kinds of stories about famous climbers who have been here.

Oppenheimer and his companions descend by way of Mickledore Chimney, glissade down the final slope, and do a bit of 'bouldering' on the way home to the hotel: 'and by the time Wasdale Head is reached we are warm and damp and dirty enough to think of nothing but cold water, dry clothes and dinner'.

The gong announces dinner: 'Everyone has plenty to tell of what the day has brought forth, but talk is not free until the first course is over.' Among the subjects then discussed are the day's adventures and the old days at Wasdale Head, the days of Ritson and Professor Wilson.

Dinner over, the company is scattered about the hotel, yet every room seems crowded. Some remain in the dining-room, discussing the possibility of new ascents with the aid of the large photographs on the walls. In the smoke room the sofa and chairs are all occupied and several men are lying on the floor round the fire, leaning against other people's legs, renewing the adventures of the day and garnishing Swiss experiences of the summer before with lively flights of imagination. . . . As coffee is passed round and the room fills with smoke, criticism, slumbers; the narratives become more imaginative, and relate to far off periods; jokes from Leslie Stephen and Mummery pass as original and raise a laugh for the hundredth time, and gradually the company settles down into a blissful dreamy state, thinking lazily of past victories and defeats that rise and pass and fade with the flickerings of the fire.

Meanwhile the more energetic may be found in the billiard room, shouting and laughing as the ball rebounds or flies off the table to the imminent danger of someone's head. 'By Jove, what a game! No wonder we couldn't play this afternoon,' the bumptious little tourist remarks to his laconic friend, 'the ball must be covered with notches.' The table is being used for a game of fives and the partners are rushing wildly backwards or forwards or into their opponents. The Bohemian stops to take off his coat—'Not that I love warmth less, but freedom more.' And now yet oftener the ivory flies off and adds to its many dinges, until at last a collision between it and an enthusiastic spectator suggests a change. 'Let's have the passage of the billiard table leg.' This is a well-known feat and all congregate round a corner of the table to watch one after another make the attempt. Only the gymnast succeeds; he begins by sitting on the table, despite the warning notice above him of a half-crown fine for such an offence; he lets himself down gently, and, suddenly twisting round, he braces his legs firmly against the cross-bars underneath; from above nothing can now be seen of him but one hand clutching the cushion, but all are watching down below to see that he does not touch the ground. After a struggle his other hand and his leg appear on the opposite side of the table leg, and a moment afterwards he is sitting breathless on the table once more, amidst loud cheers. Then the respective advantages of tall and short men in climbing are discussed, and the heights and reaches of all in the room are marked on the wall. Next the billiard room traverse is suggested, but no one responds. After much pressing the gymnast consents to try. He takes off his coat and shoes, and placing his hands on the edge of the billiard table he walks backwards up the wall to within a yard of the ceiling. Then he moves along the table and wall simultaneously with hands and feet, avoiding the framed chromolithographs as well he may. With an enormous stride he reaches from one wall to another at the corner of the room, and is just saved from upsetting some half-emptied glasses of whisky on the mantelshelf by the terrified shouts of the owners. The next corner is easier, and in the middle of the third wall he can rest his legs awhile on the window ledge. The fourth wall is more difficult again; it contains a large recess, too deep to reach from the billiard table and only a foot lower than the ceiling. All round the angle of this he must pass before he arrives at the door, which is set diagonally across the corner of the room. This is the *mauvais pas* of the performance. The gymnast cautiously brings one foot down until his toe rests on the latch hold; then, supporting himself from the corner of the billiard table with one hand, he reaches the top of the door lintel with the other, lets go with the first, swings round in the opening and catches the lintel on the opposite side also. Here he gets the first rest for his arms by jamming himself tightly in the opening with his back and legs. To complete the traverse in the orthodox way he has still to work along the passage as far as the smoke room, and this, after an uncomfortable rest, he quickly does with back against one wall and feet against the other, finally opening the smoke room door and descending to terra firma. The tales and

> visions of the company there assembled are interrupted by cheers, and those who have missed the performance unreasonably clamour for a repetition. An old hand insidiously suggests that there are three variations of the move into the doorway, and the gymnast is dragged back once more to try them. Then there are tests of balance, of hanging on the rope and lifting people with it, or wriggling through narrow chair backs, and the evening wears away inattempting or watching all kinds of mad antics.

The 'gymnast' is, of course, O. G. Jones, the strongest and supplest of them all. George Abraham recounts how, one Easter when Jones was performing the billiard room traverse, he had negotiated the doorway and was chimneying along the corridor when he came to a lath and plaster part of the wall and his feet shot tight through into the smoking room, 'much to the discomfiture of some ladies who were having tea therein'. Abraham tells the story which has gone into legend: '. . . one Christmas-time an ice-axe was arranged as horizontal bar. Some marvellous feats were shown by experts but Jones, who had been watching retiring from the end of the room, came forward and astonished everybody. He grasped the bar with three fingers of his left hand, lifted me with his right arm, and by sheer force of muscular strength raised his chin to the level of the bar three times.'

Life at Wasdale Head though was not all high jinks and horse-play. Oppenheimer's account continues: 'Outside, in the clear starlight, the literary tourist, having deserted his two companions, is walking up and down with the Oxford man, looking up in reverent silence at the dark silhouette of Great Gable, or discussing how best to enter into the spirit of the mountains.'

The Oxford man persuades him to accompany him on a climb next day:

> I am sure you would enjoy it. The views are grand, every muscle will be called into action, ingenuity has to be exercised continually to overcome obstacles, and I promise it will make you feel alive in every fibre. . . . But I see candle flickerings in some of the upper rooms, which means bed time I suppose. I warn you

by the way, that you won't find the clothes that you sent to be dried, outside your door in the morning. You'll have to hunt for your stockings amongst some four dozen pairs hanging over the stair rail, and someone else is sure to have run off with your underclothing by mistake. It's one of the amusements of the place. Good night and good luck on the morrow!'

Such [Oppenheimer concludes], is a specimen Eastertide day at Wasdale Head. For barely a week the overflowing Hotel resembles topsey-turveydom and the hills are dotted all over with irreverent pigmies. Then comes a sudden change. The climbers tramp off with knapsack and rucksack to Boot, Keswick or Windermere or drive to Seascale; once again the Hotel is left to hardy pedestrians and lovers of quietness, disturbed only by occasional coaches bringing people up from the coast for the day; once again the mountains resume their lonely spell; cragsmen will come at times but their manners will be more reserved. Tourists will appear at breakfast wearing cuffs and ties without exposing themselves to derision, and may even hire ponies and guides to Sca Fell Pike without being looked on contemptuously.

But the climber will find delight at Wastdale whether he go in or out of season, and will be puzzled to decide whether he enjoys most the wild seclusion of the place at the one time or the outlandish life and good fellowship at the other.

The picture is idealized, but other accounts make it clear that Oppenheimer's description is accurate in detail and true to the spirit of the time.

The prime mover was O. G. Jones. The decade before his arrival was dominated by cultured and academic gentlemen, and their evenings in the hotel were quiet and conversational, not unlike the long lunch-times they were accustomed to at their clubs in Manchester, Bradford and London. The exertions of the day were enough for them; after dinner they lit their pipes and stretched their legs out before the fire to reminisce about past climbs, listen to the Cumbrian tales of John Robinson and George Seatree, and debate the finer points of climbing, technical or ethical.

The 'wind of change' of the 1890s did not blow all this away. The smoke room remained a sanctuary for discussion. Haskett Smith, John Robinson, Cecil Slingsby, Professor Collie and other veterans held court there and were accorded the respect due to their seniority and experience. But as more new men arrived, and younger men, and men not always of the restrained academic temperament, the discussions became less reflective and more disputatious, and increasingly they had to be conducted against a background of rowdy uproar from the billiard room.

The decline and fall of the billiard room as a billiard room is well documented. There was a period in the early nineties when the room was adopted as a gymnasium but the table was still used for billiards. One of the gymnastic games involved clearing a corner of the table with both feet in a single vault. Early in this game's history someone fell short and his foot tore the cloth. That most tolerant of landlords, Dan Tyson, presumably saw little point in having it repaired, the way things were going. 'It marked,' George Abraham said, 'the first step in the decadence of billards at Wasdale.'

The following Easter Dr Collier and Mr A. D. Godley devised billiard fives. The game survived, even more remarkably the table and the room survived, for nearly forty years, until 1929–30 when the table was finally removed and the room was converted into a lounge.

The most detailed account of the game is given by a hero of a later generation of Lake District climbers, Bentley Beetham. It could be played either as singles or doubles. The protagonists stood at each end of the table and points were scored by getting the ball to hit the cushion at the opponent's end or, even better, into one of the pockets there. The hand was used as a racket. Beetham says there were two codes of play; one allowed barging one's opponent, the other did not; the former made for a very vigorous game, the latter for more skilful play. Both methods were dangerous to players and spectators and furnishings alike. The marble ball, travelling at great speed, frequently flew right off the table. This meant a point against the last man to touch it; it also meant a fierce missile ricocheting around an overcrowded little room. All the windows were protected by wire netting. Beetham says it was standard procedure when the ball flew off, for everyone to duck immediately. Once when this happened a loud crash was heard as the ball hit the wall, but when everyone emerged from cover the ball had disappeared. The mystery was not solved until the next day when someone noticed a neat hole in the plaster above the mantelpiece. He searched up the chimney and found the ball lodged on a shelf at the back. Beetham writes that an outline of the rules of the game 'gives no idea of the excitement and strenuosity of the game, which was really terrific. There was no form of heating in the billiard room and the air was chill. Often clouds of steam rose from the bodies of the players as they crouched round the table.'

As the game developed knock-out competitions were organized. Geoffrey Winthrop Young gives a graphic description of a visit there which must have taken place just after the turn of the century:

> During one memorable Christmas week the sky stayed steel-blue, and the rocks were all draped in dull ivory ice. It was a historic meeting of our early climbing generations. Cecil Slingsby came, who was then throwing in his immense mountaineering prestige to back the small beginnings of home climbing; Geoffrey Hastings and his adventurous brother Cuthbert; John Robinson, striding to and fro across the fells every day to our climbs from his remote home near Cockermouth, and with him Haskett Smith, to meet the next generation, Solly, the Abrahams, Herbert Reade, Oliverson, Worthington, Geoffrey Bartrum, and a host of youngsters. In the fives tournament on the billiard-table, Slingsby and I for the Alpine Club fought out a furious final with the Abraham brothers.

If the older element had, for the most part, created life at Wasdale Head in the image of their comfortable clubs at home, the new men introduced a spirit more akin to the high-spirited horseplay of the public school dormitory or the officers' mess of a fashionable regiment, where every night was mess-night. There was, however, one considerable difference from the traditional mess-night; there seems to have been little or no drunkenness at the Wastwater Hotel. E. A. Baker writes of 'long drinks that some fives-player had invented to relieve the devouring thirst provoked by that exhausting game, drinks not potent but of more than Teutonic magnitude, being consumed as fast as tankards could be refilled'; but G. T. Lowe, who was there at Easter 1895 remarks, 'It was particularly noticeable that the greater number were for the time being water-drinkers.'

There must have been much in the close confinement of the community, its sense of remoteness and separateness from ordinary life, that recalled their days at preparatory and public school. But now they had the advantages of adulthood. They were there of their own free will; they were on holiday and could do as they pleased; they had the freedom of the fells and the crags and the billiard room. It was a halcyon time and if their free and easy ways verged at times on the squalid, it was a squalor relieved always by human warmth and friendliness. Dress was informal and eccentric and interchangeable. When they returned from the fells, wet and filthy, they flung their sodden tweeds and sock and underclothes in a great heap on the landing and changed into something drier; if they had nothing to change into, they steamed gently through the evening's entertainments. 'The odour of drying garments,' George Abraham said, 'pervades the place.' At night, the wet clothing was taken to the kitchen to dry; in the morning it was every man for himself. In a wardrobe, clothes left by previous visitors were available to all.

The hotel was grossly overcrowded. Someone slept in the bath and several spent the night with the rats in the barn. One of the few house rules enjoined that billiard fives should cease at midnight, so that whoever was sleeping on the billiard table that night could prepare for bed.

The Cragsman's Equipment

The extent of the pioneer cragsman's achievement can only be fully appreciated in the light of three considerations: the rudimentary nature of his equipment, the experimental nature of his rope technique, and the frequently unstable nature of the crags themselves. In all three respects climbing in those early days was an altogether different and more formidable undertaking than it is now.

In view of the technical skill and ingenuity of many of the pioneers in their professional lives it is surprising that they were so slow to develop intelligent safety techniques for their climbing. Almost certainly they were inhibited to some extent by the feeling, which has afflicted some climbers of every subsequent generation, that there is something unfair in taking elaborate gear to the conquest of the crags.

The Alpine rope was introduced to Lake District climbing by Robinson and Seatree in 1885 and rapidly became accepted. The best rope, recommended by the experts, was that made by John Buckingham of Shaftesbury Avenue in London to the specifications of the Alpine Club; pure manilla hemp, 1¼ inches in circumference, of gentle 'lay', and available in lengths of 40, 60, 80 or 100 feet. The 80-foot variety was regarded as best for parties of three climbers.

It was only gradually that the cragsman learned the proper use of the rope. On Pillar Rock in 1885 Robinson's method was simply to fix the rope from above so that it hung down conveniently near to the route he proposed to follow, then to do the climb, if possible, without using the rope as a handhold.

Soon after, the cragsmen adopted the Alpine technique of roping themselves together; they also, unfortunately, followed the Alpine method of moving simultaneously. In the Alps it is necessary and sensible to climb simultaneously on the less difficult ground. Distances are far greater than in the Lake District and speed is important, there is less likelihood of falling and more chance of arresting a fall by digging the ice axe into the surface of the snow or ice. To transfer this method to the steep rock faces of the Lake District, though, was merely to guarantee the greater danger of the greater number, to ensure that if one man fell his companions on the rope fell too.

Early photographs, however, make it clear that this was, for some time, the normal procedure. One of the first of all rock climbing pictures (Plate 7) shows the young Ashley Abraham, already a bulky figure, attached to his younger brother Sidney by a 20-foot length of ordinary household rope and both of them spreadeagled uncertainly on steep, unstable-looking rock near Sharp Edge on Blencathra. George Abraham took the photograph in 1890. Later in the decade, when the Abrahams led the way towards more sophisticated rope work, they dubbed the picture 'How not to climb'.

The sole advantage of the rope, as used in this primitive fashion, was psychological. Haskett Smith was well aware of this. In the introduction to his book he said, 'Even in places where it gives the leader no security and to some extent actually impedes him, the moral effect of it is good. It wonderfully increases those feelings of united and ordered effort, of mutual dependence and mutual confidence, and finally of cheery subordination of self, which are not the least of the virtues or the joys of mountaineering.'

In modern rock climbing the basic rules are simple. One man climbs at a time; as he moves, his companion on the rope, stationary on some convenient ledge, protects him as best he can by keeping the rope between them almost taut; he cannot be pulled from his stance, even if the climber falls, because he is anchored in place by a rope from his waist to a 'belay', some stable projection of rock just above him.

This technique evolved very slowly. Jones and the Abrahams varied their methods according to the ground they were on. At the start of Walker's Gully, for example, Jones says: 'I mounted the wall from ledge to ledge, turning periodically at distances of four or five yards to manipulate the rope for the second man, who in his turn steadied the last man up.' They hauled in the rope by hand, and did not pass it round their backs and over one shoulder as modern climbers do for greater friction. Jones regarded himself as being 'belayed' when he was merely attached by the rope to a stationary companion. By 'belaying pin' he meant any flake of rock over which the rope could be passed to improve the chances of holding a falling man. Later, at the prompting of the Abraham brothers, he grew skilful in the art of threading the rope behind jammed stones for added protection, and came to realize the need, on difficult pitches, for the stationary man to be separately anchored to his stance. Just how primitive and ineffective the early rope techniques were, though, was tragically demonstrated on Scafell in 1903.

In some aspects of rope-work, the pioneers showed ingenuity and caution. Increasingly when a man had his sights on a particularly testing new route, he would first explore it in comparative safety from above, with a companion at the top of the route paying the rope out to him as he climbed down to study the difficulties. In 1889 the Hopkinson brothers forced a truly direct route up the first pitch of Great Gully on Dow Crag by cunning rope-craft; according to O. G. Jones's account, 'They clambered into the cave and thrust a rope through the small aperture in the roof. When a sufficient quantity had been poked up in that way, it fell over the front of the cave and was available for climbing.'

Jones was inventive in his use of the rope, and it probably saved his life more than once. On his first attempt to climb Moss Ghyll on Scafell, early in 1893, he encountered a lot of fresh snow and found it difficult to locate the 'Collie step': 'At the first attempt on the traverse I slipped and fell into the snow-bed of the gully below. The result was scarcely surprising though eminently uncomfortable. But the falling was, under the circumstances, almost part of the programme, and a rope had been fixed in the interior of the cavern, passed out through the "window", and then attached to my waist, to eliminate the danger of plunging some 400 feet down to the foot of the gully.' Jones cracked two ribs and was badly bruised, but, characteristically, he went straight back to the awkward problem, solved it and finished the climb.

The mid century fell walkers and scramblers, the climbing parsons, F. H. Bowring and men of that generation, never ventured onto the fells without a stout stick six or seven feet long, the Lake District version of the alpenstock. The fell-pole was used as a sort of third leg and was especially helpful when descending scree or steep grass or broken ground and for vaulting across streams. In most other circumstances though, as gully scrambling became climbing and both hands were needed to grasp the rock, the fell-pole became a dangerous encumbrance. Several early accounts complain of the extra hazards involved when conservative-minded climbers tried to take fell-poles with them. Haskett Smith, on his way to the Napes Needle climb in 1886, was held up for some time when his pole dropped down a narrow crack. O. G. Jones went to the rescue of two men who had got themselves into serious difficulties trying to descend one of the gullies of Glaramara with 'walking sticks tied tightly to their wrists with string'. Jones 'thought with some bitterness that this was the way that the noblest of sports acquired its notoriety for great danger'. The cross which still stands at the foot of Fleetwith Pike on the Buttermere side marks the area where an eighteen-year-old girl pitched to her death when she tripped over her fell-pole.

'Everything which can be done with the alpenstock can be done also and better with the axe,' says Clinton Dent in the Badminton Library volume on mountaineering. The arrival of the Alpinists in force on the rock climbing scene brought in the ice-axe to replace the fell-pole. The axe was essential in winter conditions, which often extend in the Lake District gullies until well past Easter, but many early climbers carried their axes in the summer too and put them to liberal, even indiscriminate, use. Collie hacked his famous step with Hastings's axe. Frequently the axe was used to form an extra, artificial hold, wedged into some accommodating crack to provide a foot or hand hold, or held strategically by the number two while the leader stepped briefly onto it to gain a better position. O. G. Jones, for example, sitting on a boulder and plotting his conquest of Kern Knotts Crack: 'Surely that must be a foot-hold ten feet up on the edge of the crack. If, while I mounted his shoulder, the second man could hold the ice-pick in a minute fissure in the face, I might manage to step onto the axe-head and reach the edge of the platform. . . . The plan commended itself to all, and we placed ourselves in position.'

The clinching reason for carrying an ice-axe even in midsummer was its great value as a 'gardening' implement. When the pioneers began their work the crags had been undisturbed by man since the beginning of time. Millennia of hard weathering, and the tenacious life-force which inspires the rough grasses and mosses and heathers of the hills, had littered all but the most smoothly vertical of rock faces with tons of loose and dangerous debris, pebbles, rocks, boulders, earth and variegated vegetation. It was the task of the leading climber to clear away all these obstacles to safe progress, while his companions waited stoically and avoided as best they could the shower of rubbish from above. The sound of rock climbing today is the metallic jangling of ironmongery and the banging of hammer upon piton; in those days it was the roar and rumble of rocks crashing to the scree below.

In the 1936 jubilee edition of the Journal of the Fell and Rock Climbing Club, Haskett Smith wrote: 'Perhaps the most remarkable change of the last 50 years is the way in which the rocks of Cumberland have been cleaned up, to the great comfort of the climber but not without loss of picturesqueness. For instance, Sergeant's Crag has lost one very delightful feature, an almost vertical wall evenly covered with a thin layer of bright green moss which was starred all over with the beautiful little Filmy fern. It was a perfect picture, but it so thoroughly lubricated the rock that the climb was impossible till J. W.

Robinson remorselessly raked it down, so that next time we attacked it, the holds were not only visible, but dry.'

The ice-axes of those days were of Alpine manufacture, sturdy but not well balanced, with wooden shafts four feet long or more. Slings had already been devised to enable the climber who needed both hands on the rock to let the axe dangle from his wrist. On the last great climb of the 'Golden Age' period, Fred Botterill took his ice-axe, although it was midsummer, and when the holds became tenuous and tiny he carried it between his teeth.

The rope and the axe were the outward signs of the cragsman; in other respects he was indistinguishable from the fell walker. There were no rigid rules about clothes, but most of them preferred strong, sensible old suits. Tweeds were warm and afforded a reassuring friction in desperate moments when knees and stomachs were brought to bear on the rock. The long Norfolk jacket, with capacious pockets, was the usual thing, sometimes with a waistcoat too. Trousers were universally of the knickerbocker type, knee breeches baggy enough to allow for the full flexing of the knees. Calves were protected by thick stockings. The climbers expressed their individuality largely through their hats, which ranged widely among flat caps, variants on the bowler and the trilby, the deerstalker and something akin to the modern Mao Tse-tung hat, and the flamboyant sombreros sometimes affected by the Abraham brothers. The knapsack of earlier times, slung across one shoulder, had been replaced by the rucksack, strapped across both shoulders but hanging uncomfortably low on the back by modern standards. It was not often worn while climbing, though; sandwiches and other essentials were generally carried in the jacket pocket.

The cragsmen took one part of their outfit most seriously. For the fell walker, his boots make the difference between a pleasant excursion and a painful endurance test; for the rock climber, the difference can be life or death.

In the first gully-climbing years, when the premium lay upon strong arms and the ability to wriggle and wrestle up narrow clefts, boots were not greatly considered. Haskett Smith and John Robinson and their companions merely wore stout country boots with a scattering of hobnails. But when climbing moved onto smaller holds in more exposed places, it became vital that a man should feel confident that his boots would cleave to the rock.

The importance of nails was quickly acknowledged. In 1885 John Robinson refused to allow Ernest Peile to venture onto the North Climb on Scafell 'as I felt responsible for his safety after promising his father I would look after him; he had no nails in his boots'. The cragsmen soon found that hob nails were not sufficient, and began a series of experiments with nails of different shapes and sizes and types of steel, arranged in varying patterns that was to continue for decades and prove an unfailing source of conversation and controversy. The detailed intensity with which the debate was carried on is illustrated by the advice of George Abraham, a leading thinker in the field: 'On a small foothold the big outside nails of the average mountain boot grip solely; the inner nails are unused, and the foot wobbles ominously, especially if held long in place. A small row, or even two, of inner nails will stop this tendency. The ideal would be to have the heads of these initial rows of inner nails on a level with the heads of the outside nails. In fact the whole of the boot is best if the nails are driven to stand out equidistant from the leather.'

They were not the first to feel the fascination of boots. Ninety years earlier Samuel Taylor Coleridge had taken a close interest, and recommended: 'Shoes, soles at least half an inch thick—the upper leather three-quarter galoshed. Nails of tempered steel must be provided, the points screws; their heads near half inch diameter, must be cut in the form of a square pyramid . . . 12 of these nails must be put into each sole, seven round the forepart and five round the heel as near the edges of the Sole as possible without endangering the bursting of the leather.'

Strong stout boots, heavy with nails, were the climbers' prime necessity throughout the 'Golden Age' and well into the twentieth century. Scarpetti, the rope-soled boots used in the Dolomites, were tried but found unsuitable for the smaller holds and smoother surface of Cumberland granite. The incut rubber soles which dominate today were unknown to the pioneers, and when they made their appearance many veterans considered them unfairly adhesive. To any modern climber who has tried nailed boots, it is a matter of wonder and admiration that the pioneers could achieve so high a standard of delicate climbing in them. It is less surprising that the more adventurous should have found it sometimes necessary, on their later and more exacting climbs, to take their boots off and climb in stockinged feet.

In one other important respect, conditions were radically different for the early climbers. Today the young man who becomes interested in rock climbing can learn the sport by joining a club or taking a course. He will find available to him information of the most comprehensive kind. The Fell and Rock Climbing Club publishes eight guide books to the climbs of the Lake District, listing and describing, sometimes in move-by-move detail, hundreds of routes up dozens of cliff faces, and clearly stating the extent and nature of their difficulties. Every major climbing ground in Britain is similarly served and the very latest routes are described in detail in the climbing magazines. And with all this help it is still quite easy to find yourself on the wrong route unless you are very careful.

The pioneers had no such help. They learnt simply by going to Wasdale Head and persuading more experienced men to take them climbing. Information came largely by word of mouth or from scanty accounts in the hotel visitors' books at Wasdale Head, Dungeon Ghyll and Buttermere. Haskett Smith's book, *Climbing in the British Isles: England*, which was published in 1894, is an A to Z of the sport, crammed with information, topographical, technical, historical, and etymological, but of little direct use to anyone seeking detailed information about individual routes. In contrast O. G. Jones's classic *Rock-Climbing in the English Lake District*, gives plenty of detail about many routes and, for the first time, attempts to classify them according to degree of difficulty. It is a vivid, lively, highly personalized account of many adventures. But it is far too big and heavy and discursive to be slipped into a jacket pocket and taken onto the crags, and it was not published until 1897, when the 'Golden Age' was almost at an end.

12 Some Personalities

'Wastdale Head was at that time a rendezvous for many amusing characters as well as for some of the most brilliant men in England.' The text is taken from the *Confessions* of Aleister Crowley, perhaps the most brilliant and certainly the most perverse and eccentric of them all.

Crowley was the son of a prosperous brewer and pious member of the Plymouth Brethren. Educated at Malvern and Tonbridge public schools, then at Trinity College, Cambridge, he showed a precocious aptitude for rebellious beliefs and outrageous behaviour. He made an early pact with the Devil, assumed an easy mastery of language, in prose and poetry, and took fierce delight in shocking people of respectable conformity. Later he was to devote his great energies and talents to the pursuit and propagation of black magic, under the permissive banner 'Do What Thou Wilt' and the self-appointed title of 'The Great Beast 666' from 'The Book of Revelation'. His adolescent interests, though, were poetry, chess and climbing.

Crowley began his climbing as a boy on the chalk cliffs of Beachy Head: 'In my play-time,' he said, 'I was either hunting flappers on the front, playing chess or climbing Beachy Head.' He was not the first to try his nerve on that great chalk cliff. Forty years earlier Edward Whymper and his brother, as schoolboys, had frightened themselves on the eastern side of the Head, and Whymper never forgot the experience: 'Since then,' he wrote after he had made his finest Alpine ascents, 'we have been often in dangers of different kinds, but never have we more nearly broken our necks than upon that occasion.'

Crowley tackled the sea cliffs with characteristic confidence: 'Beachy Head,' he wrote. 'offers rock problems as varied, interesting and picturesque as any cliffs in the world. I began to explore the face. Popular ignorance had surrounded it with innumerable absurd rumours. The general opinion was that no-one had ever climbed it. There was however a legend that it had once been done. I settled the point by walking up, smoking a pipe, with my dog (I had no woman available) in nine and a half minutes from the beach to the coast-guard station.'

He went on to work out several routes on the cliffs and their pinnacles. He sent an account to the local paper, but all it published was a powerful editorial rebuke which began with the words 'Insensate folly takes many forms'.

The Journal of the Scottish Mountaineering Club, however, did publish an article in which Crowley described climbing on chalk as dangerous and unpleasant: 'In wet weather the chalk forms a paste which clogs the boots and makes footholds impossible. In dry weather the dust takes possession of the eyes and throat. But, for all that, many of my happiest days have been spent on the face. . . . In other districts I could be no more than primus inter pares. On Beachy Head I was the only one—I had invented an entirely new branch of the sport.'

The peculiar nature of chalk led Crowley to develop a climbing style that was to prove highly appropriate to the demands of the new 'balance climbing' of Cumberland: 'One can hardly ever be sure that any given hold is secure. It is, therefore, a matter of the most exquisite judgement to put on it no more weight than is necessary. A jerk or a spring would almost infallibly lead to disaster. One does not climb the cliffs. One hardly even crawls. Trickles or oozes would perhaps be the ideal verbs.'

When he was seventeen Crowley went to Slighachan in Skye with his mother, and a group of climbers took him up Sgurr nan Gillean. The following summer, 1893, he holidayed in Langdale, performed, by his own account, some formidable feats of mixed walking and scrambling, and climbed a little with John Robinson.

His single, unhappy experience on the rope with O. G. Jones has already been recounted. His contempt for Jones was total: 'Jones obtained the reputation of being the most brilliant rock climber of his time by persistent self-advertisement. He was never a first-class climber because he was never a safe climber. If a hand-hold was out of his reach he would jump at it, and he had met with several serious accidents before the final smash. But his reputation is founded principally on climbs which he did not make at all, in the proper sense of the word. He used to go out with a couple of photographers and have himself lowered up and down a climb repeatedly until he had learnt its peculiarities, and then make the "first ascent" before a crowd of admirers. Now the essential difficulty of negotiating a pitch of any length is that one has to waste any amount of time and strength while one is finding out where the holds are. There is no credit at all in repeating a climb.'

There was probably a strong streak of envy in Crowley's attitude to Jones; certainly he was unashamedly proud of his own prowess: 'Scafell is separated from Sca Pikes by a pass called Mickledoor . . . by going down a little on one side one can climb the cliffs by the Broad Stand or Mickledoor Chimney. . . . But it had been the ambition of every climber to start from the exact top of the ridge. This was called the Direct Climb of Mickledoor; and no-one had done it. That seemed to be a shame, so I did it. This time the fat was in the fire. My good faith was openly challenged in the smoking room. I shrugged my shoulders but offered to repeat the climb the following day before witnesses—which I accordingly did. . . . I must admit that my methods were sometimes calculated to annoy; but I had no patience with the idiotic vanity of mediocrities. I took the Climbers' Record to be a serious compilation and never wrote in it without the fullest sense of responsibility. So when I found a solemn Te Deum being chanted on account of the fifth ascent of the Pillar Rock by a "lady", I took my dog to the top and recorded "First ascent by a St Bernard bitch".'

Crowley's contempt was withering and wide-ranging. He accused the Alpine Club of falsifying records, claiming ascents that had not been made and ignoring the real achievements of non-members. The Club's members, he said, were 'incompetent, insanely jealous of their vested interests and unthinkably unsportsmanlike. . . . Various old fogies, who could not have climbed the simplest rocks in Cumberland, or led across an easy Alpine Pass, had been personally conducted by peasants up a few mountains and written themselves up into fame.' He dismissed Dent's Badminton volume on mountaineering as 'full of grotesque blunders and inaccuracies'. He despised the professional Alpine guide: 'He did not know what rock climbing was judged by Cumberland standards. . . . The first-rate amateur was to the professional as a rifleman to a man with a flint axe.'

But some climbers had Crowley's whole-hearted admiration: 'They were men of education and intelligence; they had studied the physical theory of conditions; they had practised the various types of technique required to meet these conditions in detail. They were doing climbs which had never been dreamt of by any Alpine guide. The combination of Mummery, Collie and Hastings could hardly happen again in a century. Mummery had a genius for rock climbing and an uncanny instinct for mountain problems in general. Collie was brilliant all round and had an absolute scientific knowledge of materials and a feeling for topography. Hastings was a tower of physical strength and endurance, an ideal second man either as a hoist or an anchor. All three were accomplished technicians and had experience of every kind of ground and conditions.'

Crowley's greatest admiration was reserved for the man who became his closest climbing friend, Oscar Eckenstein, almost as strange as himself and every bit as strong-minded and individualistic. Most of Eckenstein's important climbing took place in Snowdonia, much of it with the great pioneer there James Merriman Archer Thomson. Mathematician and scientist by training, a railway engineer by profession, Eckenstein assiduously applied his skills to the problems of mountaineering, and made important technical contributions to the sport in the mechanics of crampons, the theory of knot-tying and the use of the new tricouni nails in climbing boots. When they first met at Wasdale Head in 1898 he was Crowley's senior by twenty years, but they formed an immediate friendship, climbed together in Mexico in 1900 and 1901, and in 1905 took part in an ill-fated expedition to Kangchenjunga in the Himalayas.

Crowley said of Eckenstein: 'He was probably the best all-round man in England but his achievements were little known because of his almost fanatical objection to publicity.' This objection, characteristic of the Pen-y-Gwyrd group, caused friction in the early years of the twentieth century between Eckenstein and the Abraham brothers, who were then bringing out a series of books about their climbing exploits.

Crowley felt that he and Eckenstein made an ideal combination: 'Eckenstein had all the civilised qualities and I had all the savage ones. He was a finished athlete; his right arm in particular was so strong that he had only to get a couple of fingers on to a sloping ledge of an overhanging rock above his head and he could draw himself slowly up by that alone. . . . He was rather short and sturdily built. He did not know the meaning of the word "fatigue". He could endure the utmost hardship without turning a hair. He was absolutely reliable. . . . He knew his limitations to a hair's breadth. . . . In the actual technique of climbing, Eckenstein and I were still more complementary. It is impossible to imagine two methods more opposed. His climbing was invariably clean, orderly and intelligible; mine can hardly be described as human. His movements were a series, mine were continuous; he used definite muscles, I used my whole body. Owing doubtless to my early ill-health, I never developed physical strength; but I was very light, and possessed elasticity and balance to an extraordinary degree.'

It is not clear whether Charles Cannan's university reading parties continued into the 1890s, but Wasdale Head's links with the academic world remained strong. Among the visitors was a senior boy from Harrow, L. S. Amery, who later became a distinguished Alpinist and a Minister in Conservative governments and earned an enduring niche for himself in the nation's history by his Cromwellian cry to the Prime Minister, Neville Chamberlain, in May 1940 in the House of Commons, 'You have sat too long here for any good you have been doing. Depart, I say, and let us have done with you. In the name of God, go!'

The young Amery was a keen gymnast and cross-country runner. His housemaster at Harrow was John Stogden, the first Alpine man to proclaim the attractions of winter climbing in Cumberland. At Christmas 1892 a younger mountaineer and teacher, R. C. Gilson, took Amery to Wasdale Head. They climbed Deep Ghyll and some of the easier routes on Pillar Rock. Then Amery was invited to join O. G. Jones and two others in an attempt on the Oblique Gully on the Ennerdale face of Great Gable. It turned out to be a typical Jones day.

Oblique Chimney had only been conquered a few days before by a party led by Dr Collier and including S. B. Winser. Jones's party for the second ascent was 'an expert Alpine climber . . . a learned classic . . . and a plucky young Harrovian with plenty of nerve and endurance in him'. The Harrovian was Amery.

They started late; the crag was plastered with ice and coated with fresh snow; a thick mist obscured everything and it took them a long time to find the Chimney. As they edged along the traverse towards the foot of the climb Amery slipped and fell ten feet before the rope held him. His hand was badly cut.

The 'learned classic' had volunteered to carry their lunches up Stony Gully and wait for them on the summit. It was already growing dark and bitterly cold when they began the climb. Amery recalled it all clearly in the first volume of his autobiography, *Days of Fresh Air*: 'At last we found our gully, a slanting cleft 20 feet deep perhaps, in a great bulging overhang of cliff. We clambered up into the heart of this and then Glynne Jones, placing feet on one side and back on the other, began with amazing skill to wriggle himself ever upwards and outwards for the best part of, I suppose, 100 feet, at the end of which a powerful kick and straddle enabled him to transfer himself to face the rock on one side of the chimney and climb out of it.' By now it was snowing heavily again. They finally reached the summit in darkness and a blizzard. The 'classic' and their lunches had long since departed. And then they misread the compass and came down via Wind Gap and Sty Head and the icy path: 'How we managed to avoid broken limbs has ever been a mystery,' wrote Jones. 'We would suddenly slip over the ice, and slide furiously down the path and into some obstruction below.'

Amery's comment on Jones is in the best traditions of gentlemanly restraint: 'He was a fine, if over-bold, climber.'

Outstanding among the distinguished men to visit Wasdale Head in these years was the brilliant zoologist Professor Arthur Milnes Marshall. A Fellow of the Royal Society and Professor of Zoology at Owens College in Manchester, he was one of a growing band of busy and eminent men who found complete relaxation in mountaineering but who were content to leave the pioneering of new routes to bolder spirits. On the 31st December 1893 the Professor was killed in a strange accident at the foot of Scafell. Together with friends he had climbed Scafell Pinnacle by way of Steep Hyhll and Slingsby's Chimney. They came down Lord's Rake, and while his companions began to climb Deep Ghyll, the Professor scrambled up the easy ridge on the other side of the Rake to find a vantage point for photographing them. No-one saw what happened next, but something caused him to slip on the snow slope, he slid down, pitched over a small cliff and fell to his death. George Abraham said it was generally supposed that he had been struck by a falling rock. W. N. Tribe, however, said: 'He apparently stepped backwards without realising the drop behind him, a thing the writer had found likely to happen when one's head is enveloped in a focussing cloth.' The disorientating effect of the focussing cloth was experienced by several photographer-climbers. Some years later in the Dolomites Ashley Abraham emerged from beneath the cloth and stepped backwards off his narrow ledge into space. Fortunately, he was roped to his brother George, who was securely belayed.

It was about this time, the early 1890s, that George and Ashley Abraham, 'the Keswick Brothers', began their long careers in climbing. Their father, George Perry Abraham, who was a professional photographer, had founded a business in Keswick in 1866. George the eldest son, was born four years later; Ashley six years after that. Brought up to succeed to the family business, they became superb photographers; and it was natural that young men of such high spirits and sense of adventure should take to the crags. For the first few years they kept apart from the mainstream development of the sport at Wasdale Head. Perhaps out of adolescent shyness they confined their climbing to unfashionable cliffs within convenient range of Keswick. In 1890 they forced a route up Sandbed Ghyll in St John's in the Vale; two years later, in Borrowdale, they made the first ascent of Walla Crag Gully—graded 'Difficult' in the current guide. This was the first rock climb ever made in Borrowdale. Two years after that, in 1894, they successfully tackled Dollywaggon Gully in Grisedale.

They rapidly coalesced into a formidable climbing team. Both were strong, vigorous and adventurous. George, though the elder, was much slighter in build; Ashley, already in his late teens approaching fifteen stone, made the perfect anchor man: 'They complemented each other completely, George more often leading, graceful, supple and balanced; Ashley, a moving column of strength and aggressive energy, in support.' In temperament as in physique, they were complementary; George was more excitable and volatile, Ashley always steady and equable. Yet they got on well together, enjoyed each other's company, and in over fifty years of climbing, mostly together, in all parts of Britain and the Alps, neither had a serious accident.

Their meeting with O. G. Jones, at Easter 1896, was providential in more ways than one; the combined strength of the three of them created a dramatic advance in climbing standards; the experience and greater sagacity of the brothers may well have helped to prolong Jones's life, for he was still falling off fairly often; and the impact of his ebullient prose and their magnificent photographs was to make the sport known to a new and far wider range of people than ever before.

13 The Dynamic Trio

O. G. Jones's climbing skill made rapid advances, largely under the guidance of J. W. Robinson. In September 1893 they made the first ascent of Sergeant Crag Gully, still graded 'Severe', and opened up one or two gully and chimney routes on the crags of High Stile overlooking Buttermere. Two days after their climb on Sergeant Crag it was repeated by two men whose names were Phillimore and Anderson, who did not know that the Gully had already been climbed, and who do not play any other part in this story, a measure of the mounting popularity of rock climbing and the modest obscurity of many of its enthusiasts.

On Boxing Day 1893 Robinson took Jones to Kern Knotts Crag, the steep and handsome outcrop on the eastern fringe of the Napes face of Great Gable with which Jones's name is forever linked. Jones described the incident, referring to Robinson as 'Nestor' in tribute to his greater experience and wisdom, and to the third member of the party, W. H. Fowler, as 'the engineer': 'The uninitiated of Wastdale often lament the secretiveness of those who know where new things exist but who keep the knowledge to themselves. Nestor is very reticent, and it is to be counted unto him for righteousness that one Christmas week, after bad weather had deprived us of all the ordinary climbing, he announced to the engineer and me that there was a fascinating little thing, the fancy of an "off" afternoon, lying conveniently close to the hotel, that he would show us how to climb. I was lying on the billiard table just then thinking of the different kinds of nothing. . . . The engineer was enthusiastic, so in the gentle rain we marched out of the inn that afternoon.'

The 'fascinating little thing' was Kern Knotts Chimney, now graded 'Difficult'. Although water was pouring down it they accomplished the climb, Jones leading, without difficulty. It was on the way down that Jones first set eyes on Kern Knotts Crack: 'Nestor, with his characteristic caution vetoed the whole affair, and vowed he would never speak to me again if I attempted to climb it. The engineer, on the other hand, thought it could not be much worse than the chimney which we had just climbed in safety, and that it might be a good thing to keep in mind for settled weather.'

Jones kept it in mind, but two years passed before he returned to Wasdale Head. In the summer of 1894 he climbed hard in the Engadine and then in the Dolomites. In May 1895 he was with the Haskett Smith brothers on Cader Idris, where they made first ascents of the East and Great Gullies on Craig Cau; and later that summer he enjoyed an Alpine season that was active even by his energetic standards.

He was back at Wasdale Head for Christmas 1895. He led his friends Mr and Mrs F. W. Hill up Kern Knotts Chimney, and noted with disapproval: 'The direct route up from the bridge has lately been simplified by an artificial step, evidently cut with a chisel. It is a pity the timid mason did not go round another way.' This time he studied that enticing crack more closely: 'On the natural bridge I halted, and looked down the smooth wall of rock facing the Styhead. The crack was straight beneath, and Hill nerved me to the sudden resolve to descend by the rope and prospect the middle portion of the climb. We had only 60 feet of rope, but I was let down carefully and at full distance found myself in a splayed-out portion above the first pitch. The bit beneath looked very awkward. . . . There was only one course available, that of climbing up again. This was not so hard as I had fancied it would be, for with the sense of perfect security in the rope that Hill carefully manipulated came freedom of movement and a bolder style.'

During this Christmas holiday Jones met Ashley Abraham.

They did not climb together then, but next Easter Jones called on the brothers in Keswick and launched their brief but formative friendship. George Abraham described the day in his book, *Mountain Adventures at Home and Abroad*: 'Without any foreword he called on us in the early hours of a beautiful April morning, after a long night journey from town. In two hours' time mutual keenness had promoted friendship, parental misgiving had been overcome, and we were off to Wastdale.'

According to George's account they met John Robinson at Sty Head and it was then that he delivered his famous warning, 'Well, Jones, if you climb that crack I'll never speak to you again!'

'After this encounter,' George continues, 'we passed across the Screes of Great Gable to the foot of the Napes. The initial climb to try our powers was to be a visit to all the ridges consecutively. Jones started first up the Eagle's Nest Ridge, watching us somewhat critically but only at the outset. In an hour and three-quarters, we had also surmounted the Needle and Arrowhead ridges and descended twice by the Needle Gully. . . . Yet that first day with Owen Glynne Jones meant much more than wrestling with those glorious crags, every muscle and sense alive to instant action as to method of rope and rock-work. Our real selves stood revealed, and a friendship was formed which proved in after years to be the most valuable possession of life.'

The new team was soon making its mark. On 20th April they climbed Scafell Pinnacle by the formidable Jones's Route from Deep Ghyll, a significant event on three counts: the first ascent of this route, now graded 'Severe (Mild)'; the Abrahams' first serious experiment in photographing high standard climbing; and the party's first use of the sophisticated combined tactics that were to stand them in invaluable stead.

Their initial aim was to follow the route pioneered by Charles Hopkinson and W. N. Tribe three years before from Deep Ghyll to the summit of the Pinnacle, but either because of the usual Hopkinson secretiveness or through his own myopia, Jones soon found himself on new ground, hopefully following the line of the long, curving crack in the great wall to the left of the ghyll. Jones described the climb in exciting detail. He was leading, with George next, giving as much protection as he could:

> I could hear another climbing party finishing an ascent of the Pinnacle by the ordinary route, their voices echoing down the ghyll and cheering me with a sense of neighbourliness. My companions were holding an animated discussion below on the subject of photography. The light was excellent, and our positions most artistic. The cameras were left in the cave at the foot of the ghyll. Ashley was afraid I meant to go up without him; but his professional instinct got the better of his desire to climb, and, shouting out to us to stay where we were for five minutes, he ran round to the high-level traverse on the other side of the ghyll, and down the Lord's Rake to the cavern. George had the tripod screw and could not hand it to his brother; so, asking me to hold him firmly with the rope, he practised throwing stones across the gully to the traverse. Then, tying the screw to a stone, he managed to project this over successfully. We composed our limbs to a photographic quiescence. Ashley had a splendid wide-angle lens, which, from his elevated position on the traverse opposite, could take in 400 feet of the cliff, showing the entire route to the summit. It was his turn to take the lead. 'Mr Jones! I can't see you, your clothes are so dark.' I apologized. 'Will you step out a foot or two from that hole?' I was in a cheerful mood and ready to oblige a friend, but the platform was scarcely two feet square, and to aquiesce was to step out a few hundred feet into Deep Ghyll. For this I had not made adequate preparation and told him so. 'Well, will you take off your coat?' That I could do with pleasure, and for a while his instructions were levelled at George. He was in an awkward place and was much cramped in ensuring safety, but Ashley was dissatisfied and insisted on his lifting the left leg. This gave him no foot-hold to speak of, but in the cause of photography he had been trained to manage without such ordinary aids. . . . The ghyll had become rather gloomy and we had a lengthy exposure. I was glad to slip on my jacket again and draw in the rope for George's ascent.

The result is the photograph, Plate 12.

His plate satisfactorily exposed, Ashley abandoned the cumbersome equipment and joined his companions on a tiny ledge high on the face. Jones continued the climb:

> The others fixed themselves to a little belaying pin-while I attempted to swarm up the vertical corner. A couple of feet above their heads I found that the only available holds were sloping the wrong way. They could be easily reached but were unsafe for hauling, and after clinging for some minutes without advancing an inch I was compelled to descend and reconsider the problem.

Jones searched for an easier alternative but without success:

> I returned to the corner and prepared for another attempt. This time Ashley gave me a shoulder at a slightly lower level on the ghyll side of the ridge. A trying drag upwards with very scanty fingerholds brought my knees onto a satisfying hollow in a little ledge, and steadied by the two side faces of the sloping slab I stepped up and on to it. . . . The other two men came up with a little assistance from the rope, and we cleared away the loose stones from our platform. It shelved badly downwards and offered no guarantee of safety in case I fell from the next vertical bit. But George sturdily rammed his brother close against the wall and intimated that the two would accept the responsibility of fielding me if necessary. I mounted their shoulders and reached up at arm's length to a sharp and firm edge of rock. A preliminary grind of my boot into a shoulder-blade and then a clear swing out on the arms, a desperate pull-up with knees and toes vainly seeking support, and at last the upper shelf was mounted. . . . Boot scratches were now numerous, both along the ridge and by the left. We took the finish hand over hand, and reached the pinnacle cairn in five minutes.

It was an excellent first season for the trio. The Easter weather was unusually fine; the rock was dry and warm; they climbed well and happily on the Screes as well as around Deep Ghyll, and on the last day of the holiday Jones decided their form was strong enough for a look at the legendary Collier's Climb on Scafell. Pioneered by the prehensile Dr Collier three years earlier, this route, and particularly its initial pitch, had acquired a reputation sufficiently fearsome to inhibit a second attempt. According to Jones, 'Queer tales were told round at the inn of men who were flung back over the Rake's Progress after rising only ten feet. Even Dr. Collier was reported to have said he never wished to see the place again.'

On 22nd April 1896 Jones and the Abrhams edged their way along Rake's Progress. Once again, Jones takes up the story:

> There could be no possible doubt of the place. A thin crack rose direct from the Progress, overhanging for the first ten feet, then leaning back a trifle towards the left. A yard or two to the left of this a square corner led directly up so as to join the crack just below a thin chimney, that started some twenty feet above our heads. To get to this chimney was the difficulty. . . . We decided to take the corner. A. was to stand on a small ledge about a foot above the Progress, and brace himself firmly enough to hold my weight. G. acted as a sort of flying buttress for his brother, and paid out my rope with extreme care. From A.'s shoulders I could just reach a high handhold with the left. But one grip at that height was useless, as the body had to be lifted up on to the rib of rock separating the two clefts. A. then padded his head with a handkerchief beneath his cap, and begged me to stand on it. However steady a young man may be, there are times when his friends think him weak in the head. Such a time was this, and I anxiously asked him if he could hold it perfectly still while I used it. 'You may do anything except waltz on it,' was the encouraging rejoinder, and I promptly placed my left foot on his parietal. 'That's all right,' the tough young head called out, 'you may stay there all day if you like.' This was reassuring but I had come out to climb and meant to move on. Yet for the life of me I could not see what to do next. The left foot required a lift before the high handhold could be employed, and there was nothing for it to rest against except the square corner of the recess. Two or three times I tried hard to grip the corner with the toe of my boot, but ineffectually. Then A., seeing my trouble, reached up a hand and held my boot on an infinitesimal ledge. It felt firm and I trusted to it. With the first movement upwards my right hand felt a charmingly secure depression in the rib above, and, swinging clear from A.'s head, I dragged up on to the buttress and felt that the game was half won already.

This was combined tactics carried to a new extreme. The next moves showed how quickly Jones had learned the wisdom of ingenious rope management:

> The rib was easy to ascend for a foot or two, till indeed it terminated at the small chimney above. But caution was the instinct uppermost in my mind, and the climb to the grassy

> platform above might, in spite of appearances, prove nasty. Casting around for some means of anchoring on my own rope, I saw that in the crack to my right a bunch of small stones were firmly jammed, and that daylight could be seen behind them.... The others were as yet unroped. Calling to them to let go the rope, I drew up the free end by my teeth and my 'unemployed' hand, and let it fall straight down the hole to them. If a fall occurred now in trying the next few feet I could only tumble three or four yards.

In his 'Mountain Adventures', George says: 'This was the first time our leader had followed our advice on this point; we had tested its efficiency several times previously, and the use of this security proved the secret of many a succeeding success.'

The Abraham brothers had to return to work in Keswick next day, but Jones had a few more days of holiday left. On his final day, 'feeling strong after a fortnight's scrambling', he returned to Kern Knotts Crack with two companions from the hotel. 'Surely,' he thought, 'if the Crack could be done at all now would be the time, with weather and physical fitness corresponding.' He knew from his top-roped reconnaissance the previous Christmas that all would go well once he was above the 'sentry-box', a third of the way up the climb.

Combined tactics and a strategically held ice axe helped him to attain the sentry-box platform. He then made three attempts to surmount the short, 'splayed-out' section above; each time he was forced back by a projecting block at the top of the niche. While he rested on the platform, his companions quickly climbed Kern Knotts Chimney—the other side of the Crack and much more easily negotiable—and lowered the rope to him: 'I flung away my coat and tied on to the rope. . . . With renewed confidence the fourth attempt was successful. When the first twelve feet were passed I found two wedged stones a short distance above my head. These forced my body out of the crack altogether, but they offered respectable holds during the process.'

The rest was easy and Jones was quickly at the top. It was a first ascent of a kind, though the current guide book dates the true first ascent one year later when Jones led H. C. Bowen up the Crack without a top-rope protecting him. Subsequently Jones became so expert that it was claimed he could climb up the Crack and down the Chimney in seven minutes.

The Crack is short, only 70 feet, but sheer and dramatic and difficult; its current rating is 'Very Severe (Mild)'. Before this no climb had ever been subjected to such careful and intensive investigation, and there were probably many, especially among the veterans, who shared Crowley's view that the tactics were unfair and damaging to the tradition of pure climbing exploration.

In June 1896 the Abraham brothers teamed up with John Robinson and F. W. Jackson to conquer the steep, uncertain rock of Iron Crag Chimney, near Shoulthwaite Ghyll. A. H. Griffin describes this as 'a remarkable *tour de force* which has been comparatively rarely repeated'. The current guide says of the final 40 feet: 'This pitch is fundamentally unsound.'

The following Christmas brought the dynamic trio, Jones and the two Abrahams, together again. It was a severe winter, but bitter cold and ice-coated rock merely inspired Jones to greater effort. On the Great Pitch of Pillar's Shamrock Gully, he was saved from serious accident by his rope-craft. George Abraham told the story:

> The groove proved excessively difficult, but the hopeful look of the ledge, and probably our encouragement, tempted our friend upwards against his better judgement. About 25 feet above us no progress was made for some time, and after considerable delay we called up to him inquiringly. No answer came; but at last the oppressive silence was broken by the words: 'I cannot get up or down safely!' The position was alarming for the jaws of the gully dipped deeply below, and, though the rope was secured to us and the great boulders, a fall would have been serious. A few moments later Jones, with remarkable foresight and judgement, espied a small piece of jutting rock no bigger than the top of an egg-cup. This was just above him on the right, but it was possible to swing the rope up to and over it; and he began the ascent thus secured. We paid the rope out from the cave and all went well for a time. Then suddenly there was a cry of warning, and something of a more solid nature appeared. 'Hold tight!' was the startled shout, and Jones came swinging

> in pendulum fashion across the wall with astonishing impetus. The rope held over the belay, and he crashed pell-mell amongst us in the bed of the cave. We collapsed like ninepins, sprawling in all directions. In the mêlée the rope flew out of my hand, and I well remember how Jones sat up presently on the snow, rubbing his bruises and accusing me of losing my head and the rope simultaneously.

When he had recovered his breath, Jones returned to the attack. He persuaded the brothers to form a human ladder, George on the shoulders of Ashley, then climbed over them both to force a pitch that is still described as 'severe, strenuous and unpleasant'.

'Our indomitable leader', as George Abraham calls him, carried on climbing, despite a rising storm, driving sleet and approaching darkness. They became hopelessly lost and finally had to rappel down to the Shamrock Traverse on a doubled rope in the Alpine fashion. It was pitch dark by now and the High Level path around the shoulder of Pillar mountain was so icy that they roped together. Again they got lost and it was a long time before they found Black Sail and the path back to Wasdale Head. The hotel was dark and locked when they reached it after midnight. 'Thus ended,' wrote George, 'the most memorably exciting day I have ever known.'

14 Triumph and Tragedy

These were the halcyon days of the 'Golden Age' The community of the Wastwater Hotel was an established and thriving tradition; every season the frontiers of the sport were perceptibly advanced; tragedy, ultimately inevitable, lay in the future.

The Lake District led the way. The most advanced and difficult climbs were done there, and when such climbs were accomplished elsewhere it was by men trained at Wasdale Head. Their influence was most strongly felt in Scotland. In February and March 1894 a powerful party went to the Western Highlands and laid open the boundless possibilities of the area. In Glencoe Collie, Collier and Solly made the first route on Buachaille Etive Mòr, Collie's Climb; they went on to discover a number of routes on the buttresses of Bidean nam Bian; then they moved north to Ben Nevis and made the first ascent of the formidable Tower Ridge. When Collier and Solly had to leave, Geoffrey Hastings joined Professor Collie for further advanced exploration in Glencoe. 'This brief but exciting campaign of Collie and his companions,' say Clark and Pyatt, 'marked the beginning of a new era in Scottish mountaineering.'

Other Wasdale men, Haskett Smith and O. G. Jones prominent among them, carried the new skills to the dark cliffs of North Wales. But here the real impetus was to come from a local man, James Merriman Archer Thomson. A school-teacher at Bangor, he paid a brief visit to the Lake District in

1890 and climbed Deep Ghyll, but it was not until four years later that he began what Clark and Pyatt call 'two seasons of exploration in the mountains of Snowdonia, particularly in those surrounding the Ogwen Valley, which were to revolutionise Welsh climbing'.

In other places too the sport was emerging with little or no reference to Wasdale Head. Crowley and Mummery had climbed the chalk cliffs of the south coast before they knew Cumberland; a few years later A. W. Andrews began to explore the granite cliffs of Cornwall, wearing tennis shoes and accompanied by his sister; most important of all, the 1890s saw the invention of gritstone climbing in the Peak District by James William Puttrell.

Small in stature, sturdily compact, Puttrell had much in common with the 'hard men' of the 1950s, whose training on gritstone enabled them to carry rock climbing into a new dimension. The short, steep cliffs of the Peak District lie within easy reach of the great industrial regions of south Lancashire and Yorkshire, Derby and Nottingham. As climbing progressed from the guts-and-muscle methods of the gully era to the more balanced and balletic techniques required on the open faces, training on gritstone became almost an essential qualification for the would-be 'tiger'. In their history of Peak District climbing, *High Peak*, Eric Byne and Geoffrey Sutton effectively support their claim that every leading pioneer in the sport since 1914 has been outcrop-trained, the great majority of them on gritstone.

Puttrell lived and worked in Sheffield. As a manager for the silversmiths Mappin and Webb he enjoyed neither the means nor the leisure that came so easily to most of the Wasdale Head men. But the urge to climb was strong in him, and in the 1880s he began to risk the wrath of the Peak District gamekeepers and farmers, which in itself called for considerable courage, and to explore the crags of Wharncliffe, just north of Sheffield.

At first he went out alone; then he persuaded a silversmith friend, W. J. Watson, to join him. Together they turned Wharncliffe Crags into 'a veritable gymnasium', then switched their attention to Rivelin Edge, and then, in 1890, to the long escarpment of Stanage Edge.

Puttrell was a cheerful and companionable man. In forays to the Lake District and North Wales he made friends with O. G. Jones, the Abraham brothers and Archer Thomson. He persuaded Jones and the Abrahams to visit the Peak and sample gritstone climbing, but they were not impressed enough to go again. He was more successful a few years later when he introduced that all-embracing adventurer, Lehmann Oppenheimer, to the excitements of gritstone.

In 1897 Jones and the Abraham brothers continued to carry all before them. At Easter they were in North Wales, climbing on Cader Idris and Lliwedd. Jones had arranged to climb in Cumberland and left them with a final warning, 'Don't do Slanting Gully'. The Abrahams, of course, chose to follow his Kern Knotts Crack example rather than his advice and immediately went out and climbed it.

Jones travelled overnight to Coniston to meet Godfrey Ellis, and on the morning of 23rd April they set off with an eighty-foot rope to tramp over to Wasdale Head by way of a climb on Dow Crag, Central Chimney, which is now graded 'Severe (Mild)'. A few days later Jones led the first ascent of Kern Knotts West Chimney with C. W. Patchell as his companion, and the following day, supported by H. C. Bowen, he made the first ascent of Kern Knotts Crack without benefit of top rope. After a few more days' climbing, Jones and Bowen felt fit enough to tackle their main objective, C Gully on the Screes above Wastwater, a long and awesome route which gets harder as it gets higher and which is currently graded 'Very Severe (Mild)'. They had to deal with wet conditions in the gully and shattered, unstable rock on its walls. Bowen fell off climbing the final pitch, but Jones had the rope tight and all was well. By two o'clock in the afternoon, as Jones expressed it, 'The C Gully was to acknowledge itself vanquished from beginning to end'.

That summer Puttrell forsook his gritsone edges for a while to climb with the Abraham brothers in Cumberland. They met by appointment at Sty Head tarn on the morning of 12th July, climbed Central Gully on Great End, and lunched at the top on meat pies and Carslbad plums. They walked across to Mickledore, then picked their way along Rake's Progress to prospect for a possible new line in the area of Collier's Climb. They found a new and easier way up to Collier's ledge, then sought a variation off to the right. Puttrell's account was published in the Journal of the Yorkshire Ramblers' Club: 'We anticipated meeting difficulties hereabouts, and certainly were not disappointed, for we found it required some degree of nerve to leave the spacious ledge and tackle the small crack running up the precipitous face of rock above. Trouble we certainly had, but it was trouble which, perforce, must and did yield to the cautious skill of our leader.'

At the top of an oblong pinnacle they built a small cairn and deposited a card in it recording their visit. They sat down to admire the view and sang so loudly that people on the scree 150 feet below them thought they were calling for help. Then they climbed on: 'The great rock chimney which we entered, and which my companions did me the honour of naming the "Puttrell Chimney", needed care and finesse of touch—especially on the leader's part—to make progress possible without damaging the parietals of those immediately beneath, but it provided a splendid finish to a splendid climb.' Named the Keswick Brothers' Climb in honour of the Abrahams, this exposed route is currently graded 'Very Difficult'.

The following Christmas O. G. Jones took a large party to investigate his friends' discovery, recommended it 'for its beauty and its sustained interest', and devised a variation finish to avoid some scrambling on rough scree. He also at this time made the first attempt on what is now called Botterill's Slab in the same area of Scafell Crag. He was forced back by ice and the smoothness of the rock after about 40 feet, but remarked, 'It will probably go some day when conditions are more favourable.'

After this Jones went to the Alps for winter climbing in the Bernese Oberland, but the next Easter he was back at Wasdale

Head. On 10th April 1898, with W. J. Williams, he climbed Jones's Route on Dow Crag; nine days later, with G. T. Walker, he created Jones's Route Direct from Lord's Rake to the summit of Scafell Pinnacle; and three days after that he made two new routes on the same day on Scafell Crag, Jones and Collier's Climb, which was pointed out by Collier and climbed by Jones, and Pisgah Buttress which he climbed with the Abraham brothers. It was a period of intensive achievement. All the routes were difficult, but much the most impressive was Jones's Route Direct from Lord's Rake.

The only previous attempt to find a way from the entrance to Lord's Rake to the summit of Scafell Pinnacle had been defeated eleven years earlier when a party led by Charles Hopkinson was beaten back by ice-glazed rock after 150 feet. Jones wrote: 'What this earlier party found impossible in the winter of 1887, Mr G. T. Walker and I, in April 1898, favoured by the best of conditions, were just able to overcome.'

Jones and Walker had had a full day's climbing and it was already late afternoon: 'In spite of the late hour I could not refrain from a trial trip. . . . At the point where the earlier party found the direct ascent barred by smooth ice on the wall, we had a council of war. It resulted in my throwing down my boots to Walker, and then crawling up 50 feet of, perhaps, the steepest and smoothest slabs to which I have ever entrusted myself. This brought me to a tiny corner where I essayed to haul in the rope attached to my companion. But he also had to remove his boots. . . .' More difficulties lay ahead and darkness was falling as they reached the foot of the last two pitches: 'Standing on Walker's shoulders I screwed myself out at the right-hand top corner of our waiting-room and started along a traverse across the right face of the nose. The toes of the feet were in a horizontal crack, the heels had no support, and the hands no grip. It was only by pressing the body close to the wall, which was fortunately a few degrees away from the perpendicular, and by sliding the feet along almost inch by inch, that the operation could be effected. It was with no small sense of relief that the end was reached in a few yards, and a narrow vertical fissure entered that gave easy access to the top of the nose. Then we put on our boots again and hurried.'

'It is thus possible,' Jones concludes, 'to reach the summit of the Scafell Pinnacle by a route up the buttress quite independent of either of the great ghylls that flank it.' This is the authentic voice of the new climbing. There were still some difficult gully routes to be conquered, but the future direction of climbing was now clearly indicated. The current guide grades the route 'Severe' and describes it as 'an important break-away from gully and chimney climbing, executed in stockinged feet'.

The Easter holiday, going so marvellously, nearly ended in disaster for Jones. Attempting to repeat his climb of the notorious C Gully on the Screes, he fell when shattered rock on the final pitch broke away under his weight, and was only saved by the rope. George Abraham gave a characteristically excitable account: '"Promise me you'll never climb the C Gully on the Screes! It's a deadly place!" Such were the words spoken one Easter evening at Wasdale Head by my late friend O. G. Jones. We had come back from a strenuous day on the Pillar Rock, to find the famous enthusiast looking paler than the snows on the Pillar's peak. He was bruised and battered, and had his arms in bandages; it was at last evident that the mountains had asserted their supremacy.'

Jones was fully recovered in time for his summer season in the Alps, climbing first around Chamonix, then from Zermatt, where W. M. Crook met him: 'I was standing outside the Monte Rosa Hotel in the main street of Zermatt, one bright sunny day, when early in the afternoon Jones, with his two guides, came in. He had been frequently doing two peaks in one day (I believe he had once done three). All the party showed signs of wear and tear, but Jones was the freshest of the three. His face and hands were as brown as berries, covered with dust and sweat; his clothes were literally in rags, torn to pieces on the rocks. Yet in a few minutes he had washed, changed into the garb of civilization, and reappeared as fresh in body and as vigorous and vivacious intellectually as if he had undergone no fatigue at all. Twenty hours physical work did not appear to take as much out of him as five hours does of humbler mortals.'

Only a few days later the climbing community suffered a severe blow. Dr John Hopkinson, the leader of the brilliant band of Manchester brothers, fell to his death on the Petit Dent de Veisivi, and three of his children, a son and two daughters, perished with him. The effect on John's four surviving brothers was shattering. Many years later Katharine Chorley, the daughter of Edward, wrote: 'The tragedy shadowed all our mountaineering lives, even those of my generation. . . . As for my father, he never climbed seriously again.'

The following Christmas found O. G. Jones back at Wasdale. The weather was continuously atrocious, so he walked over one day to Keswick with the Abraham brothers to investigate Iron Crag Chimney, which they had pioneered with John Robinson a few years before. They persuaded the Abrahams' father, George Perry Abraham, to go with them despite the weather and the evil reputation of the climb. They reached the foot of the Chimney later than they intended and it was streaming with water. Someone suggested that only two of them should attempt the climb, but Jones said 'All or none', so they roped up and set off, with Jones in the lead, the brothers following, and their father in the rear. It was another Jones epic; the Chimney was a waterfall, the rain fell unceasingly, it was bitterly cold and darkness was falling. At one stage they prepared to spend the night in the inhospitable Chimney. But Jones finally forced his way to the top, climbing over Ashley to master the last pitch. As he stepped onto the summit a large boulder, which had sustained his weight briefly and uncertainly a few moments before, came away and crashed down the Chimney. Mr Abraham senior escaped by inches. Finally, when they all gathered at the top, it was pitch dark and still raining and a fierce wind was blowing. Jones shouted, 'Coil the rope and then we'll do a sprint', and disappeared into the night. On the way down Mr Abraham asked his sons, 'Is he subject to fits?'

Jones had one overwhelming objective in mind at this time, Walker's Gully on Pillar Rock.

He was thirty-one and at the peak of his powers. His daring was as great as ever, but more closely matched now by his skill. Throughout the autumn term he had maintained his Alpine fitness by hard exercises with dumb-bells. Sheer muscular strength had always been at his command. It was now reinforced by more delicate qualities of suppleness, balance and precision, by a new mastery of rope-craft, and by a sure confidence in movement at the limit of the physically possible.

Walker's Gully was a worthy challenge. It had been attempted many times but never conquered. More than one party had reached the foot of the last, ferocious pitch, only to be turned back there.

Two things were essential for Jones's attempt, the right companions and the right weather. He was forced to wait. 'The Christmas of 1898,' George Abraham wrote, 'was marked by heavy rain and unseasonable conditions. Several large parties of climbers had come to the hotel and, after a day or two of smoking and grumbling, had departed; until, at the New Year, Mr Jones and myself were the only climbers left there. To keep ourselves in training, we struggled up through the powdery snow of the Central Gully on Gable Crag, performed many rash feats at the end of the barn and the billiard table, besides leaving a considerable quantity of our clothing on the "Mosedale Boulder".'

They reconnoitred the top of Walker's Gully and found that the conditions brought one advantage; snow on the slopes above the top of the Gully held all the loose stones so firmly in place that the usual hazard of stone-falls from above was eliminated. George paid out the rope while Jones went to the edge of the Gully and peered down. All he could see was 'icy over-hanging rock and the mist-filled abyss far below', but he concluded that there was a chance if they could find a good third man.

A few days later A. E. Field arrived at the hotel and agreed to join them. They waited several days for an improvement in the weather but it did not come. So early in the morning of 7th January 1899 they set off up Mosedale in a tremendous downpour of rain and sleet. Faith was rewarded; as they gained the soft snow on Looking Stead, the clouds rolled away and the rain relented; by midday they were at the foot of Walker's Gully.

Jones's account of the climb has become a classic:

> The precipice was a grand study in black and white, its immense slabs shiny black with a thin veneer of ice, and decorated artistically with snow festoons and long slender icicle tassels. Verily the giant had donned his coat of mail, and meant to do his best to repel our attack; but his preparations were incomplete. A little more ice on the middle obstacle, a little further loosening of a splinter of rock at the top pitch, and we should have been driven back unsuccessful. Maybe he thought us too wise to attempt the climb under such adverse conditions; but we were not, and that mistake spelt his defeat.
>
> We roped at the foot of the crags, and I started up by the left of the gully. The direct route could have been taken with greater ease, but a solid jet of ice-cold water was shooting straight down the middle, and we preferred to keep dry a while longer. I mounted the wall from ledge to ledge, turning periodically at distances of four or five yards to manipulate the rope for the second man, who in his turn steadied the lvst man up. It is easier, not to say far more pleasurable, to climb than to describe the process.
>
> Keeping up the wall for 60 feet, we were then able to traverse along a narrow terrace into the gully, and the hard work began in earnest. Vertically upwards sprang the great cleft, with massive boulders many tons in weight dividing it into separate storeys like the rungs of a gigantic ladder. On our heads dripped the water thawing from the upper rocks, uncomfortable at first, but preferable to the vagrant falling stones that haunt the locality in the summer time. There was no drift of snow that might help us up the first few feet of each pitch. The side walls were clothed in wet ice. We wriggled up yard by yard, working closer together now for mutual aid. So long as the gully remained narrow, we were safe, for it was easy to hold in by leaning across from side to side.
>
> Then came the first overhanging bit at the middle pitch, and

while Field braced firmly in the innermost recesses, steadying my rope, the second man balanced himself astride the gully, outstanding on the slenderest of ledges. Then I clambered on to his shoulders to reach the outer edge of the roofing-stone that overhung our course. Its upper surface was steeply sloping, and a jet of water plumping on to its centre radiated out a spray of icy liquid from which there was no escape. Sharp was the word, for strength and courage languish rapidly under such penetrating influences. But I could find nothing to hang on to, so smoothly lubricated did every hold seem, until an aperture was discovered in the roof through which a loop of rope could be passed from below. This served excellently, and I hastily drew myself up with its aid. The others followed with greater speed though they could not dodge the waterfall, and we stayed a moment to wring out our coats before continuing the assault.

If variety were charming, we had charmed lives. Up the next ladder we went, through one obstacle, over the next and 'chimneying' up between the third and the great wall, the leader using the shoulders and heads of his companions, their upstretched hands steadying his precarious footholds, and their expert advice supporting him all through. And with it all the most sublime views outwards and upwards and downwards of Nature's simple and severe architecture, designed and executed in her grandest style.

At last we came to the final obstacle, the limit of previous exploration. We had arrived at a little platform deep in the mountain, and three enormous boulders, one on top of the other, overhanging more and more near the top, had to be circumvented. There was no way behind them; the only possibility was to work up one side wall and climb past them. I flung off my boots and Norfolk jacket, expecting to give the second man a bad time standing on his shoulders at the take-off, and attempted to climb up a narrow fissure in the left wall. Unhappily it proved to be useless, and we were all supremely uncomfortable when it was discovered that I should have to descend again.

Next the right wall was tried and I blessed the previous three months' monotonous training with heavy dumb-bells. The strain on the arms was excessive. Fortunately, there was no running water there, or the cold would have been unendurable. At the worst corner, by hanging on with the right hand, and with the left looping part of my rope through the recess at the side of the boulder, a good grip was improvised. Of natural holds there were none on that smooth, icy wall and the loop was a perfect boon. Even a perfect boon is hard to utilize when hands and toes are benumbed and all one's muscles are racked with prolonged tension. But the loop served its purpose, and after a few more struggles in the crack a ledge was reached from which it was evidently an easy scramble to the head of the gully.

'Réussi—parfaitement—messieurs—send up my coat and boots.' The gasping message was finished in English to save delay, but I shiveringly waited many minutes in soft snow before the rope could be untied and the articles in question slung up on it. A cherished pair of socks fell out of the coat pocket as it was hauled over the edge of the top boulder, and took a preliminary clear drop of two or three hundred feet. It gave us quite a shock at the time, for we thought it was a packet of sandwiches.

Then my companions came up, with an enviable surplus of warmth and energy. We raced up the steep snow and rock that remained above us, and did not halt till we had crossed the fell and descended to our starting point near the foot of the Pillar Rock. There we sat in a protected corner, and I put my frozen feet into others' pockets, my dignity into my own, while we ate the crushed remnants of our lunch and discussed the day's excitements. When the grateful diffusion of animal heat had brought sensation to my extremities, and the spare energy of the whole party had spent itself in dragging on my boots, we started off again and made our way over the snow-covered fells down to Wastdale.

Walker's Gully was Jones's crowning contribution to Lake District climbing. Today it is graded 'Severe (Hard)'. The guide book describes it as 'a superb climb up an impressive gully' and warns that the 'last pitch may be found Very Severe by a short man'. Jones was a short man and the conditions in which he made the climb were forbidding in the extreme.

Next Easter Jones, the Abraham brothers, Mr and Mrs F. W. Hill and J. W. Puttrell were at Ogwen Cottage in Snowdonia and made new climbs around Twll Du, on the eastern buttress of Glyder Fach and the northern buttress of Tryfan. At Whitsun Jones was again at the Cottage. In the summer he returned to the Alps, climbing first at Zermatt, then crossing to Arolla to meet his friend and fellow-teacher at the City of London School, F. W. Hill.

They made a number of climbs, then on 28th August they set off with three guides to traverse the Dent Blanche, intending to climb up by the West Arete, which had been done only twice before. W. M. Crook walked part of the way with them and later recalled that Jones was in ebullient mood, reminiscing about previous climbs, more concerned with his Alpine than with his Cumbrian achievements, and looking eagerly forward to a projected visit to the Himalayas with the Abraham brothers.

At the foot of their climb Jones and Hill and the three guides roped together. High up on the ridge they were halted by a small but steep buttress and Furrer, the leading guide, decided to climb straight over it rather than try to turn it on the flank. Hill's account of what happened next was published in the *Alpine Journal*:

> When I reached the level of the others, Furrer was attempting to climb the buttress, but, finding no holds, he called to Zurbriggen to hold an axe for him to stand on. Apparently he did not feel safe, for he turned his head and spoke to Jones, who then went to hold the axe steady. Thus we were all on the same level, Vuignier being some 25 or 30 feet distant from them and also from me. Standing on the axe, which was now quite firm, Furrer could reach the top of the buttress, and attempted to pull himself up; but the fingerholds were insufficient, and before his foot had left the axe his hands slipped, and he fell backwards on to Zurbriggen and Jones, knocking them both off, and all three fell together. I turned to the wall to get a better hold, and did not see Vuignier pulled off, but heard him go and knew that my turn would soon come. And when it did not I looked round, and saw my four companions sliding down the slope at a terrific rate, and 30 feet of rope swinging slowly down below me.

Hill had a terrible journey before he reached safety. He managed to turn the buttress on the right and gain the summit, but on his way down the South Ridge he was overtaken by a fierce storm and forced to spend the nigh crouched against a boulder. The next day was only slightly better and he had another night in the open, without food or drink, before reaching Zermatt fifty hours after the accident.

The four bodies were recovered and O. G. Jones was buried at the little Roman Catholic church at Evolena. The Anglican chaplain from Zermatt read the English burial service. Among those present were two men who had been with Jones on his first visits to Wasdale Head nine years earlier, Dr Sumpner and W. M. Crook.

The death of Jones was given full and extensive coverage in the English press. The accident was described in detail and widely compared to the Matterhorn disaster, especially over the breaking of the rope. Many tributes were published, notably by W. M. Crook and the Alpinist Harold Spender, who wrote of Jones, 'He went where no other men would go. He had become easily the best rock climber in England.' In the *Westminster Gazette* one of his fellow teachers wrote: 'If ever a man brought an exhilarating atmosphere into a public school common room without violating any traditions worth maintaining, that man was Owen Glynne Jones. He was the very ideal of *mens sana in corpore sano*, and we all felt that in him we had a colleague bright, scholarly, manly and brave. After school hours it was refreshing to see him devising some new form of training both legs and arms for future conquests in the Alps, and older men, whilst wearily entering from their class-rooms, smiled at his feats with chair or table.' The *Morning Leader* sent a reporter to his lodgings in Denmark Hill in South London, where his landlady, Mrs Edwards, said, 'he was such a perfect gentleman in all his ways', and added, 'I always knew he must come to this end, and he knew it too. He used to say so and say it was the death he would choose.'

Most of the papers accepted that the deaths were caused by pure accident, but some reports were more critical. One correspondent described Jones as 'quite careless of life'. The *Echo*, under the headline 'Precipitated into the Abyss', said: 'The practice of roping together, supposed to be necessary for safety, is also obviously a source of extreme danger.' And the *Manchester Guardian*, though a constant friend of adventure and exploration, took a stern editorial view: 'Many climbers hold, we think rightly, that to take the risk of such places is bad mountaineering, bad mountaineering being a kind of gambling with nature for your life, while good mountaineering means the unfailing maintenance of a clear balance of precaution over risk, the very worst that can happen only bringing into action a safeguard prearranged to meet it.'

15 The End of an Era

O. G. Jones was thirty-two when he was killed, at the height of his physical powers, unsurpassed in skill and undiminished in his appetite for climbing. His great achievements in the Lake District were the product of a few holiday visits between the end of 1895 and the beginning of 1899, just over three years. Had he lived, he could have expected many more years of active lead climbing and would certainly have carried the sport forward at an accelerating pace.

His death delayed progress but did not bring it to a halt. Inspired by his example, his friends went on searching for fresh challenges. And a new generation of enthusiasts, inspired by his book, began to explore crags that had been largely neglected until then, Gimmer Crag and Dow Crag, the cliffs of Bowfell and Buttermere.

So many new faces were now appearing at Wasdale Head that the hotel decided to install a professional French guide. 'A First Class Dauphiné Guide and Climber', the advertisement proclaimed, 'has been engaged, who will conduct climbers on the various Climbs in the District at a moderate charge.' The guide, Gaspard, remained a regular though shadowy figure at Wasdale Head until the First World War. Each summer he returned home for an Alpine season, but for the rest of the year he was available at the hotel for the safe conduct of beginners up the easier routes. Gaspard was no 'tiger'; he made no new routes and seldom ventured onto the more severe 'courses'. But he was a proficient cragsman, and a safe and reliable guide, slow, careful, taciturn. He came to know the crags intimately and was an expert in mountain rescue. Each evening, while the climbers talked or hurled themselves about the billiard room, Gaspard went to work on forty pairs of boots, cleaning off the day's dirt, rubbing them with dubbin or sperm oil and hammering new nails where necessary.

Many of the newcomers though were too good to need Gaspard's help. The Thompson brothers from Newcastle-on-Tyne discovered a new 'Difficult' route on Scafell Pinnacle, which was given their name. Two more brothers, Claude and Guy Barton of Leeds, climbed C Chimney on the Overbeck crags of Yewbarrow in September, 1899, and two years later, accompanied by L. F. Meryon, conquered one of the last great gully problems of the area, Savage Gully on the north face of Pillar Rock, a climb which is still graded 'Very Severe (Mild)'.

Another band of brothers, the Broadricks of Windermere, were the most promising of all. R. W. Broadrick was born in 1872, educated at Haileybury and Trinity College, Cambridge, and became a teacher at Fettes College in Edinburgh. His younger brother, H. C. Broadrick, had the same academic training and also became a teacher. Both were tall and long of reach, both were keen athletes, and in the few years in which they climbed together, between 1899 and 1903, their achievement was considerable, especially on Dow Crag. In April 1899 they made the first buttress climb on the crag, Broadrick's Route on B Buttress, which is graded 'Severe (Hard)' and described as 'steep, exposed and delicate'. In September of the next year they made another route of comparable quality, Broadrick's Route, North Gully, and two years after that, with F. E. Edwards, they climbed Broadrick's Crack, which the guide book rates 'Severe (Hard)'.

R. W. Broadrick was also a formidable fell walker. Early one morning in September 1902 he set off with Mr Dawson of Sale to see how far they could travel across the mountains in twenty-four hours. They left Rosthwaite at 3.32 a.m., deposited their cards on the summit of Great Gable, traversed Kirk Fell and Pillar Mountain, and dropped down to the Wastwater Hotel for breakfast. They tramped over Lingmell shoulder to Scafell Pike, crossed Great End and Bowfell, and descended to the Old Dungeon Ghyll Hotel for another meal. From here their route took them down Langdale, over Red Bank to Grasmere, up Fairfield, then over Dollywaggon and Helvellyn to reach Thirlspot in time for tea. They were on the summit of Blencathra at 7.55 p.m. and, despite thick mist, reached the summit of Skiddaw at 10.40. Soon after midnight they passed through the silent streets of Keswick and at four minutes past three, 'tattered but triumphant', they were back in Rosthwaite. They had covered seventy miles and recorded 18,500 feet of ascent.

For a while after the death of their great friend, the Abraham brothers concentrated their efforts on the Scottish Highlands. In May 1900 they travelled north with two Peak District gritstone men, J. W. Puttrell and Professor E. A. Baker. Baker describes how they carried the news of the relief of Mafeking into Glencoe: 'We mounted a pair of ice-axes in front of the wagonette, and drove the 13 miles to Kingshouse with a handkerchief of ample breadth and sanguinary dye flying from this flagstaff.'

Their objective was the Crowberry Ridge on Buachaille Etive Mòr, which Scottish experts considered impossible. After a long wait for fine weather, they succeeded, with George Abraham leading, Baker second, then Puttrell, and Ashley Abraham bringing up the rear and taking photographs.

Next year the two gritstone men, joined this time by Lehmann Oppenheimer, made another break-through route in Scotland, the first ascent of the Ben Nuis Chimney on the Isle of Arran. Puttrell led and found the route so difficult that a rescue party from Brodick had almost reached them by the time they gained the top. In fact, the climb was not repeated until 1955, when it was done with the aid of pitons.

In the Lake District during these years the Abraham brothers concentrated their attention on Pillar Rock. In October 1900, with four other climbers, they made the first ascent of the Great Doup Buttress. The following May, with C. W. Barton and

J. H. Wigner, they found a superb and varied route up the west face, the New West Climb which, although it is graded no higher than 'Difficult (Hard)' has become one of the best-loved of the classic climbs.

The Abrahams had attempted the route a few months earlier but had been defeated by a storm of hail and sleet. When they returned on 26th May 1901, the Rock was bathed in spring sunshine. They roped up with George first, Ashley next, Dr Wigner third and Claude Barton as the last man. All went well until about 150 feet up they had to traverse left along a ledge to reach the foot of a steep chimney. George Abraham considered the problem:

> Though grassy, it was fairly continuous for several feet; but just before it reached the bottom of a long, steep chimney there was a gap about a yard wide. Foot-holds and hand-holds were at the time 'conspicuously absent', the latter being masked by vegetation, so one had to move along the ledge in a sitting position, with both feet dangling like useless ornaments over an absolutely sheer drop. However, the position was at least safe for those of a steady head until the break in the ledge was reached, and here the leader spent a long time in meditation before crossing this really awkward passage. There were two small hand-holds where the rock had broken away, but no foot-holds were available until the farther side of the gap could be touched by the left foot. To launch boldly out from the ledge, with such slender support for the hands only, needed both care and coolness, and everybody felt relieved when the leader swung himself safely across into the foot of the chimney. . . . A large fallen rock had become jammed in the foot of the vertical chimney, and this proved a good starting point for what is probably the most interesting part of the climb. Before proceeding the rope was belayed round this jammed stone; it would evidently prove an ideal safeguard in case of a slip. The leader found the second climber's shoulder of much assistance, and even his head was used as a step to bring hand-holds within reach. We wriggled slowly one by one up this narrow chimney for some 40 feet before a resting place could be found, and our direct passage was stopped by some enormous overhanging slabs.

From here a traverse to the right took them onto slightly easier ground, and so to the summit. It was the first new route on the west face of Pillar Rock since the day, seventy-five years before, when the shepherd John Atkinson clambered up the easy ledges of the Old West route. The Abrahams and their two companions descended into the Jordan Gap and ran down the screes to the spot where they had begun their climb four hours earlier: 'We lay on the rocks tasting all the joys of glorious conquest. Gazing up at those gigantic crags, which had not yielded without many anxious and exciting moments, we felt we had gained a new friend whom to know was to love.'

New crags in new dales were being discovered. Lehman Oppenheimer inspired the exploration of the Buttermere crags. In 1899 he stayed at the Fish Hotel with his Mancunian friend G. H. Craig, and they attempted Stack Ghyll on the Warnscale face of Haystacks only to be defeated by the chock-stone on the first pitch. They were back there at the end of the year with another friend, Tom Shaw, and on the last day of the old century they succeeded despite very slimy conditions. Shaw led and managed to turn the first pitch by keeping out on the wall to the right. They had no trouble with the easier chimneys above this, until they came to the final pitch, which has another chock-stone barrier. Oppenheimer described their methods: 'Shaw tried back and foot work but the cave was too wide. The walls were too clean cut for climbing on, so he stood on Craig's shoulders while I held the rope from the back of the cave. In this position he searched for some time for a handhold, and at last gave a spring, scraped the top of the cave wall with his edge-nails, and struggled out under the corner of the boulder.' The climb is graded 'Severe'.

Soon after this Craig and Oppenheimer had a frightening moment on the North Climb of Pillar Rock. Oppenheimer was leading: 'There was a perfectly easy traverse to the east but I soon ran out the length of the rope on it. Craig could not follow me, the descent into Savage Gully being too risky without a rope above, so I tried to climb straight up the Gully on to the Nose. . . . Just as I was pulling over the top jammed stone my hands slipped on some greasy rock and down I went. Craig had firm hold of the rope, but he was some 30 feet away round the Nose, and after a rapid and exhilarating descent I swung down the gully like a pendulum and came back against the rock with a bang. It was one of those incidents which strengthen friendships, but which nevertheless I was not anxious to repeat. My cap came off in the fall and we found it later in the day, 300 feet below, at the base of the rock. Craig escaped with a finger scraped by the rope, I suffered even less, and was ready for another try in a few minutes.'

Oppenheimer had had several attempts at Savage Gully on Pillar Rock and in June 1901 he was there again with Peter Thompson. Thompson was leading and when Oppenheimer found himself unable to manage a delicate traverse he volunteered to go up to the Nose the easy way and drop a rope to safeguard his friend. Thompson then climbed the final two pitches in stockinged feet and Oppenheimer reassures his readers: 'To disarm cavillers the rope was not taken in as he climbed up until he reached me.' Within three months the Gully was climbed by the Barton brothers without a top rope.

In May 1902 the partnership of Shaw, Craig and Oppenheimer made its greatest contribution to the sport on a crag which had not been touched until then. Craig and Shaw had noticed Bowfell Buttress some years earlier. Now with Oppenheimer, G. R. West, C. Hargreaves, and 160 feet of rope they set off from Fell Foot farm in Little Langdale to see if it would 'go'. Shaw led with Craig second and Oppenheimer as the last man with the usual role of scraping away all the loose stones and debris to make the climb 'clean' for their successors. It is a long climb for the Lake District 350 feet, and it took them a long time, but when they had finished they had created another classic route comparable in many ways to the Abrahams' New West on Pillar. Both are graded 'Difficult (Hard)'; both derive their excellence not from the severity of any particular pitch but from their sustained difficulty and interest over varied and exposed ground; both climbs quickly increase in difficulty if the weather is anything less than good.

Directly across Mickleden from Bowfell another fine and

neglected cliff drew the attention of the new generation. Since 1882, when Haskett Smith clambered up its North-west Gully, Gimmer Crag had been ignored. With the arrival of 'slab and wall' climbing though it came into its own. At Easter 1901 Andrew Thomson of Kendal and E. Rigby began to explore the crag, and in November of the following year, with John Sandison of Bromley in Kent, they made the first ascent of Gimmer Chimney, graded 'Very Difficult'. In April 1903 Rigby and Sandison, accompanied by Darwin Leighton of Kendal, climbed A Route, which is now graded 'Very Difficult (Hard)'. In the course of these explorations they conquered the redoubtable Amen Corner, with Rigby leading: 'As a matterof fact,' Andrew Thomson confessed, 'only the leader actually climbed it; the others all came off and were hauled up ignominously. The pitch is certainly not more than 15 feet in height, but presents difficulties quite unique. It is simply a right-angled corner with a narrow crack in the right-hand wall; but, and it is here that the "shoe pinches", both walls overhang. It was ultimately climbed by gripping the edge of the crack with both hands, and *walking* up the left wall, the body being almost in a horizontal position. The strain on the arms is terrific, and one gets into a position with a hand actually on the double hand-hold by which the final pull-up is effected, yet too exhausted to do so. There is one redeeming feature about it and that is, there is no real danger, for if the rope is held in the corner one would fall upon a soft grass ledge.' This method of climbing later came to be called the 'layback'.

Lesser crags were being explored at this time too. Just south of Keswick, Claude E. Benson worked out a series of practice routes on the outcrops of Castle Head. And in the hollow of Glaramara Thomson, with other Kendal men and Millican Dalton of Essex, discovered that it was possible to combine rock climbing and potholing in the caves of Dove's Nest. Dalton's love of caves grew on him so powerfully that for many years between the wars he lived in one on Castle Crag in Borrowdale during the summer and made a living by acting as a guide to tourists under the self-awarded title, 'Professor of Adventure'.

He maintained his troglodyte existence until shortly before he died in 1947 at the age of eighty.

The feeling was growing that the main crags, Pillar, Scafell and Great Gable, had been worked out. For the first but by no means the last time, many climbers thought that the limit of the possible had been reached. George Abraham began his account of the New West climb for the Climbers' Club Journal with the words: 'Perhaps 'tis a rash and dangerous act to even think of a new climb amongst our higher Cumberland fells; for have not both experts and novices decreed that Wasdale is an exhausted centre?'

Invariably in the history of climbing when such fears have been expressed, they have been promptly belied by some break-through. In 1903 the break-through was made by Fred Botterill in a slab climb of the greatest delicacy and exposure on Scafell Crag. It was the last great climb of the 'Golden Age' and the most difficult of them all. It is the only climb of the period which is now graded 'Very Severe'.

Botterill was the first of the long and distinguished line of men who were trained on Pennine gritstone and went on to create new frontiers on the bigger cliffs of the Lake District and Snowdonia. Clark and Pyatt definitively expound the advantages of gritstone training: 'In the first place, the gritstone rock had a roughness of texture and a lack of in-cut holds which encouraged the development of balance climbing rather than the push-and-pull methods which had previously been universal.... Secondly, the gritstone crags were low, averaging some 50 feet or so, and thereby allowing explorations to be made while safeguarded by a "top-rope" from above; a method, usually impracticable on the greater cliffs, which gave greater scope for experiments and for the discovery of just where the borderline lay between the possible and the impossible.'

Fred Botterill was brought up and lived in Leeds. In early youth he acquired a taste for scrambling and climbing in the Rocky Valley at Ilkley. In 1903 he spent the Whitsun holiday at Wasdale Head with two friends, H. Williamson and J. E. Grant. For a few days they contented themselves with climbing the standard courses, then, on the morning of 3rd June, they walked up to Scafell Crag and started to investigate the steep slab which flanks the Central Buttress on the left. Botterill was a member of the Yorkshire Ramblers' Club, and he sent his account of the climb that followed to the club's Journal. At first he tried the crack which is formed where the slab meets the face of the buttress but he found this impossible. So he tried again about 12 feet to the left on the face of the slab itself:

> Clearing away the moss from little cracks here and there I managed to climb slowly upwards for about 60 feet. The holds then dwindled down to little more than finger-end cracks. I looked about me and saw, some 12 feet higher, a little nest about a foot square covered with dried grass. Eight feet higher still was another nest and a traverse leading back to where the crack opened into a respectable chimney. If I could only reach hold of that first nest what remained would be comparatively easy. It seemed to be a more difficult thing than I had ever done but I was anxious to tackle it. Not wishing to part with the axe I seized it between my teeth and with my fingers in the best available cracks I advanced. I cannot tell with certainty how many holds there were; but I distinctly remember that when within two feet of the nest I had a good hold with my right hand on the face, and so ventured with my left to tear away the dried grass on the nest. However, the grass removed from the ledge, a nice little resting place was exposed—painfully small, but level and quite safe. I scrambled on to it, but on account of the weight of the rope behind me, it was only with great care and some difficulty that I was able to turn round. At last I could sit down on the nest and look around me.
>
> The view was glorious. I could see Scafell Pike and a party round the cairn. Far below was another group intent on watching our movements, a lady being amongst the party. I once read in a book on etiquette that a gentleman in whatever situation of life should never forget his manners towards the other sex, so I raised my hat, though I wonder if the author had ever dreamed of a situation like mine. I now discovered that our 80 feet of rope had quite run out and that my companions had already attached an additional 60 feet. Further, I began to wonder what had become of my axe, and concluded I must unthinkingly have placed it somewhere lower down. There it was, stuck in a little crack about five feet below me. Not knowing what was yet to come I felt I must recover it, so I lowered my-

self until I could reach it with my foot. I succeeded in balancing it on my boot, but in bringing it up it slipped and clattering on the rocks for a few feet took a final leap and stuck point downwards in the Rake's Progress. Standing up again I recommenced the ascent and climbed on to the second nest *à cheval*, from where, after a brief rest, I began to traverse back to the crack. This was sensational but perfectly safe. As usual I started with the wrong foot, and after taking two steps was obliged to go back. The next time I started with the left foot, then came the right, again the left, and lastly a long stride with the right, brought me into the chimney. The performance was what might have been called a *pas de quatre*. Complimentary sounds came from my companions below, but without stopping to acknowledge these I pulled myself up ten feet higher on to a good grass-covered ledge to the right of the crack, smaller but very similar to the Tennis Court Ledge of Moss Ghyll.

'How is it now?' my companions inquired. 'Excellent,' I replied, 'a good belaying pin and just room for three. Do you feel like following?' Without answering me the second man commenced the traverse to the chimney edge whilst I carefully belayed the rope. Up he came in splendid style and without stopping, taking only a quarter of the time it had taken me. He then untied and we threw down the 140 feet of rope to our third, who were joined us. We hailed a climbing friend who was watching from the Progress and invited him to join us, but he very generously refused and said he would hover near lest we might not be able to advance further and so require the aid of a rope from above. We next christened our berth 'Coffin Ledge', built a cairn on it and left our names on a card.

Starting off again a long stride with the left foot took the leader back into the crack, and a stiff climb of 20 to 30 feet landed us all into an extraordinary chimney, which though only wide enough to comfortably admit the body sideways ran right into the crag for about 15 feet. Like the crack below it leaned to the left at an angle of 70 degrees or so. About 25 feet up, chock-stones and debris formed a roof, and suspended in the middle some six feet below it, were three more chock-stones. When the second man had joined me he exclaimed with astonishment; 'What a place. How can we get out?' 'Wait a bit,' I answered, although I could not then see a way. However, I went as far as I could into the crack and with restricted use of back and knee climbed upwards until the level of the suspended chock-stones was reached; from there a narrow ledge rendered these easily

> accessible. They were securely wedged and safe to stand upon. The ledge continued along out of the crack until the most outward chock-stone of the roof was within reach. This I seized with both hands, and a steady pull upwards landed me into the Puttrell Chimney of Keswick Brothers' Climb.

The climb was a *tour de force* on a number of counts: for its continuous exposure and the very long run-out of the rope; for its sustained delicacy, requiring smooth and careful movement from one tiny hold to the next; and also for the fact that it was accomplished by a man wearing thickly nailed boots and carrying, until he providentially dropped it, an ice-axe. If O. G. Jones had pioneered this type of climbing with his ascent of Scafell Pinnacle from Lord's Rake in 1898, Botterill now clinched the development and pointed clearly to the way rock climbing must evolve.

In the event though the evolution was long in coming. It was many years before Botterill's Slab was climbed again and new routes of comparable quality began to emerge.

In the preface to his book, Lehmann Oppenheimer wrote: 'It was a fact of which all frequenters of Wasdale Head were proud that, in spite of the extreme difficulty of some of the climbs and the great number of ascents—well over ten thousand, I should estimate—which had been made up till then, no roped party had ever met with any serious accident in the District. Unhappily in 1903 a great catastrophe took place on Sca Fell, which destroyed our boast and robbed many of us of mountaineering friends.'

The accident happened on Monday, 21st September, a day of strong and blustery wind. It was sixteen years now since Edward Hopkinson had climbed down the face of Scafell Pinnacle and built his cairn on the ledge 165 feet above Lord's Rake, and though many had tried, no-one had succeeded in reaching the cairn from below. On that Monday morning four young men made a further attempt; R. W. Broadrick of Windermere, the schoolmaster and marathon fell runner who had some 'Severe' routes on Dow Crag to his credit; Henry Jupp of Croydon; Stanley Ridsdale of Kew Gardens, London;

and A. E. W. Garrett of Wallington in Surrey. They were all climbers of experience. They spent the morning climbing on Scafell Crag, then they lunched with another party of climbers, led by W. E. Webb.

The account in the *Manchester Guardian*, telegraphed by a correspondent, said:

> After luncheon each party separated to make climbs at different points separated by about 200 yards. The ascent which the ill-fated party endeavoured to make was that of the Scawfell Pinnacle from Lord's Rake. This is recognized by climbers as the most difficult piece of ground on Scawfell. . . . The climb is what is known as a 'face climb'. It is in every way a very perilous task and was made all the greater on Monday by the strong gusts of wind which were prevalent on that day all up and down the valley. Mr Webb and his companions relinquished their task owing to the slippery state of the ground and the high wind and set out to return to the hotel. While retracing their steps they were horrified to find lying at the foot of the Pinnacle their four friends, from whom they had been but a short time separated. Mr Ridsdale alone was alive, but he was utterly unable to give any account of the accident. He was only able feebly to point towards his three friends as a direction to Mr Webb and his companions to attend to them first.

Before he died a few hours later Ridsdale was able to give some account of what had happened: 'We were going up, Broadrick was first, Garrett second, myself third, and Jupp last. Then Broadrick and Garrett changed places. Broadrick said he was tired. Garrett slipped.'

The route the four men were attempting was not finally conquered until April 1912, when the formidable team of Siegfried Herford and G. S. Sansom were approaching the height of their form. It is now graded 'Severe' and described as 'justifiably the most popular route on the Pinnacle face'. The cause of the accident or precisely where it took place will never be known. It seems likeliest that something happened, perhaps a slip or a sudden violent gust of wind, to dislodge Garrett as he was moving up to take over the lead from Broadrick, possibly on the delicate ground about 140 feet up on what is now called Herford's Slab. What is clear is that the drill of careful and adequate belaying of the rope was not being carried out, so that the fall of one man brought the death of all four.

It was the worst accident in British climbing history until December 1954, when five climbers were killed on Ben Nevis. It marked the end, for the time being, of the Lake District's leadership in the sport, the end of the 'Golden Age'.

16 Exeunt omnes

On Boxing Day 1903 a journalist from Keswick, Alex Goodall, tried to glissade down a snow slope at the top of Deep Ghyll, lost control and plunged headlong down the gully. His body was found on the screes below Scafell Crag at the place where R. W. Broadrick and his three companions had been found and where, ten years earlier, Professor Milnes Marshall had fallen to his death.

The accidents, the Broadrick tragedy especially, had a traumatic effect on climbing at Wasdale Head. It was several years before the sport recovered momentum. Leadership passed to Snowdonia, where Geoffrey Winthrop Young had begun to form his brilliant group at Pen-y-Pass. And when climbing revived in Cumberland under the inspiration of Siegfried Herford and G. S. Sansom, the development was cut brutally short by the First World War. Their greatest climb, the conquest of Central Buttress on Scafell Crag, took place in April 1914.

Early in 1904 the Alpinist Harold Spender wrote a letter to the *Manchester City News*: 'On these English heights dozens of young fellows without any experience of mountains or real respect for their dangers, risk their lives every Christmas and Easter in gay adventure on the heights. There is a very strong and partly a healthy prejudice against the importation of guides, and, of course, there are no natives who possess the necessary capacity. But if guides are not employed, the parties ought at least to observe some proportion between their experience and their climbs. As far as I have observed, there is no sense of any such obligation, and it is simply due to good fortune that there have not been many more accidents. How long is this to go on, and how many more young lives are to be lost?'

At last the full danger of the sport was realized. Men had been killed in the Lake District mountains before this, but not while rock climbing. Cragsmen had been killed in climbing accidents, but not in the Lake District Partly through their skill and caution, and partly, perhaps, by sheer beginner's luck, no roped climber had ever been killed on the crags of Cumberland. Now the proud record was lost, and when in 1907 the Fell and Rock Climbing Club of the English Lake District was formed, safety was one of its prime preoccupations.

The Fell and Rock was a latecomer among climbing clubs. The Scottish Mountaineering Club had been formed in 1889; for the men of Snowdonia, the Climbers' Club came into being in 1897; the Yorkshire Ramblers' Club was already in existence; and in 1902 a number of gritstone enthusiasts met at a Manchester hotel and created the Rucksack Club. At Wasdale Head though, the great advances of the 'Golden Age' sprang from free, spontaneous and quite unorganized efforts. The Fell and Rock Club was only formed when the sport had lost its first impetus and was passing through a fallow period.

The role of the Alpine Club in this story and much of the history of climbing in the twentieth century suggest that there is something about organized societies, with their rules and journals, their regular meets and annual dinners, which can be inhibiting and even inimical to the progress of rock climbing. Perhaps the sport is too individualistic to benefit from rigid codes and organized encouragement. In every generation the pioneer 'tigers' are young men, often of rebellious outlook and impatient of their seniors, operating in small groups. Clubs tend to come under the control of men who are no longer in the 'front line' of the sport, and whose aim is to preserve things as they were in their young days. They resist change and condemn new ideas. The Alpine Club in the closing decades of the nineteenth century was the first but not the last body to damage both the sport and itself by its narrow, restrictive and reactionary attitude.

The first volume of the Fell and Rock Club's Journal defined the chief objective as: 'To encourage and foster under the safest and most helpful conditions the exhilarating exercise and sport of Fell Rambling and Rock Climbing in the Lake District.' That most clubbable of men, Ashley Abraham, was appointed the club's first President, and at the first annual dinner, held at the Commercial Hotel in Kendal, he pronounced the basic creed to loud applause: 'I am a rock climber and lover of our Lakeland fells first, and a mountaineer afterwards.' He also spoke these cautionary words: 'Lack of discretion is a great evil in rock climbing, but there is another evil equally great, and that is competitive climbing. This has been the fundamental cause of most of our home accidents, and for this reason I mention it tonight. In almost every party there is, by common consent, one man better and more capable of leading than any of the others. When that man is beaten it is time to turn back.'

The list of the club's senior members amounted to a roll-call of the surviving heroes of the 'Golden Age'. J. W. Robinson and George Seatree were the honorary vice-presidents. The honorary members included Haskett Smith, Cecil Slingsby, Norman Collie, Charles Pilkington, Geoffrey Hastings, George Abraham and, most senior of all, C. A. O. Baumgartner, who had climbed Pillar Rock fifty-seven years before.

Although the 'old guard' faded from the foreground of the story after the early 1890s, they were still climbing vigorously. Colonel 'Rusty' Westmorland, the son of Tom Westmorland, the pioneer 'Pillarite', remembers being taken walking in the area of Grisedale Hause when he was eleven years old, in the year 1897, and his thrill when they met 'four real climbers with ropes'. They were Haskett Smith, J. W. Robinson, Geoffrey Hastings and Ellis Carr, who had just been foiled in an attempt on Chock Gully on the cliffs of Dollywaggon Pike. They all walked down Grisedale together, and Westmorland says, 'When passing a rock we used to call Elephant Rock, near Elm

How, Haskett Smith showed us what he could do on it with a running start and maintained his momentum to the top.' The Chock Gully route was, in fact, eventually conquered by Westmorland himself in 1910.

Haskett Smith made his last new route in the Lake District in April 1908, at the age of forty-nine. Haskett Gully, on the crags which enclose Mirklin Cove just over a mile to the west of Pillar Rock, was a climb in the old style, a steep and slimy gully with some short but difficult pitches. Lehmann Oppenheimer and a Cornishman, H. Scott Tucker, accompanied Haskett Smith, and Oppenheimer gives account of the garrulous ascent. Half way up they gathered in a cave at the foot of a steep, 15-foot wall. Tucker wedged himself firmly against the rock and held Oppenheimer. Then Haskett Smith clambered onto Oppenheimer's shoulders and called for the ice-axe so that he could test the ledges above him: '"Give me the *escarbadientes*, or I suppose I ought to say *palito*", for at breakfast time Craig had been speaking about the coarseness of the English word toothpick, and enlarging on the superior politeness of the Spanish language. "*Palito—piolet*—or *piolito* would perhaps be a more suggestive portmanteau word", said Haskett Smith, but his philological ingenuity did not help him to find the holds, and we had to resort to ingenuity of another kind.' The weather closed in on them but failed to halt the flow of pedantic reflection. At the top they consoled themselves with 'a thermal bottle full of hot soup'. The current guide says, 'The climb is about 300 feet long, and one, at least, of the few short pitches in it is severe. It is a very unpleasant climb, mossy, wet and loose.'

The Fell and Rock Climbing Club suffered an early bereavement. During its inaugural year its best-loved member, John Wilson Robinson, died after an operation for 'an internal ailment'. He was buried on 23rd August 1907, in the cemetery of the Friends Meeting House at Pardshaw, near Cockermouth. The club formed a Memorial Committee, under the chairmanship of Haskett Smith, and they organized the building of the cairn which stands to this day to beckon climbers along Robinson's High Level Route to Pillar Rock. In a nearby boulder a bronze memorial tablet was set and Cecil Slingsby spoke a final tribute.

This was a sad blow, and Dr Joseph Collier of Manchester had died the year before. But for the most part, the early cragsmen were blessed with longevity. Tom Westmorland of Penrith died in 1909, and the next year an even earlier 'Pillarite', C. A. O. Baumgartner, died at the age of eighty-five. F. H. Bowring, the man who introduced Haskett Smith to the pleasures of 'chimney-sweeping', lived in Hampstead for the last twenty years of his life, reading extensively in the original Greek, Latin, Italian and several oriental languages. When he was over ninety, fearing that his sight might be declining, he began to commit the whole of the *Iliad* to memory. He was ninety-four when he died.

The First World War robbed the sport of several leading spirits. Siegfried Herford enlisted as a private in the 24th Royal Fusiliers (Sportsmen's Battalion) and was killed by a rifle grenade in France in January 1916. The two surviving sons of John Hopkinson died in France; and one of Cecil Slingsby's sons, Lawrence, a climber of great promise, won the M.C. at the Battle of the Somme but was killed by a shell soon afterwards. Lehmann Oppenheimer enlisted in the Artists' Rifles in 1915, motivated, in part, by 'the desire to wipe out the ignominy of inheriting a German name'. He was commissioned and served with distinction as a machine gun officer in France. In June 1916 a poison gas shell burst near him and he died shortly afterwards of bronchitis and pneumonia. He was forty-eight.

Fred Botterill lived until 1920, but lacked the dedication to extend his great achievement of September 1903. In 1906 he led a party, which included his gymnast brother, Arthur, and Lehmann Oppenheimer, up the North-west Climb on Pillar Rock (by Taylor's Chimney), which is graded 'Very Severe (Mild)'. The next year, with Oppenheimer and several others, he climbed Warn Ghyll on Haystacks, which the guide says 'is Severe and has an evil reputation'. In April 1909, with J. Hazard, he discovered a pleasant new route on the Napes face of Great Gable, Abbey Buttress, graded 'Very Difficult'. In September of that year he was climbing as second to Thomas James Rennison, who was eager to lead Eagle's Nest Ridge. They gained the ledge 50 feet above the Dress Circle, Rennison climbed another ten feet or so, paused, and then suddenly, without any cry of warning, fell clear. Botterill had been carefully paying out the rope from the ledge below and passing it, for additional friction, around the 'belay' of a rough knob of rock. He crouched to take the force of Rennison's fall, but when the impact came, the rope snapped on one of the sharper angles of the belaying rock and Rennison fell to his death. Botterill never climbed seriously again. G. S. Sansom later wrote of him: 'Botterill was unambitious; he was a very beautiful climber and could have done as much as Herford, or later Kelly, had he tried.'

George Seatree, originally of Penrith and later of Liverpool, who was affectionately known as 'la'al paddock', the little rabbit, was President of the club from 1908–10, and with his family gave the club devoted support until his death in 1928.

The same year saw the death of Cecil Slingsby. He had carried on climbing in Norway and the Alps, Scotland and the Lake District, well into the twentieth century, and his hospitable homes, at Craven in Yorkshire and later at a house in Westmorland which overlooked Morecambe Bay, had seen many gatherings of the men of the older generation—Haskett Smith and Norman Collie, Geoffrey Hastings and Godfrey Solly, the Hopkinsons and the Pilkingtons and many others. 'They gathered,' Geoffrey Winthrop Young wrote, 'for annual meetings at his home on the moors, a picturesque setting, intensely human, with his beautiful wife and "a sun-drift of wide-blue-eyed children with soft mischievous voices".' Winthrop Young was later to marry one of those children, Eleanor.

Slingsby was another convivial man, an active member of the Alpine Club and the Yorkshire Ramblers' as well as being President of the Fell and Rock in 1911 and a faithful supporter throughout. His last climb, the North Climb on Pillar, was a remarkable occasion. The year was 1919. Raymond Bicknell led and Slingsby, celebrating his seventieth birthday, came second and moved and handled the rope, according to Winthrop Young, 'with an instantaneous precision that was an example for any modern school'. And Winthrop Young, last man on the rope, was finding out what standard of climbing he could aspire to on an artificial leg of his own devising. He had lost a leg in the fighting on the Italian front.

In his late seventies, Slingsby's memory failed him completely and he spent his last days at a nursing home in Sussex. In the summer of 1928, while her husband was in the Alps testing his artificial leg on longer routes, Eleanor went to visit her father. They sat in the garden of the nursing home, and an old man who had been reading the paper nearby called across, 'Slingsby, there's something in the *Telegraph* just up your street. A fellow with one leg has climbed the Matterhorn.' Eleanor said that it must be Geoffrey, her husband. She was not sure how much her father could understand any more, but he paused for a moment and said, 'Magnificent, magnificent! Of course, he shouldn't have done it, you know!'

The Abraham brothers continued to climb adventurously and propagate the sport with vigour. George published many books about their climbs in the Lake District, Scotland and North Wales, the Alps and the Dolomites, and Ashley travelled widely to lecture and display their mountain photographs. The business in Keswick flourished, particularly after they began making postcards of their pictures. George looked after the shop while Ashley managed the wholesale side of affairs. Their rock climbing was still concentrated on the Wasdale Head area, even after C. D. Frankland and Bentley Beetham had revealed the possibilities of the Borrowdale crags, and it was a normal day for them to load their rucksacks with twenty pounds of camera equipment (an Underwood whole-plate camera, a dozen glass-plate slides, two lenses and a tripod) and walk from Keswick to Great Gable for a long day of climbing and photography, before walking back to Keswick that night. To the end their favourite climb of all remained the New West on Pillar Rock, and this was the last climb that they made together, in 1936.

In the early years of the century they took, with customary enthusiasm, to the new sport of motoring. A motor journey was a sporting event in those days, particularly in the Lake District where the higher roads had rough, unmetalled surfaces and steeper gradients than today. In this field the Abrahams notched at least two first ascents for the internal combustion engine, Hardknott and Wrynose passes.

Haskett Smith continued to climb for many years with undiminished verve and verbosity. In 1913 he was in the Canadian Rockies. In the twenties Dorothy Pilley Richards climbed with him in the Lake District and wrote: 'Forty years on, he carried, in everything, in his humour, his crisp anecdote, his apt quotation, his waistcoats, cut-away and whipcords, the spirit of 40 years back. On a climb with him "Silence while the leader advances" was decidedly not the rule. The idea rather was to give all the party a full stream of verbal as well as moral support.'

He shared a flat near Olympia in London with a sister, and they lived modestly on independent means that were only just sufficient. Although a qualified lawyer, Haskett Smith did little or no legal work and is said to have been highly offended on the one occasion when a solicitor sent him a brief. He was a member of several learned societies, and wrote many articles about his great interests, etymology and genealogy. His wit remained sharp. When told that Winthrop Young had been appointed to a readership in comparative education, he said, 'It is good to hear that the comparatively educated, of whom there are so many, are to have something done for them at last.'

Right up to the late 1930s he regularly joined the London branch of the Fell and Rock Climbing Club on country walks, and never showed signs of fatigue. In 1936 he agreed to climb Napes Needle to mark the fiftieth anniversary of his conquest of the pinnacle.

Easter Sunday was the day appointed for the jubilee ascent. On Good Friday, Haskett Smith, now seventy-six years old, was driven from London to Wasdale Head in a small open car, and when he finally climbed out after the long journey his limbs were creaking and his eyes streaming. The President of the Fell and Rock Climbing Club, R. S. T. (now Lord) Chorley, and the editor of the club's Journal, G. R. Speaker, were there to greet him. Next day they set off to take him for a trial climb on Pillar Rock, but he could only get as far as Robinson's Cairn. Sunday dawned cold and gusty with occasional snow flurries but, though Haskett Smith was in poor shape with his eyes badly inflamed, the party set off slowly up the track to Sty Head and then along the climbers' path to the foot of Napes Needle.

An audience of 300 had gathered around the Dress Circle and Needle Gully for the occasion. R. S. T. Chorley led the climb, which followed the original route of 1886, and, with help from the rope above him and with G. R. Speaker carefully guiding his feet from below, Haskett Smith gained the famous summit for the last time. Someone called out, 'Tell us a story', and he shouted back, 'There is no other story. This is the top storey.' Chorley made a short speech of admiration and affection, the old gentleman replied briefly, and thought it possible that he might not be able to repeat the climb again in another fifty years, the company sang 'For he's a jolly good fellow', and then the climbers descended and returned to the hotel where Haskett Smith said his last farewell to the mountains of Cumberland. He died in 1946.

Soon after this Chorley and Speaker officiated at another jubilee climb. Godfrey Solly, the discoverer of Eagle's Nest Ridge on Great Gable, had kept himself fit over the decades by climbing in the Alps, the Caucasus and the Canadian Rockies. In April 1939 at the age of eighty, he went to Pillar Rock to mark the fiftieth anniversary of his first ascent, and the companion of that ascent in 1889, the Reverend Edmund Freeman of Whitehaven, went with him. They planned to do the easy Slab and Notch route, but because a fall from there can have serious consequences, Speaker said they should rope up. Solly said that was quite unnecessary. Fortunately there were two novice climbers in the party, and Speaker argued that the rope should be used for their sakes. At this Solly conceded the point but insisted that, in that case, he should be allowed to lead, which he proceeded to do 'with cheerful ease'. He died three years later.

'Of all the whole-hearted mountaineers I have known,' wrote Winthrop Young, 'Collie alone remained to the end wholly and passionately absorbed in the mountain world.' Professor Norman Collie climbed in many mountain ranges, in Norway and the Lofoten Islands, in the Alps of Europe, the Canadian Rockies and the Himalayas, as well as in his native Scotland where, in 1920, he encountered the famous ghost, the Grey Man of Ben Macdhui, who, he claimed, walked with him to the top of the mountain. A scientist of the greatest eminence, a man of deeply civilized accomplishment, his consuming passion was for mountains. He wrote: 'Even if I never again had a chance of climbing a first class peak in the Alps, I would return there to live the lazy, delightful, disreputable life in a tent, near the ice and the snows and the pine woods, to smell the camp fire, lie on my back all day amidst the grass and the flowers, listening to the wind and looking at the sky and the great silent peaks.'

He ended his days gazing upon the mountains he loved most of all, the Cuillin of Skye, where he had first fallen under the thrall of climbing. In 1940, two young fighter pilots, training for the Battle of Britain, spent a few days' leave at Sligachan Inn at the foot of the Cuillin. One of them, Richard Hillary, destined for fame and an early death, wrote in his book *The Last Enemy*: 'We were alone in the inn save for one old man who had returned there to die. His hair was white but his face and bearing were still those of a mountaineer, though he must have been a great age. He never spoke, but appeared regularly at meals to take his place at a table tight-pressed against the window, alone with his wine and his memories. We thought him rather fine.' It was, of course, Norman Collie. He died in November 1942 at the age of eighty-three.

The last survivors of the 'Golden Age' were the Keswick brothers. Ashley Abraham climbed until he was seventy-two and died three years later. George was still climbing in the

Alps when he was seventy-five and did not die until the spring of 1965, in his ninety-fourth year. Ashley's son, Geoffrey Perry Abraham, carried on the business for a while, but when he retired the shop, which had been there for more than a hundred years, was taken over by George Fisher for his climbing shop.

One direct link with the 'Golden Age' still remains. Colonel 'Rusty' Westmorland, who lives in Threlkeld, was fifteen years old when he made his first climb in the Lake District, on Pillar Rock in 1901. To mark the jubilee in 1951 he led the North Climb; ten years after that, he led the New West; and in 1971, at the age of eighty-five, he climbed Pillar Rock again, this time by the Old West route by which the Rock had first been conquered 145 years before.

Rock climbing has changed greatly in the seventy years since the 'Golden Age' came to an end. It is still, as it always will be, a minority sport, but while its devotees numbered no more than a few dozen in 1903, there are now reckoned to be 50,000 in Britain and perhaps 250,000 or more in the world. What was merely a holiday pursuit for busy professional men has become for some a full-time occupation, and livings are earned by teaching climbing, writing about it, filming it and taking part in prestigious expeditions. It had even become, through the occasional 'live spectacular' on television, something of a spectator sport. Standards have risen, in skill and daring and technique, and the leading heroes of later generations have carried their expertise, nurtured on gritstone and refined on 'Borrowdale volcanic', to the conquest of more and more difficult cliffs on ever steeper and higher mountains, first in the Alps and now in the Himalayas. The sport has become totally democratic. Working-class lads from Glasgow and Salford brought a new kind of toughness into climbing and even the ancient bastions of the Alpine Club and Himalayan exploration have fallen before the boots of Hamish MacInnes, Joe Brown and Don Whillans. The spirit has become more intense and more competitive and, often, more vituperative. When the 'tiger' of today goes to the crags, he goes armed with a library of detailed information to guide him, an armoury of sophisticated equipment and techniques to safeguard him, and a mountain rescue service to come to his aid in time of serious trouble.

The crags remain, cleaned of their loose rocks and vegetation and criss-crossed now by hundreds of routes yet, for the most part, just as they were when Haskett Smith first surveyed them with an appraising eye. Despite repeated fears, they are still not 'climbed out'. And there are still many who climb them for the old, original reasons—to escape for a while from everyday worries and preoccupations, to enjoy the freedom of the fells and the physical fitness that comes from hard exercise on the crags and, above all, to experience again that '*stretched and anxious* state of mind favourable to depth of pleasurable Impression'.

17 Postscript

This book was first published in 1972 and has been out of print since 1976.

When the idea of a new, paperback edition was raised it seemed a sensible idea to revise the original edition, correcting known errors, incorporating extra material where necessary and amending the emphases in the light of subsequent thoughts and developments. To do this, however, would have meant resetting the entire text which would have been an expensive undertaking. So in the interests of keeping the retail price as low as possible it was decided to reproduce the 1972 text by photographic process and add a brief 'postcript' chapter to deal with corrections and amendments.

First, the factual errors. On page ten I describe Professor Norman Collie as 'the discoverer of neon and X-ray photography'. He was certainly a distinguished scientist and a creative pioneer in both these fields but I now believe that to call him 'discoverer' is to overstate his claims to fame. On the top line of page fifty the date – the day when 'Steeple' Jackson set off for his final and fatal attempt on Pillar Rock – should read '1st May' instead of '30th April'.

Some members of the Fell and Rock Climbing Club have complained that I give 1907 (on page 173) as the year of the Club's foundation. They said it should be 1906. It is a moot point, depending on whether you date it from the preliminary meetings and enrolment of its first members or from the completion of these arrangements and the first general meeting which was held at the Wastwater Hotel on March 30 1907. An account of the Club's formation in the first issue of its *Journal* gives the date as 1907, and that is authority enough for me.

If it had been possible to revise the original text I would, as a chief priority, have modified the claim that the sport of rock climbing was born at Wasdale Head in the early 1880s. I still believe that *British* rock climbing was born there and then, the creation of Haskett Smith and his friends and followers. There were occasional, individual forays on to steep rock in North Wales and Scotland and the Pennines in the same period, but it was at Wasdale Head that Britain's first rock climbing community began to meet regularly, expand in numbers and grow in skill and confidence year by year.

None the less, as Doug Scott makes clear in his book *Big Wall Climbing* (Kaye and Ward, 1974), another school of dedicated cragsmen was emerging in the Eastern Alps before 1880 and tackling routes in the last two decades of the century that were as technically hard as those in the Lake District and considerably longer and more formidably exposed. Scott says that young German and Austrian climbers, mostly from middle-class backgrounds in the big cities, 'wanted to escape the restrictions society was imposing upon them'. If so, then the motivation was clearly much the same as that of their contemporary British counterparts. Speaking of the period after 1875, when most of the major summits in the Eastern Alps had been gained, Scott writes: 'This was the golden age of big wall rock climbing when classic lines of ascent went up with beautiful directness from the base to the summit. These routes consisted of superb pitches of sustained difficult free climbing, of short sections of aid climbing round exhilarating overhangs and committing rope moves across blank walls.'

Scott's book came out two years after *The First Tigers*. It was, in Dr Johnson's phrase, 'pure ignorance' and not Cumbrian chauvinism that led me to give the sole credit to the men of Wasdale Head. Rock climbing was virtually bound to emerge, along with other adventure sports, in the closing decades of the nineteenth century and it now seems to me that it did so more or less simultaneously and quite independently in the Eastern Alps and in the Lake District.

The First Tigers deals with the development of the sport up to 1903. No new primary sources for that period have appeared since the book came out and it now seems unlikely that there will be any more. The closest in relevance, though it deals with a slightly later period, is *Climbing at Wasdale Head before the First World War* (Castle Cary Press Ltd., 1982), a scholarly presentation of the climbing diaries and articles of George S. Sansom. The diaries were found soon after Sansom's death in 1981. They cover the period from 1907 when he first went to Wasdale Head to early 1914 when he supported Herford on the first ascent of Central Buttress. He met several of this book's heroes including A. E. Field and the Abraham brothers and it was the youngest Abraham, John, who introduced him to climbing. 'I was very impressed,' Sansom wrote, 'with Mr Botterill's elegant, effortless climbing; in fact I have never seen a neater climber.' And of Herford he said: 'We soon became friends, a friendship which lasted until his death in the war. I do not think we ever had a quarrel or serious disagreement, and I felt his loss greatly. He was tall, slim and graceful in movement.' Herford and Sansom both loved the Lake District: 'For some reason, which I do not understand, the Wasdale mountains were friendly whilst the Welsh ones seemed hostile.'

A few people have complained the *The First Tigers* gives too much weight to the activities and opinions of Aleister Crowley. More than thirty years after his death his powerful personality can still arouse resentment and hatred. He was, as I think this book makes clear, an abrasive and often offensive man. He was also a good climber and an effective writer, prepared to speak his mind with no regard to consequent unpopularity. His strictures on the Alpine establishment, for example, and on the behaviour of Owen Glynne Jones were fiercely stated but he could defend them with example and argument. He was there, however briefly, at the time and his comments offer a challenging corrective to most of the other source material.

In the dozen years since *The First Tigers* came out the sport has continued to flourish and expand and Lake District climbers have continued to play a leading role. The most amazing thing is the way standards, at the upper limits, go on rising though it is hard to see how the pace of development can be maintained for very much longer. O. G. Jones classified the routes of his day in four grades; today there are eighteen separate categories, seven of them in the Extremely Severe group. The lead climbers of the 1980s climb more than their pioneer predecessors and train harder and take the sport much more seriously. The golden rule of the 'Golden Age' at Wasdale Head was 'the leader must not fall'. With the gear and methods of the time it was an eminently sensible axiom. But the men who are making new Lakeland routes today hold that if a man is not falling off frequently, then he is not climbing at or near the limits of his ability. Modern protection techniques – the running belays which ensure, on the whole, that if the leader falls he does not fall more than a few feet – make it possible for the determined climber to come off, try again, fall again and simply go on trying until he finally succeeds. Such assurance gives a great boost to confidence but it is not always possible to arrange a guaranteed protection and when this happens the moden 'tiger' has to call on his own resources of skill and strength and courage. The leading figures of today display a determination and fanaticism that would have shocked Haskett Smith and surprised even O. G. Jones.

Despite this, I believe that the conclusions in the final paragraphs of *The First Tigers* still hold good. Rock climbing is too slow and detailed and introspective to become a spectator sport and as a result it has been spared the mass interest and massive injections of money that have brought games like tennis and soccer to their present depths of greed and rancour and bad manners. The majority of rock climbers still operate in the middle reaches, between the grades of Very Difficult and Very Severe. They climb for holiday adventure and escape. They are knowledgeable about the history of their sport and like to go back from time to time, to the classic routes of the last century.

Most important of all, Lake District climbers have remained loyal to the original spirit of free climbing. They use the latest techniques to catch them if they fall but they use only the rock itself for their climbing. In the Dolomites and Yosemite and other parts of the world climbers employ sophisticated 'engineering' methods to haul themselves up faces that might otherwise be impossible, hammering in pitons, standing in slings, pulling up on loops of tape. Such methods are rarely seen in the Lake District and roundly condemned when they do appear.

The crags themselves are little changed. Many of the old routes have become harder because the passage of countless feet has made small holds smoother and more rounded. In some places, like Kern Knotts Crack, holds have disappeared altogether. Here and there, in the particularly hard places where Extremes are being made, you will see splodges of white around the handholds where climbers have dipped their fingers in chalk to keep them dry. But for the most part nothing has altered and climbers can still go to Pillar Rock and Scafell Crag and a dozen other cliffs and find out almost exactly what it felt like to Fred Botterill and Godfrey Solly and the other bold spirits of Wasdale Head when they were creating these climbs nearly a hundred years ago.

Bibliography

Abraham, George D. (1907). *The Complete Mountaineer.* Methuen & Co. Ltd, London.

(1910). *Mountain Adventures at Home and Abroad.* Methuen & Co. Ltd, London.

(1919). *On Alpine Heights and British Crags.* Methuen & Co. Ltd, London.

(1933). *Modern Mountaineering.* Methuen & Co. Ltd, London.

Amery, L. S. (1939). *Days of Fresh Air.* Jarrolds (London) Ltd.

Baker, E. A. (1933). *The British Highlands with Rope and Rucksack.* H. F. & G. Witherby, London.

Benson, C. E. (1902). *Crag and Hound in Lakeland.* Hurst and Blackett Ltd, London.

Bogg, Edmund, *see under* Lowe, G. T.

Budworth, Captain Joseph (1792). *A Fortnight's Ramble to the Lakes.*

Byne, Eric, and Sutton, Geoffrey (1960). *High Peak.* Secker and Warburg Ltd, London.

Chorley, Katharine (1950). *Manchester Made Them.* Faber and Faber Ltd, London.

Clark, Ronald W. (1953). *The Victorian Mountaineers.* B. T. Batsford Ltd, London.

(1956). *Six Great Mountaineers.* Hamish Hamilton Ltd, London.

Clark, Ronald W., and Pyatt, Edward C. (1957). *Mountaineering in Britain.* Phoenix House Ltd, London.

COLERIDGE, S. T. (1956). *The Collected Letters*. Clarendon Press, Oxford.

CREW, PETER (1968). *Encyclopaedic Dictionary of Mountaineering*. Constable & Co. Ltd, London.

CROWLEY, ALEISTER (1970). *Confessions*. Jonathan Cape, London.

DE QUINCEY, THOMAS (1948). *Recollections of the Lake Poets*. John Lehmann Ltd, London.

DENT, C. T. (1892). *Mountaineering*. The Badminton Library, Longmans, Green & Co., London.

GRAY, THOMAS (1951). *Journal of a visit to the Lake District*. Oxford University Press.

HASKETT SMITH, WALTER PARRY (1894). *Climbing in the British Isles: England*. Longmans, Green & Co., London.

HILLARY, RICHARD (1944). *The Last Enemy*. Macmillan & Co. Ltd, London.

HOPKINSON, SIR ALFRED (1930). *Penultima*. Martin Hopkinson Ltd, London.

JONES, OWEN GLYNNE (1897). *Rock Climbing in the English Lake District*. Longmans, Green & Co., London.

LARDEN, WALTER (1910). *Recollections of an Old Mountaineer*. Edward Arnold & Co., London.

LOWE, G. T. (1896). *Climbs in Lakeland*, published in EDMUND BOGG'S *From Lakeland and Ribblesdale*, 1898.

MCMULLEN, R. T. (1893). *Down Channel*.

MASON, A. E. W. (1926). *A Romance of Wastdale*. Hodder and Stoughton Ltd, London.

MILLWARD, ROY, and ROBINSON, ADRIAN (1970). *The Lake District*. Eyre and Spottiswoode Ltd, London.

MONTAGUE, C. E. (1923). *Fiery Particles*. The Cloister Press.

MOORMAN, MARY (1957). *William Wordsworth*. Oxford University Press.

MUMM, A. L. (1938). *The Alpine Club Register 1877–90*. Edward Arnold & Co., London.

NICHOLSON, NORMAN (1955). *The Lakers*. Robert Hale Ltd, London.

NOYCE, WILFRED. *See under* PYATT, EDWARD.

OPPENHEIMER, LEHMANN J. (1908). *The Heart of Lakeland.* Sherratt and Hughes.

PYATT, EDWARD C., and NOYCE, WILFRED (1962). *British Crags and Climbers.* Dennis Dobson, London.

PYATT, EDWARD C. *see also* under CLARK, RONALD W.

QUILLER-COUCH, ARTHUR (1944). *Memories and Opinions.* Cambridge University Press.

ROBINSON, ADRIAN, *see under* MILLWARD, ROY.

ROLLINSON, WILLIAM (1967). *A History of Man in the Lake District.* J. M. Dent & Sons Ltd, London.

SALE, HENRY S. (1908). *On Cambrian and Cumbrian Hills.* C. W. Daniel Co. Ltd, London.

SEATREE, GEORGE (1923). *Lakeland Memories.* R. Scott, Penrith.

SUTTON, GEOFFREY, *see under* BYNE, ERIC.

UNSWORTH, WALTER (1968). *Because it is There.* Victor Gollancz Ltd, London.

Wastwater Hotel, Wasdale Head. The hotel visitors' book.

WEST, THOMAS (1778). *A Guide to the Lakes.*

WORDSWORTH, WILLIAM (1835). *Guide through the District of the Lakes.* The Tantivy Press.

YOUNG, GEOFFREY WINTHROP (1951). *Mountains with a Difference.* Eyre and Spottiswoode Ltd, London.

PERIODICALS

Climbing Guides to the English Lake District, edited by J. Wilkinson, published by the Fell and Rock Climbing Club, 1967–70.

Journals of the Alpine Club.

Journals of the Climbers' Club.

Journals of the Fell and Rock Climbing Club of the English Lake District.

Journals of the Scottish Mountaineering Club.

Journals of the Yorkshire Ramblers' Club.

Index

Abraham, Ashley P.; as photographer, 110, 134–5, 139, 161; on Blencathra, 119; as climber, 134, 139–41, 144, 162; temperament, 134; meeting with Owen Glynne Jones, 136; in Scotland, 161; as first President of the Fell and Rock Climbing Club, 174; later years of, 178, 181; *see also* Abraham Brothers

Abraham Brothers, 11, 101, 104, 116, 123, 131, 147, 156, 178; as photographers, 10, 134, 138, 178; with Owen Glynne Jones, 11, 120, **134–58, 13:–44**; as climbers, 120, **134**, 178; on Scafell: Pinnacle by Jones's Route, **138–40**; Collier's Climb, 140–2, Keswick Brothers' Climb, **148**, Pisgah Buttress, 149; in Iron Crag Chimney, 143, 151; on Pillar Rock: Shamrock Gully, 143–4, Great Doup Buttress, 161, New West Climb, **161–3**, 178; in Peak District, 147; in North Wales, 147, 155; on Great End, 148; in Scotland: Crowberry Ridge, Buachaille Etive Mòr, 161; as writers, 131, 178; as pioneer motorists, 179

Abraham, Geoffrey Perry, 182

Abraham, George D.: as writer 17–18, 55, 104–5, 113, 115, 117, 133, 138, 143–4, 150, 152, 162; as photographer, 119; as climber, 134, 139–41, 143–4, **152–5**, 161, **162–3**; temperament of, 134; meeting with Owen Glynne Jones, 138; with the Fell and Rock Climbing Club, 174; later years of, 178, 181–2; *see also* Abraham Brothers

Abraham, George Perry, 74, 134, 151

Abraham, Sidney, 119

Accidents, 3, 6, 172–3; in the Alps, 61, 102, 151, 156–8; in the Dolomites, 133–4; in the Lake District, 2, 44–5, 50, 60–1, 65–7, 92–3, 120–1, 133, 143–4, 150, 163–4, 169–71, 177; in Scotland, 171

All the Year Round, 68–9

Alpine Club, 8, 45, 52, 64, 71, 76, 109, 116, 118, 130, **173–4**, 177, 182
  Journal, 7–8, 45, 53, 76, **156**
  Register, 11

Alps, **5–9**, 26, 43, 44, 51, 52, 62, 70, 71, 77, 81, 87, 93, 95, 106, 109, 119, 134, 148, **150–1, 155–7**, 178, 180, 181, 182; Wetterhorn, 5; Mont Blanc, 5, 9, 95; Matterhorn, 6, 61, 62, 79, 178; Monte Rosa, 8; Meije, 52; Dent de Requin, 97; Grépon, 97; Dent Blanche, 102, 105–6, 156; Petit Dent de Veisivi, 151

Ambleside, 25, 35

Amery, L. S., 10, **132–3**

Andrews, A. W., 51, 146

Angler's Rock, *see* Ennerdale

Archer Thomson, James Merriman, 130, **145–6**, 147

Arran, Isle of, 15, **161**

Artificial aids, *see under* Techniques

Atkinson, John, 35–6, 163

Baddeley, M. J. B., 19, 103

Baker, Professor E. A., 116–17, 161

Baker, G. P., 93

Ball, John, 44

Barker, Miss A., 43

Barn-door traverse, 108

Barton Brothers, 164
Barton, Claude W., 160
Barton, Guy, 160
Bartrum, Geoffrey, 116
Baumgartner, C. A. O., **36–8**, 40, 42, 63, 174, 176
Beachy Head, 51, 127–8
Beetham, Bentley, 115–16, 178
Ben Nevis, 15, 88, 171; Tower Ridge, 145
Benson, Claude E., 165
Bicknell, Raymond, 177
Bidean nam Bian, 145
Black and White, 90
Black Sail, 41, 144
Blencathra, 28, 161; Sharp Edge, 119
Boots, *see under* Equipment
Borrowdale, 25–6, 31, 74, 134, 178
Botterill, Arthur, 9, 176
Botterill, Fred, 123; training on gritstone, 166; on Botterill's Slab, Scafell, **167–9**; on North-west Climb, Pillar Rock, 176; in Warn Ghyll, Haystacks, 176; on Great Gable: Abbey Buttress, 177, Eagle's Nest Ridge, 177; end of serious climbing, 177
Botterill's Slab, *see under* Scafell
Bowen, H. C., 142, 147
Bowfell, 159, 161, 164; Bowfell Buttress, 3, 59, **164**
Bowring, F. H., 67, 82, 121; at Wasdale Head, 1, 56–7; education and career of, 57; appearance of, 57–8; on Pillar Mountain, 72; on Scafell, 73–4; on Great Gable, 74; last years of, 176
Braithwaite, J., 36
Briggs, W. A., 93
British Medical Journal, The, 66
Broad Stand, *see under* Scafell
Broadrick Brothers, 10, **160**
Broadrick, H. C., **160**; *see also* Broadrick Brothers
Broadrick, R. W., **160–1**, **16;–70**, 172; *see also* Broadrick Brothers
Browne, T. H. Murray, 42
Buachaille Etive Mòr; Collie's Climb, 145; Crowberry Ridge, 161
Budworth, Captain Joseph, 27–9
Buttermere, 34, 37, 41, 62, 72, 121, 125, 136, 159, 163

Cader Idris, 57, 105, 147
Canadian Rockies, 179, 180, 181
Cannan, Charles, 58, 82, 131
Carr, Ellis, **91–2**, 93, 174
Castle Head, Keswick, 165
Caucasus, 45, 93, 97, 180
Chalk cliffs, 146; *see also* Beachy Head
Chorley, Katharine, 12, 65, 86–7, 151
Chorley, R. S. T. (later Lord), 180
Cliffe, J. H., 46
Climbers' Club, 8, 173
Journal, 166
Clothing, *see under* Equipment
Colebank, J., 36
Coleridge, Samuel Taylor, 16, 24, 30, **31–4**, 35, 59
Collie, Professor J. Norman, 10, 11, 12, 82, 105, 114, 174, 177; as climber, 80–1, 90, 92–3, 97; on Collie Step, Scafell, **96–7**, 122; encounters Owen Glynne Jones, 98, 99; descriptions of, 81, 130, 181; in Norway, 81, 181; in the Himalayas, 97, 181; in Scotland: on Collie's Climb, Buachaille Etive Mòr, 145, Bidean nam Bian, 145, Tower Ridge, Ben Nevis, 145, Ben Macdhui, 181; last years of, 181
Collier, Dr Joseph, 115, 176; description of, **93**; on Pillar Rock, 93; on Scafell, **93**, 140, 149; in Piers Ghyll, 93; on Great Gable, 132; in Scotland, 145
Combined tactics, *see under* Techniques
Coniston, 18, 35, 41, 80
Coniston Old Man, 27
Conway, W. M., 7–8

Coolidge, Rev. W. B., 53
Cornish cliffs, 51
Craig, G. H., 163–4
Crib Goch, *see under* Snowdon
Crook, W. M., 105, 150, 156, 157
Crowley, Aleister, 10, 12, 143, 146; writings of, 18, 63, 101–2, 127, 129, 130, 131; on Beachy Head, 51, **127–8**; education and character of, 127; climbing style of, 128, 131; in Skye, 128–9; in the Lake District 129–30
Cuillin, the, 52–3, 80, 90, 95, 181; Sgurr Alasdair, 52; the Inaccessible Pinnacle, 53; Sgurr nan Gillean, 80–1, 128
Cumberland Paquet and Wares Whitehaven Advertiser, The, 35–6
Cundill, Major Ponsonby, 42
Cust's Gully, *see under* Great End

Dalton, Millican, 165–6
de Quincey, Thomas, 30, 34, 39
Deep Ghyll, *see under* Scafell
Dent Blanche, 102, 105–6, 156
Dent de Requin, 97
Derwentwater, 26, 28
Dixon, Professor, 100
Dollywaggon Pike, 27, 161; Dollywaggon Gully, 134; Chock Gully, 174–5
Dolomites, 125, 133, 178
Dove's Nest caves, 165
Dow Crag, 11, 79–80, 159, 169; Great Gully, 20, 89; Easter Gully, 80; East Buttress, 80; Hopkinson's Crack, 80
Dungeon Ghyll, Old Hotel, 125, 161
Dymond, C. W., in Mickledore Chimney, 42; on Slab and Notch, Pillar Rock, 43

Echo, The, 157
Eckenstein, Oscar, **130–1**
Edwards, F. E., 160
Elliott, Rev. J. M., 41
Ellis, Godfrey, 147
Ennerdale, 35, 36, 37, 47, 59, 61, 62, 77, 103
Equipment, 3, 77, 110, **118–26**, 131, 182–3
  Artificial aids, *see under* Techniques
  Boots, 12, 73, 100, 110, **123–5**, 131, 146
  Clothing, 57–8, 63, **123**, 179
  Rucksack, 123
  Fell-pole, 46, 47, 49, 58, 77, **121**
  Guide books, 4, 19, 35, 42, **125–6**, 182
  Ice-axe, 54, 77, 110, 119, **121–3**; for use of ice-axe *see* Techniques
  Rope, 31, 47, 61, 73, 81, 110, **118–119**; for use of rope *see* Techniques
Eskdale, 33, 39
Evolena, 157

Fairfield, 87, 161
Fell and Rock Climbing Club of the English Lake District, 173, 174, 175, 179, 180
  Guide Books of, 59, 92, 96, **125**, 143, 160, 175, 176
  Journal, 77–8, 122–3, 174
Fell-pole, *see under* Equipment
Fell-running, 52, 160–1, 169
Fell-walking, 19, 23, 27–34, 44, 46–47, 57, 62, 87
Field, A. E., 152–5
Fleetwith Pike, 121
Fowler, W. H., 136–7
Frankland, C. D., 178
Freeman, Rev. Edmund, 180
Freshfield, Douglas, 8
Furrer, the guide, 156

'Gardening', 20, 64–5, 68, **122–3**, 164, 167
Gardiner, Frederick, 18, 45, 52
Garrett, A. E. W., 170
Gaspard, the guide, 159–60
Gilson, R. C., 132

Gimmer Crag, 11, 159, 165; North-west Gully, 59, 165; Gimmer Chimney, 165; Amen Corner, 156
Gipsy Journal, 102–3
Gladstone, William Ewart, 61
Glaramara, 121, 165
Glencoe, 15, 145, 161
Glyder Fach, 155
Godley, A. D., 115
Goodall, Alex, 172
Grading and description of routes, **19–21**, **125–6**, 182; publication controversy, 94–5
Grant, J. E., 166–9
Grasmere, 25, 30, 161
Gray, Thomas, **24–6**, 27, 31
Great Doup, *see under* Pillar Mountain
Great End, 44, 161; Cust's Gully, 20, 88; Central Gully, 59, 148; South-east Gully, 59
Great Gable, 4, 50, 62, 63, 67, 83, 110, 113, 160, 166, 178
  Ennerdale Face of, 59, 61, 77; Oblique Chimney, 101–2, 132–133; Central Gully, Gable Crag, 152
  Kern Knotts Crack, 3, 17, 20, 122, 137, **142–3**; Kern Knotts Chimney, 17, 20, **136–7**, 142, 143
  Napes face of, 5, 62, 67, 74, 138, 176–7; Eagle's Nest Ridge, 3, 20, **93–4**, 138, 177, 180; Arrowhead Ridge, 20, 95, 138; Needle Gully, 67, 138; Needle Ridge, 68, 138
  Napes Needle, 5, 20, **67–8**, 75, **77–9**, 90, 98, 99–101, 103, 105, 121, **179–80**
  Westmorland Cairn, 43
Grépon, 97
Gritstone, 51, **146**, **166**, 173, 182

Hall, Richard W., 63
Hargreaves, C., 164
Haskett Smith, Edmund, 2, 59, 68, 89
Haskett Smith, Walter Parry, 5, 10, 12, 36, 38, 51, 63, 69, 74, 76, 82, 84, 91, 98, 110, 114, 116, 124, 174–5, 176, 177, 183; at Wasdale Head, 1–2, **56–61**, 114, 116; background and personality, 1, 56, 59–60, 65, 98, 179; on Great Gable, 5, 67–8, 77; on Napes Needle, 5, 6, **7–8**, 75, **77–9** (first ascent), 121, **179–80** (jubilee ascent); with John Wilson Robinson, 11, 63, 67–8, 79–80; writings of, 16, 50, 57–8, 60, 64, 77–9, 92, 97, 99, 103, 104, 119, 122–3, 125; first ascents in 1882, 59; on Pillar Rock, **60–1**, 68, 79, 89, **90–1** (first ascent, North Climb); on Scafell, 68, 79, 89–90, 95; on Dow Crag, 79–80, 89; on Sergeant Crag, 80; on Pavey Ark, 80; in North Wales, 137, 145; on Gimmer Crag, 165; Haskett Gully, 175
Hastings, Cuthbert, 116
Hastings, Geoffrey, 70, 77, 116, 122, 174, 177; on Scafell, 71, 75–6, 89–90, 96–7; on Great Gable, 79; on Pillar Rock, 89, 90, 92–3; on Dow Crag, 89; in the Alps, 97; on the Screes, Wastwater, 97; in Himalayas, 97; description of, 130; in Glencoe, 145
Haystacks: Stack Ghyll, 163; Warn Ghyll, 176
Hazard, J., 176
Helm Crag, 27, 28, 87
Herford, Siegfried W., 89, 170–1, 176; on Central Buttress, Scafell, **172**
Helvellyn, 28, 44, 161
High Stile, 136
Hill, F. W., 137, **155–6**
Hill, Mrs F. W., 137, 155
Himalayas, 45, 156, 181, 182; Nanga Parbat, 97; Kangchenjunga, 131
Hinchcliff, Thomas, 44
Hodgson, John, 47–8
Hopkinson, Albert, 85; education

and career, 87; on Scafell Pinnacle, 88–9; *see also* Hopkinson Brothers
Hopkinson, Alfred, 85; education and career, 86; recollections of, 87–8; *see also* Hopkinson Brothers
Hopkinson Brothers, 65–6; background and upbringing of, 85; education and careers of, 85–7; early mountain experiences of, 87–9; friendship with Pilkington family, 88; on Ben Nevis, 88; routes named after them, 88; in the Lake District, 88–9; as climbers, 89; on Great Gully, Dow Crag, 120
Hopkinson, Charles, 85; education and career, 86; on Scafell Pinnacle, 88–9, 138, 149; *see also* Hopkinson Brothers
Hopkinson, Edward, 10, 66, 85, 151; education and career, 86; description of, 86–7; on Tryfan, 88; on Ben Nevis, 88; on Scafell Pinnacle, 88–9, 169; builds Hopkinson's Cairn, **89**, 169; effect of brother John's death on, 151; *see also* Hopkinson Brothers
Hopkinson Family, 11, 12–13, 66, 85–9, 177
Hopkinson, John, 10, 85, 176; education and career, 85–6; on Tryfan, 88; on Ben Nevis, 88; death of, 151; *see also* Hopkinson Brothers
Hutchinson, Sara, 32, 34

Ice-axe, *see under* Equipment *and* Techniques
Inaccessible Pinnacle, the, 53
Iron Crag Chimney, 143, 151

Jackson, the guide, 74
Jackson, Fred, 71
Jackson, F. W., 143
Jackson, Rev. James ('Steeple'), **46–50**, 96
Johnson, Dr Samuel, 18, 25
Jones, Owen Glynne, 10, 12, 17, 121, 159; with the Abraham Brothers, 11, 17, 120, **134–5**, 137–44, 147, 151; writings of, 16–17, 19, 94, 100–1, 125–6, 136–7, 139–40, 140–2, 149–50, 153–5; grading of climbs by, **19–21**; climbing style of, 65, 104–5, 129, 152; character and background of, **98–106**, 157; at the Wastwater Hotel, 106, **112–113**, 114; use of rope, 120–1, 143–4
in Iron Crag Chimney, 151
in North Wales, 105, 137, 145, 147, 155
in Sergeant Crag Gully, 136
in the Alps, 102, 105–6, 137, 148, 150–1, 155–7; death in, 102, **156–7**, and obituaries and press comment on, 157–8
in the Peak District, 147
on Dow Crag: Central Chimney, 147; Jones's Route, 149
on Great Gable, 101–2, 132–3, 152; Napes Needle, 98, 100–1, 105; Kern Knotts Crack, 122, 137, 138, **142–3**, 147; Kern Knotts Chimney, 136–7; Kern Knotts West Chimney, 147; Napes face of, 138
on High Stile, 136
on Pillar Rock, 105, 120; Shamrock Gully, 143–4; Walker's Gully, **152–5**
on Scafell, 17, 101, 120–1; Pinnacle by Jones's Route from Deep Ghyll, **138–40**, by Jones's Route Direct, **149–50**, 169; Collier's Climb, 140–2; Keswick Brothers' Climb, 148; Botterill's Slab, 148; Jones and Collier's Climb, 149; Pisgah Buttress, 149
on Wastwater Screes, 140; C Gully, 147, 150
Jones, Robert, 29
Jupp, Henry, 169–70

Kangchenjunga, 131
Kendall, 11, 25, 92, 165, 174
Kern Knotts, *see under* Great Gable
Keswick, 10, 17, 18, 25, 27, 28, 30, 32, 74, 114, 134, 138, 142, 151, 161, 172, 178
King, J. E., 58
Kirk Fell, 4, 160
Koecher, Miss, 100

Langdale, Great, 59, 129, 161
Langdale, Little, 164
Larden, Walter, 8
Leighton, Darwin, 165
Lewkowitch, 102
Lingmell, 4, 57, 69, 72, 73, 161
Lingmell Gill, 42
Lliwedd, 53–5, 147
Longman, William, 44
Lorton, 62, 67, 71
Lowe, G. T., 107, 117

McMullen, R. T., 14–15
Maitland, Mr, 49
Manchester City News, 172–3
Manchester Guardian, 13, 18, 83, 157–158, 170
Mason, A. E. W., 10, 83
Mason, J., 75–6
Matterhorn, 6, 61, 62, 79, 178
Meije, 52
Meryon, L. F., 160
Mickledore, *see under* Scafell
Mickledore Chimney, *see under* Scafell
Milnes Marshall, Professor Arthur, 10, 133, 172
Mirklin Cove, 175
Mont Blanc, 5, 29, 95
Montague, C. E., 83–4
Monte Rosa, 8
Morning Leader, 157
Mosedale, 9, 49, 103, 152, 153
Moss Ghyll, *see under* Scafell
Mumm, Arnold, 52, 58
Mummery, A. F., 9, 51, 70, 92, 97, 111, 130, 146

Nanga Parbat, 97
Nicolson, Sheriff Alexander, 53
North Wales, 1, 7, 8, 45, 46, 57, 87, 95, 105, 130, 145–6, 166, 178; Pen-y-Pass, 15, 172; Snowdon, 36, 53, 61; Pen-y-Gwryd, 53, 54, 109, 131; Lliwedd, 53–5, 147; Cader Idris, 57, 105, 147; Tryfan, 88, 155; Ogwen Valley, 146; Glyder Fach, 155
Norway, 70, 77, 81, 87, 181

Ogwen Valley, 146
Oliverson, C. H., 116
Oppenheimer, Lehmann J.; as writer, 17, 108–14, 169; education of, 108; as artist, 108; as climber, 108; on gritstone, 147; on Arran, 161; on Haystacks: Stack Ghyll, 163, Warn Ghyll, 176; on Pillar Rock: North Climb, 163–4, North-west Climb, 176, Savage Gully, 164; on Bowfell Buttress, 164; in Mirklin Cove, 175; death of, 176
Otley's *Guide to the Lakes*, 35
Owen, Henry, 53, 54

Packe, Charles, 44, 57, 69, 84
Pall Mall Budget, The, 90
Parker, A. G., 80
Patchell, C. W., 147
Pavey Ark: Great Gully, 59; Little Gully, 80
Peak District, 18, 51, 57, 146–7
Peile, Ernest, 71–4, 124
Pendlebury, Richard, 17–18, 45–6
Pendlebury, William, 18, 45–6
Pen-y-Gwryd, 53, 54, 109, 131
Pen-y-Pass, 15, 172
Petit Dent de Veisivi, 151
Petty, 66–7, 74
Photography, 119, 133–4, 138, 139, 161, 178
Piers Ghyll, 42, 65–6, 67, 69, 73, 88
Pilkington Brothers: on Pillar Rock, 43, 52; guideless climbing in the Alps, 52; in the Cuillin, 52–3; on the Inaccessible Pinnacle, 53; in Piers Ghyll, 65–6

Pilkington, Charles, *see* Pilkington Brothers
Pilkington Family, 11, 88, 177
Pilkington, Lawrence: as fell-runner, 52; describes first ascent of the Inaccessible Pinnacle, 53; accident in Piers Ghyll, 66, 88; *see also* Pilkington Brothers
Pike o' Stickle, 22
Pillar Mountain, 4, 5, 37, 42, 160; Great Doup, 50, 72; High Level path, 144, 175–6; Robinson's Cairn on, 175–6, 180; Great Doup Buttress, 161
Pillar Rock, 5, 35, 40, 42, 43, **47–50**, 52, 62, 63, 65, 72, 79, 89, 92, 96, 105, 118, 130, 132, 150, 161, 175, 180; first ascent of, **35–6**; early ascents of, **36–8**; accidents on, 60, 65, 92–3, 143–4, 163–4
by Savage Gully, 91, 160, 163, 164
by Shamrock Gully, 143–4
by Walker's Gully, 65, 72, 90, 120, **152–5**
Curtain route, 47
New West Climb, 3, **162–3**, 164, 166, 178, 182
North Climb, 60, **90–1**, 163–4, 177–8, 182; by Hand Traverse, 20, **91–2**, 92–3; by Stomach Traverse, 68; by the Nose, 90, 91, 92, 93, 163–4
Old Wall route, 37
Old West route, 36, 74, 163, 182
Slab and Notch route, 20, 43, 45, 47, 48, 72, 180–1; by Pendlebury Traverse, 17–18, 20, 45–6, 52, 58, 72
West Jordan climb, 59; Central Jordan climb, 59; East Jordan climb, 68
Pope, Rev. J., 61
Prior's Guide, 42
Puttrell, J. W.; on gritstone, 51, 146–7; background of, 146; as climber, 147–8; on Scafell, 148; in North Wales, 155; in Scotland, 161
Pyrenees, 1, 44, 57, 69

Quiller-Couch, Arthur, 10, 82–3

Radcliffe, Mrs Ann, 28
Raven Crag Gully, 16–17, 84
Rawnsley, Canon, 19
Rennison, Thomas James, 177
Reade, Herbert, 116
Red Pike, 103
Ridsdale, Stanley, 169–70
Rigby, E., 165
Ritson, William, 36, 37, **39–41**, 42, 45, 50, 72, 111
Rivelin Edge, 147
Robinson, 34
Robinson, John Wilson, 11, 69, **71–4**, 114, 116, 124, 129, 138, 151, 174; on Great Gable, 17, 63, 67–8, 74, 77, 101–2, **136–7**; on Pillar Rock, 62, 63, 65, 72, 74, 79, 91, **92–3**, 118; background of, 62; as fell-walker, 62; character of, 62–3; on Scafell, 63, 68, 73–4, 79, 96–7, 101; appearance of, 63; on Dow Crag, 79–80; on Sergeant Crag, 80, 122–3, **136**; on Wastwater Screes, 97; on High Stile, 136; in Iron Crag Chimney, 143; death of, 175; Robinson's Cairn, 175–6
Robinson's Cairn, *see under* Pillar Mountain *and* Robinson
Rocky Valley, Ilkley, 166
Rope, *see under* Equipment *and* Techniques
Rosthwaite, 74, 160, 161
Rucksack, 123
Rucksack Club, 173
Ruskin, John, 6, 18, 27

St Sunday Crag, 42
Salt, Henry S., 50
Sandbed Ghyll, 134
Sandison, John, 165
Sanson, G. S., 89, 170, 172, 177
Saturday Review, 44
Scafell, 5, 32–3, 83, 89, 110–11, 166; accidents on, 2, 120, 133, **169–171**, 172

Botterill's Slab, 3, 21, 88, 148, 166, **167–9**
Mickledore, 5, 41, 42, 83, 129, 148
Broad Stand, 5, 20, **32–3**, 38, 41, 44, 66, 73, 103, 129
Collier's Climb, 17, 20, **140–2**, 148
Deep Ghyll, 19, 20, 42, 58, 59, 71, 75–6, 103, 132, 133, 138, 139, 140, 172
North or Penrith Climb, 20, 41, 42, 72, 73, 124
Steep Ghyll, 20, 73, 101, 110, 133
Mickledore Chimney, 42, 66, 73–74, 83, 111, 129
Rake's Progress, 68, 73, 140, 141, 148, 168
Moss Ghyll, 84, **95–7**, 110, 120–1, 168
Hopkinson's and Tribe's Route, 88
Lord's Rake, 133, 139, 149, 169, 170
Keswick Brothers' Climb, 148; Puttrell Chimney on, 148, 169; Jones's finish on, 148
Jones and Collier's Climb, 149
Pisgah Buttress, 149
Central Buttress, 167, 172
Scafell Pinnacle, 74, 76, 79, **88–9**, 110–11, 133, 149, 169, 170; by Deep Ghyll, 20, 75–6, 79; by Jones's Route Direct, **149–50**, 169; by Jones's Route from Deep Ghyll, **138–40**; by Steep Ghyll, 20, 68, 89–90 (Slingsby's Chimney), 110, 133; by Thompson's Route, 160; from Jordan Gap, 68; from Lord's Rake, 170–1; Herford's Slab, 170; Hopkinson's Cairn, 88, 89; Hopkinson's Gully, 88, 89
Scafell Pike, 4, 41, 42, 114, 161
Scottish Highlands, 7, 18, 145, 161, 177, 178, 181; Ben Nevis, 15, 88, 145, 171; Glencoe, 15, 145, 161; Buachaille Etive Mòr, 145, 161; Bidean nam Bian, 145
Scottish Mountaineering Club, 173
Journal, 53, 96, 128
Screes, Wastwater, 3, 41, 83, 140; C Gully, 17, 20, 147, 150; Great Gully, 97
Seatree, George, 36, 38–41, 49, 62, 63, 71, 118; on Pillar Rock, 38, 47, 72, 74, 79; on Scafell, 73–4, 79; on Great Gable, 74; later years of, 174, 177
Sedgwick, Professor, 39
Sergeant Crag, 80, 122–3; Sergeant Crag Gully, 136
Sgurr Alasdair, 52
Sgurr nan Gillean, 80–1, 128
Shaw, Tom, 163, 164
Skiddaw, 22, 28, 161
Skye, Isle of, 15, 53, 80, 81, 128–9, 181; *see also* Cuillin
Slighachan, Skye, 128, 181
Slingsby, Lawrence, 176
Slingsby, W. Cecil, 77, 97, 114, 116, 174, 176; description of, 69–70; education and upbringing of, 70; in Norway, 70–1, 81, 177; in the Alps, 70–1, 177; at Wasdale Head, 71; in Deep Ghyll, 71, 75–76; on Dow Crag, 89; on Scafell Pinnacle, 89–90; use of combined tactics, 90; on Pillar Rock, 90, 91, 177–8; on Great Gable, 93–4, 95; last years of, 177–8
Snowdon, 61; Crib Goch ridge, 36, 53
Solly, Godfrey Allan, 95, 116, 177; career of, 91; on Pillar Rock, 91–92; **180–1** (jubilee climb); on Great Gable: Eagles' Nest Ridge Direct, **93–4**; in Scotland, 145
Southey, Robert, 30
Speaker, G. R., 180
Spender, Harold, 157, 172
Stanage Edge, 147
Steep Ghyll, *see under* Scafell
Stephen, Leslie, 9, 44, 111
Stocker, A. H., 53–5, 80
Stogden, John, 44–5, 132
Sty Head, 26, 102, 133, 137, 138, 180

Sumpner, Dr W. E., 99–101, 102–3, 157

Techniques, 3, 118, 183
à cheval, 168
Alpine, **51–2**, 119, 144
artificial aids, 47, 48, 49, 61, 131, 137, 161
combined tactics, 75, 77, 90, 94, 98, 100, 122, 138, 140, 141, 142, 144, 149, 151, 154, 162, 175
hand traverse, 91–2
layback, 165
simultaneous movement, 119
stockinged feet, climbing in, 100, 125, 149, **154–5**, 164
stomach traverse, 68
use of ice-axe, 5, **96**, 103, 119, 121–3
use of rope, 17, 48, 49, 54, 61, 68, **73**, 75, 76, 77, 83, 93, 96, 100, 102, **118–21**, 140, 142, 143–4, 167–9
belay, **119–20**, 140, 143–4, 171
top-rope, 94, 120, 137, 142, 164
Thompson Brothers, 160
Thompson, Peter, 164; *see also* Thompson Brothers
Thomson, Andrew, 165
Times, The, 6, 13
Tribe, W. N., 88, 133, 138
Tryfan, 88, 155
Tucker, H. Scott, 175
Tyndall, Professor, 44
Tyson, Dan, 1, 72–3, 108–9, 115
Tyson's Farm, 56, 83
Tyson, W., 36

Vegetation on crags and removal, *see* 'Gardening'
Victoria, Queen, 6, 61
Vuignier, the guide, 156

Walker Family, 11
Walker, G. T., 149–50
Walker's Gully, *see under* Pillar Rock
Walker, Horace, 92, 95
Walker, J. E., 62
Wall, T. W., 53–5
Walla Crag Gully, 134
Walpole, Horace, 24
Wasdale, 4, 35, 39, 40, 45, 66, 72, 100, 110, 136, 138, 151, 166
Wasdale Head, 1, 2, 3, 5, 9, 10, 11, 13, 18, 32, 36, 38, 39, 51, 55, 56, 58, 59, 65, 66, 69, 71, 72, 75, 77, 79, 82, 83, 90, 94, 95, 97, 101, 102, 105, 106, **107–17**, 125, 127, 131, 133, 134, 137, 144, 145, 146, 147, 148, 150, 157, 159, 166, 169, 172, 173, 178, 179
Wastwater, 100
Wastwater Hotel, 1, 2, 3, 13, 39–40, 44, 45, 49, 50, 69, 72, 77, 106, 144, 145, 152, 160; visitors' book at, **41–2**, 52, 88, 89, 100, 125, 129; life at, **107–17**; billiard room at, **111–13**, 117, 152; billiard fives at, 111, 115–16; billiard room traverse, **112–13**; French guide at, 159–60
Watson, W. J., 146–7
Webb, W. E., 170
West, G. R., 164
Westminster Gazette, 157
Westmorland, Annie, 43
Westmorland, Edward, 43
Westmorland, Colonel Horace ('Rusty'), 174–5, 182
Westmorland, Mary, 43
Westmorland, Thomas, 43, 174, 176
Wetterhorn, 5
Wharncliffe Crags, 146
Whitehaven News, 48
Whitehead, Dr 42
Whymper, Edward, 6, 95, 99, 127–8
Wigner, Dr J. H., 162–3
Williams, W. J., 149
Williamson, C. N., 69, 90
Williamson, H., 166–9
Wills, Alfred, 5
Wilson, Lieutenant, 36, 42
Wilson, Professor John, 39, 110, 111
Windermere, 10, 18, 25, 26, 114, 160
Windy Gap, 103

Winser, S. B., 93, 132
Winthrop Young, Eleanor, 177, 178
Winthrop Young, Geoffrey, 12, 69, 116, 172, 177, 178, 179, 181
Woolley, Hermann, 89
Wordsworth, Dorothy, 30
Wordsworth, William, 4, 24, 29–31, 39

Y Boulder, 9, 110, 152
Yewbarrow, 4, 41, 103; Central Chimney, 160
Yorkshire Ramblers' Club, 167, 173, 177
Journal, 148, 167–9

Zurbriggen, the guide, 156
Zermatt, 6, 150, 155, 156, 157

Index to Postscript

Abraham Brothers, 186
Abraham, John, 186
Alps, 185, 186

Botterill, Fred, 186, 188

Collie, Professor J. Norman, 184
Crowley, Aleister, 186-7

Fell and Rock Climbing Club of the English Lake District, 184-5
Field, A. E., 186

Grading and description of routes, 187-8
Great Gable, Kern Knotts Crack, 188

Haskett Smith, Walter Parry, 185, 187

Herford, Siegfried W., 186

Jackson, Rev. James ('Steeple'), 184
Jones, Owen Glynne, 186, 187

North Wales, 185, 186

Pennines, 185
Pillar Rock, 184, 188

Sansom, G. S., 186
Scafell, 186, 188
Scott, Doug, 185
Scotland, 185
Solly, Godfrey Allan, 188

Techniques, 185, 187, 188

Wasdale Head, 185, 186, 187, 188